KENYAN RUNNING

KENYAN RUNNING

Movement Culture, Geography and Global Change

JOHN BALE
and
JOE SANG

FRANK CASS
LONDON • PORTLAND, OR.

First published in 1996 in Great Britain by
FRANK CASS PUBLISHERS
Crown House, 47 Chase Side, Southgate,
London N14 5BP

and in the United States of America by
FRANK CASS
c/o ISBS, 920 NE 58th Avenue, Suite 300
Portland, Oregon 97213-3786

Website: www.frankcass.com

British Library Cataloguing in Publication Data

Bale, John, 1940–
    Kenyan running : movement culture, geography and global
change
    1. Running – Kenya 2. Athletics – Kenya 3. Athletics – Kenya –
    Social aspects 4. Athletics – Kenya – History
    I. Title II. Sang, Joe
    796.4'2'096762

ISBN 0-7146-4218-5

Library of Congress Cataloging-in-Publication Data

Bale, John
    Kenyan running : movement culture, geography, and global change /
John Bale and Joe Sang.
        p. cm.
    Includes bibliographical references (p.   ) and index
    ISBN 0-7146-4684-9 (hardcover). – ISBN 0-7146-4218-5 (pbk.)
    1. Runners (Sports)–Kenya. ". Running–Social aspects–Kenya.
    3. Track-athletics–Social aspects–Kenya. I. Sang. Joe.
    II. Title.
    GV 1061.23.K4B35   1996
    796.42'096762–dc20   96-12789
                                                                CIP

Printed in Great Britain by
Anthony Rowes Ltd, Eastbourne

This book is dedicated to
Alice Bale
and
Monica Sang

Contents

Figures

Tables

Acknowledgements

We are happy to acknowledge the help of a number of people and organisations in the production of this book. Thanks for permission to reproduce various illustrations are offered to *Athletics Weekly* for Figure 1.1, to Rhodes House Library, Oxford, for Figures 1.2 and 4.2, to Jan Agertz for Figure 1.3, to Jan-Erik Karlberg for Figure 1.4, to Ismael Kirui for Figure 1.7, to Frank Cass (publishers) for Figure 3.1, to Hans Huber AG Buchhandlung Verlag (Bern) for Figure 3.2, and to Cassell Publishers for Figure 3.3. Figure 4.1 is reproduced by permission of the Syndics of Cambridge University Library. We must thank Rex Collings (publishers) for permission to reproduce Figure 4.4, the Elsa Conservation Trust for Figure 4.5, Reebok Ltd for Figure 5.1, the Athletic Department, Iowa State University for Figure 5.5, Walter Abmayr for Figure 7.1, and Nation Newspapers Limited (Nairobi) for Figures 7.7 and 7.8. In the case of a small number of illustrations it has been impossible to trace copyright holders. If any such omissions can be located we will be pleased to acknowledge them in subsequent editions of this book.

John Bale started writing *Kenyan Running* in the Spring of 1994 while he was a visiting professor at the University of Jyväskylä in Finland. He is very grateful to Pauli Vuolle, Kalevi Olin and their many colleagues in the Faculty of Sport and Health Sciences for their support and help in providing a congenial environment in which to embark upon such a venture. Many thanks are also given to Tuija Kilpeläinen for her superb organisational skills and excellent company. He would also like to thank Lena and Olof Moen, Samuel Gichaba and Reuben Ndunga for their hospitality and help in Göteborg. Finally, he is grateful to Michael Popkin for finding time to discuss life in Kenya in the 1940s and 1950s.

Joe Sang worked on various parts of the book as a research student at Keele University in the early 1990s. He would like to thank everyone who helped him during that period. He particularly appreciates the assistance of Mike Kosgei, Kipchoge Keino, Kiptalem Keter and Mike Boit. The other athletes and sports officials who directly or indirectly helped in this project are also warmly thanked. For assistance while at Keele he must thank Tom Kiptanui, Anne Too, Jack and Joanna LeLan, Wilson Matunda, Oscar Koitaba, Chris Sum and all his other friends. Finally his heartfelt gratitude goes to his brothers Paul, James, Hilary and Peter, sisters Chebet and Lucy, and to his father who, having been Kenya's first Sports Commissioner, provided many insights into Kenyan athletics.

We are both very grateful to Heikki Herva for allowing us access to his data on world athletic trends. Andrea Abbas, Leslie Crouch, Allen Guttmann, John Hoberman, Andrew Huxtable, Tony Isaacs, Joel Kirui, Simon Naylor, Anders Närman, Cynthia Nekesa, Bob Phillips and David Terry read (or at least talked about) various versions or parts of the book. We greatly appreciate their many insightful comments, additions and corrections. Most of their suggestions have been incorporated into the text. We would also like to thank staff at the Kenya National Archives, Nairobi, and those of the libraries of Birmingham University, the School of Oriental and African Studies (University of London), Rhodes House (Oxford University) and the Royal Geographical Society for help and co-operation. We are grateful to the Keele University inter-library loans team for their efficient service. Maralyn Beech and Andrew Lawrence from the Geography Department at Keele deserve special thanks for their excellent photographic and cartographic work respectively. Despite all this help, however, it is the authors who take sole responsibility for what follows.

John Bale,
Joe Sang,
October 1995.

Preface

Ex Africa semper aliquid novi (Pliny)

Africa is often viewed as an emerging continental giant on the modern sporting stage. Such a view is a gross oversimplification. It is true that there is a growing number of African stars in boxing, football and track and field athletics. Most African countries, however, have not made a significant impact on modern Western sports; the African impact has been selective and patchy. On the other hand, the occidental impact on African sports has been overwhelming.

In recent years the success of footballers from Nigeria and Cameroon has attracted the attention of television viewers and football fans – as well as a number of overseas coaches and trainers. The entry of these countries into the final stages of World Cup competitions has also provided fertile fodder for the foreign press. All too often, however, the emergence and success of African countries in sports is 'explained' in stereotypical and sometimes racist terms. The idea and image of the uninhibited 'natural' athlete dies hard. The fact that such athletes are culturally 'produced' is invariably ignored. This book seeks to correct the balance.

There are few English-language books on sports in Africa. There are even fewer detailed studies of sports in particular African countries. This book, the first to explore in detail the emergence and significance of a single sport in one particular African country, focuses on track and field athletics in Kenya. Like the west African footballers mentioned above, Kenyan runners have caught the imagination of the world of sports since they burst on to the world stage in the 1960s. And Kenyan running itself has become an imaginative world in the mental map of the Western sports fan and the general public.

This book does not present lists of performances or biographies of the stars. The success of most of the athletes mentioned in the text can be discovered in more conventional statistical gazetteers and histories of world track and field athletics. We prefer to adopt a more interpretive approach. Kenya is seen as part of a global system of culture in general and of sport in particular. It is this, in a sense, which forms the theoretical basis of our book; that is, global rather than Kenyan processes need to be examined in order to 'explain' modern Kenyan track and field athletics.

Although this book is not a conventional study in sports history, our approach necessarily requires an historical overview and we far from ignore the years leading up to the recent decades in which Kenyan athletic power has been so publicly visible. Indeed, *Kenyan Running* could be seen as the first attempt to write a history of Kenyan athletics. However, we prefer to see our book as an interdisciplinary endeavour. We feel that such a study needs to consider what Kenyan running 'means' from philosophical and sociological perspectives, but within a geographical framework which situates such body culture in the contexts of colonialism, modern globalised athletics, and the Kenyan state itself. We seek to 'read' Kenyan athletics (as well as to present readings of what various people have written about it) in the context of both Kenyan 'movement culture' and the changing global sports system. In doing so we try to avoid exaggerating the disciplinary distance between geography, history and sociology. In order to flesh out our study we also utilise the insights provided by authors from the fields of travel writing, sports studies, anthropology and development studies. The diverse practices of colonialism – of which track and field athletics was part – require diverse sources for their study.[1]

In the chapters which follow we will describe the roots of Kenyan running and the way in which it has 'developed' – or 'failed to develop', depending on which way it is viewed. The first two chapters provide a background to what follows. Chapter 1 briefly describes the emerging occidental awareness of the modern Kenyan athlete from the mid-1950s to the present day. It hints at some of the issues surrounding the establishment of Kenya as an athletic power but basically aims to alert the reader to the significance of Kenyan athletics at the present time. Chapter 2 delves more deeply into the character of modern Kenyan running and why it is considered important as a social and national phenomenon. We review the statistically measurable performance indicators which are so central to sport in the nations of the modern world. We situate Kenya within the geographical mosaic of African and world athletics, employing the basic geographical tool of the map to reveal how significant the country's athletes really are. We also discuss the role of sport in the boosting of nations and in the bonding of their peoples.

In Chapter 3 we start our historical review in which we examine the antecedents of modern Kenyan track and field. We first look at the folk-games and sport-like activities of earlier times, the body-cultural forms which modern sport has largely replaced. We observe the images of Kenyan body cultures which were communicated to the European public by travel writers in the early twentieth century, and the extent to which those images are congruent with present-day athletic competences.

Chapter 4 traces the emergence of modern athletics in Kenya, illustrating how different agencies and ideologies contributed to the inclusion of track and field in the school curriculum, in the training of police and army personnel, and in the world of Kenyan competitive sports. It also shows how pre-modern and modern forms of movement culture coexisted in the inter-war period, prior to the hegemony of modern track and field. We also suggest that the landscape of modern sport is a symbol of colonial power.

In Chapter 5 we acknowledge that, today, track and field athletics in Kenya is part of a shrinking world. We explore the character of the global system of sport by highlighting the gradual globalisation of Kenyan athletics (and athletes). While we have not presented this book as a deeply theoretical treatise, the theory around which it is loosely constructed is made most explicit in Chapter 5. Basically, we do feel that the global structures of sports and society are important in explaining the present character of Kenyan athletics but that human agents are not passive pawns at the mercy of these structures. We hope that the role of both the structures and the agencies are given appropriate attention throughout the pages which follow.

Explanations of the apparent success of Kenyan runners are shrouded in myth. Chapter 6 examines some of these myths, often based on crude environmental and racist assumptions. We also identify the marked regional variations that are found in the national map of the 'production' of Kenyan running talent. We show that it is not simply that *Kenya* is part of a world athletics system but that *one small part of Kenya* 'produces' most of its star athletes. We try to find out what is so important about this particular region of the country and those who live there.

The book concludes with Chapter 7 and a consideration of the extent to which Kenya's recent athletic history can be viewed as a form of 'cultural imperialism', 'development' or 'under-development'. We also consider whether, through track, road, and cross-country racing, Kenyans can be said to display resistance to Western cultural influences in movement culture. We note, furthermore, that through their running some athletes are involved in loosening the ties which have traditionally bound them to their nation. We are cautious in predicting what will happen to Kenyan athletics in the future. We conclude by noting that, although achieving athletic results and records is not the only route for Kenyan athletic 'development', it is the route which it is most likely to take.

Reference

1. Young, *Colonial Desire*, p. 159.

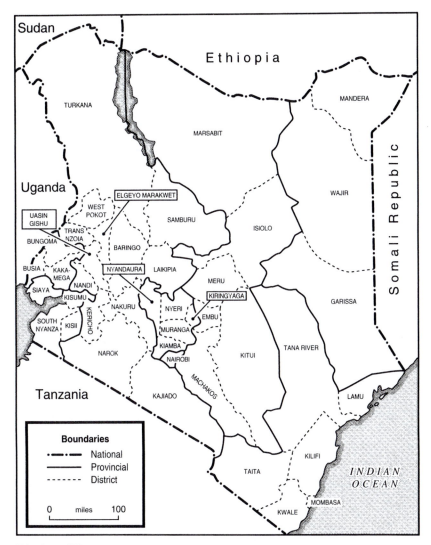

Districts of Kenya.

1

Black Athletes at the White City

The romanticizing of the African champion ... has served to
link exotic physiological states with the racial alien and his
alleged biological advantages.

JOHN HOBERMAN, *Mortal Engines*

The 1948 Olympic Games, hastily organised at London's Wembley
Stadium in a still shell-shocked Europe, had revived the spirit of
Olympism after the Second World War, albeit at a somewhat low-key
level. Although the world had to wait until the 1952 Games for the post-
war emergence of sport as a more global phenomenon, the London
Games did, nevertheless, illustrate how the geographical margins of
Olympism had penetrated the colonies of the British imperial realm.
Athletes competed in track and field events from the far-flung areas of
the Empire – Jamaica, Trinidad, Singapore and India, for example. Most
black African nations did not possess a National Olympic Committee
and some of their athletes therefore competed under the flags of their
'mother countries' – notably France and Britain. The 1952 Olympic
Games at Helsinki pushed the Olympic margins further; they readmitted
Germany and pitted the USA against the USSR – a Cold War in spiked
shoes – but they also illustrated the seemingly inexorable colonisation of
the world by the spirit of *citius-altius-fortius* – the Olympic ideal. In
these post-war spectacles, the presence of black athletes from the British
Empire became increasingly evident.

In London, Wint and McKenley, British- and American-trained
Jamaicans respectively, had won gold and silver medals in the 400
metres sprint; in Helsinki the Jamaican team won the 4 × 400 metres
relay. Other black athletes from the British colonies, while not attaining
Olympic success, were, by the early 1950s, achieving performances
worthy of inclusion in the world-ranking lists.[1] It was recorded that
Nigerian athletes featured among the top 50 performers in the world in
the 100 metres, the long jump and, most notably, the high jump. Joshua
Majekodunmi from Nigeria was placed second in the high jump at the
1950 Empire Games and was ninth at the Helsinki Olympiad. He was

the first black African athlete to feature in the world top 50 over a sequence of years during the late 1940s and early 1950s. But athletes of African origin were not noted for their performances in distances above 800 metres (with the noteworthy exceptions of the north Africans, El Ouafi who had won the 1928 Olympic Marathon, and El Mabrouk and Mimoun who competed in the 1952 Olympics, all running in the colours of France). Moreover, track and field athletes from the countries of east Africa were only conspicuous because of their absence.

Despite the evident globalisation of the Olympics, most track and field events in the decade following the Second World War were still dominated by white athletes. Yet basing his information on a study of the Helsinki Games, Professor Ernst Jokl of the University of Kentucky noted that 'Africa harbours a great athletic reserve army which has not yet been fully mobilized for the Olympic contests'. Athletes from the African nations, he continued, 'are bound to play an increasingly important role in the Olympic Games in the future.'[2] Jokl's prediction was accurate. Forty years later the track events of the Olympics were to be dominated by athletes from one of Britain's former east African colonies, Kenya. At the Barcelona Olympics of 1992 Kenyans won two gold medals, four silver, and two bronze in track events ranging in distance from 400 to 10,000 metres.

In this book we examine the evolution and extent of Kenya's apparent power in track and field athletics.[3] We ask how such athletic 'success' and 'development' can be measured but, at the same time, expose the ideology of such a 'quantitative' approach to sport. In addition, we attempt to counter the mythology of Kenyan running by suggesting that the present state of Kenyan track and field athletics cannot be 'explained' by a single cause. Instead it requires an understanding of the globalisation of sport and the integration of Kenyan athletics into a global system – a central feature of its modernisation.

Athletics and Empire

Although subsequent chapters will delve into the early years of the twentieth century, our story starts in 1954, the year of the British Empire and Commonwealth Games in Vancouver, British Columbia. The Empire Games, as they had traditionally been known, were one of a number of sub-Olympic sports gatherings which, while subscribing to the faster-higher-stronger ideology of Olympism, were politically or geographically selective in terms of the nations invited to compete. Of course, the Empire Games were an unashamed glorification of the

British imperial ethos and until 1954 most of the 'black' colonial nations were effectively excluded from participation. Indeed, to this day, the Commonwealth Games have only once been held in a nation where the majority of the population is black – Jamaica in 1966. No predominantly black nation has yet hosted the Olympics.

In effect, the Empire Games (and other events like them) served to continue a traditional imperial ideology which had been based on two incompatible principles.[4] The first was the ideal of 'fair play' which presented all colonial subjects, irrespective of colour, with the opportunity of taking part in the Games. Alongside it, however, the second principle of the racial superiority of the Anglo-Saxons predicted that the 'lesser breeds' would occupy the minor placings and not seriously threaten the supremacy of the whites from the 'Old Commonwealth'. In the rather cosseted world of track and field athletics these principles did not seriously clash until the mid-1950s.

The Vancouver Games were the first intercontinental sporting event in which a Kenyan track and field team had participated. The team was made up of some sprinters, middle- and long-distance runners, a couple of high jumpers and a javelin thrower. On the way to Vancouver the team broke its journey in London in order to take part in the annual Amateur Athletic Association (AAA) championships, held at the venerable White City Stadium, constructed for the 1908 Olympics. The British sporting public was not entirely unaware of a black athletic presence. They had, of course, heard of Jesse Owens. Indeed, in the 1948 Olympics the British representative who gained fifth place in the long jump was Prince Adegboyega Adedoyin from Nigeria. Their champion sprinter, Emmanuel McDonald Bailey, was a West Indian who had represented Britain in the 1952 Olympics. Arthur Wint, the Jamaican gold medalist at 400 metres in 1948, had been in the Royal Air Force and studied at a London teaching hospital. Bailey and Wint were familiar on British tracks. In the British athletic psyche, however, black athletes were meant to be long jumpers, high jumpers or, most likely, sprinters (that is, runners in events up to, but certainly not beyond, the half mile). The black athlete excelled in the explosive events, was 'quick off the mark', but lacked stamina.[5] After all, in 1954 the world records for the 100 metres, 200 metres, 400 metres and long jump which were held by black athletes. The athletic *cogniscenti* might also have been aware that four Nigerians had cleared a world class height of 6 feet 6 inches (1.981 metres) in their national championships two years earlier. In Britain, the patronising press claimed that only one of the four had any knowledge of high-jumping technique, reinforcing the racist notion that black athletes depended on 'raw talent'.[6]

The middle- and long-distance running events had traditionally been dominated by the northern and central Europeans. The British still held Sydney Wooderson, the English archetype, in much affection; the Swede, Gunder Hägg, had held the mile record until broken by Roger Bannister, and the 'flying Finn', Paavo Nurmi, was still venerated as the greatest distance runner of all time. In Helsinki the French north African, Mimoun, had been unable to beat the Czech, Zatopek.

At the time of the 1954 AAA championships, news coming out of Kenya would have been more concerned with the Mau Mau uprisings which were raging there than with anything connected with sport. Not surprisingly, the press build-up to the championships hardly heralded a Kenyan running presence. In his preview in the *Manchester Guardian*, the respected athletics correspondent, Larry Montague, did refer to the potential of 'a remarkable young high jumper from Kenya' named Jonathan Lenemuria who had cleared 6 feet 7 inches (2.007 metres) in Kampala, Uganda, but failed to even mention that some of the colony's runners would be competing.[7] The preview in *The Times* of London made no mention of the Kenyans at all.[8]

The featured race of the Friday night of the AAA meeting in the 1950s and 1960s was traditionally the six miles championship. On this occasion the assembled crowd was ready to savour the running of the charismatic English runner, Gordon Pirie. However, spectators were somewhat surprised to find an unknown and barefooted Kenyan named Lazaro Chepkwony lining up for this event, during the course of which he contributed an erratic series of fast laps and in doing so confused some of the British runners (Figure 1.1). He ran with the leading group, during which time he was 'taken to heart by the spectators'[9] until pulling a muscle in the fifteenth lap and dropping out. From a British perspective, his 'unscientific' approach, whereby fast bursts were interspersed with laps of a slower pace, and the fact that he was unable to complete the race, was exactly what would be expected of the African novice and confirmed the prevailing view that black runners were unsophisticated. If they were runners at all they were sprinters.

The following day, in front of a crowd of 30,000 spectators, the three mile event featured another Kenyan who lined up alongside the Oxford University graduate and member of the élite Achilles Club, Chris Chataway. Assembled with him were a coterie of British middle distance runners including Chataway's adversary, Fred Green of Birchfield Harriers. The Kenyan competitor was Nyandika Maiyoro, the national champion from Kisii district in Nyanza province. His best time was over half a minute slower than the existing world record. As the gun signalled the start of the race Maiyoro sped into the lead and opened up an enormous gap, at times amounting to about forty metres ahead of the British runners. At the mile mark he led his pursuers by over four seconds, a feat met by the British crowd with a combination of amazement and amusement. He hung on to the field, however, and in a competition in which Green and Chataway both broke the world record, finished in third place, beating the Kenyan record with a time of 13 minutes 54.8 seconds.

Figure 1.1. Lazaro Chepkwony, leading the great British runner Gordon Pirie, during the AAA six miles championship, Friday evening, 9 July 1954 – the first occasion that a Kenyan distance runner had raced in Europe (courtesy of *Athletics Weekly*).

Less visible, but arguably more significant, were the performances of the Kenyan field event athletes. The javelin thrower, Kiragu, like Maiyoro, finished third. The same position was occupied by Lenemuria in the high jump, using the Western roll style, and another Kenyan jumper, Maritim was in fifth place. In this event the two Kenyan jumpers outperformed all of the British entries.

The reaction to the performances of Maiyoro and Chepkwony can be illustrated by some comments in the report of the championships carried in the pages of the liberal *Manchester Guardian*. The six mile event was said to have been 'bedevilled' by Chepkwony's sudden bursts; the first half of the three miles was 'made confusing' by Maiyoro's 'ludicrously fast pace'.[10] The report in *The Times* stated that it was 'inevitable' that Maiyoro would eventually be overtaken by Green and Chataway.[11] These comments reflected not only the athletic and social prejudices of the period but also the lack of seriousness with which the British public, at least, perceived the challenge of the African runners. They also reflected the problem of how the Western writer could coherently represent the apparently strange reality of the African runner.

A much more sympathetic attitude towards Kenyan distance running was evidenced by the editor of *Athletics Weekly*, P. W. Green, who noted that

> it was the unusual and unexpected form by some of the coloured runners in the distance races which provided much food for thought. Never again shall we nurse the idea that the coloured races (sic) are no good at anything beyond a mile. Maiyoro of Kenya, with as near the perfect action as I have seen, would, with the right training and competition, be a match for any runner in the world.[12]

In relation to the high jump (where five Africans finished in the first six competitors) *The Times* reporter was moved to comment that 'altogether, the men from Nigeria, Kenya and Uganda made their presence felt at the meeting, even if they failed to capture any titles'.[13] Indeed, on the evidence of the performances in this meeting, the high jump could be said to have been Kenya's strongest athletic event.

The events at the White City had projected Kenyan track and field onto a global, as opposed to a national or continental, stage but the AAA championships were only the prelude to the August celebrations in Vancouver. The 1954 Empire and Commonwealth Games are probably best remembered for two things. First, it was in Vancouver (in what had been billed as the 'mile of the century') that the first four-minute miler, Englishman Roger Bannister, defeated John Landy, the Australian who had improved on Bannister's world record. The second reason for remembering Vancouver is for the collapse of the English marathon runner, Jim Peters, while in sight of the finishing line and a considerable distance ahead of the next runner. Buried beneath these headlines were the performances of the Kenyan athletes. Maiyoro was again the most prominent, achieving fourth place in the three miles. He did not dash to the front, as in the London race, but stayed with the pack, taking the lead with one lap to go but being outsprinted by an English trio led by Chataway, but again setting a new Kenyan record. His time was 13 minutes 43.8 seconds. Subsequently Maiyoro was patronisingly dubbed 'the popular Black Jack from Kenya' by one of the most respected athletics reporters of the day.[14] But other Kenyans did not go unnoticed. Chepkwony was seventh in the six miles and eleventh in the three miles, Maboria was sixth in the javelin, Maritim and Lenemuria finished eighth and tenth respectively in the high jump, and the national team finished fourth in the 4 × 440 yards relay. Other Kenyan athletes competed in the heats of the half mile and the 120 yards hurdles. The Kenyan team was certainly not made up solely of distance runners.

Yet it seems that it was, in fact, a runner who left the most indelible imprint on the minds of the English athletics *aficionados*, perhaps because of the greater visibility of track events over those such as the high jump and javelin which are held on the infield. The McWhirter twins, editors of the short-lived *Athletics World*, noted that although 1954 had been the year of the four-minute mile, there were many who felt 'that the most significant item was the appearance of the great distance runner from Kenya, Nyandika Maiyoro'. There was also a hint that this was a sign of things to come; it was reported that back in Kenya two 15-year-old boys had run under 15 minutes 30 seconds for three miles in the 'Kenyan Goan Sports'.[15]

Kenyans did not win any medals in Vancouver. They were noted by dedicated track fans but not by the world's sporting public. Kenyan athletes did not appear, therefore, to be natural-born athletic marvels who could emerge out of Africa and easily defeat the best the Empire had to offer. Nor can it be said that Kenya was the most successful African nation at the Games, given the success of the Nigerian and Ugandan athletes who, between them, occupied the first three places in the high jump. Kenya was not, therefore, projected into the medal table – that is, the list of nations and their medal tallies published in most national daily newspapers throughout the Commonwealth (and, in the case of the Olympics, the world). The medal table is, therefore, the medium which gives greatest visibility to national, as opposed to individual, success in sport. The lay public may not read the detailed results but they are often exposed to the list of countries and the number of medals their athletes win. Unofficial though they are, these tables are beloved by the media who have featured them regularly since the 1930s. The medal table advertises the relative ranking of nations in such sporting spectacles to a wide audience.

The Olympic Games of 1956 in Melbourne witnessed the re-emergence of Maiyoro. He performed with little success in the heats of the 1,500 metres and did not qualify for the final. In the 5,000 metres, however, he was placed seventh but this time beat Chataway by almost ten seconds. In 1958 a Kenyan team competed at the Empire and Commonwealth Games held in Cardiff and, before doing so, paid another visit to London's White City Stadium to compete in the AAA event. This time Maiyoro followed the leader and was rewarded with second place in the British championships and yet another Kenyan record, this time 13 minutes and 34.8 seconds. Other Kenyans enhanced their nation's visibility. Arere Anentia, won another three miles event with Kanuti Sum placing third. Joseph Leresae was third in the high jump (beating the Nigerians), Kiptalam Keter was seventh in the half-mile, and Bartonjo Rotich qualified for the final of the 440 yards hurdles. At Cardiff, the Kenyan team improved significantly on their Vancouver achievements. Although Maiyoro did not run particularly well (he failed to qualify for the final of the mile and fell behind the field after 2.25 miles in the three miles), some of his compatriots showed that Kenya was developing a group of serious athletes who could compete without embarrassment in a variety of events in international competition. Anentia and Sum were third and sixth respectively in the six miles, Rotich was third in the 440 yards hurdles, and Leresae fourth in the high jump. It can again be clearly seen from these performances that Kenya was not turning out an assembly line of distance runners but possessed a relatively well-diversified track and field team. The bronze medals of Anentia and Rotich signalled a landmark in Kenya's athletic history since they were the first medals won by Kenyan athletes in major international competition.

Olympic honours

The 1960 Olympics were held in Rome. Kenya entered a number of athletes and Maiyoro, unquestionably a pioneer of Kenyan distance running and an increasingly well-known figure in Kenya (Figure 1.2), brought his career to a climax with an impressive sixth place in the final of the 5,000 metres in a new African record time of 13 minutes 52.8 seconds. This was the fastest time ever recorded by a black athlete.

Seraphino Antao, from the coastal city of Mombasa (and of Goan ancestry), was a semi-finalist in the 100 metres and Rotich achieved a similar standard in the 400 metres hurdles. Kenyans also competed in the 10,000 metres and the marathon. From an African perspective, however, the games were most significant because of the signal given to the world from Kenya's east African neighbour, Ethiopia, through the devastating victory of Abebe Bikila in the marathon.

Figure 1.2. Nyandika Maiyoro was the first world-class Kenyan runner. He is seen here (left) opening a new dormitory, named after him, at Kabianga College in Kericho in 1960, With him is the college Principal, J. M. Popkin (from the correspondence and papers of J.M. Popkin, Rhodes House Library, Oxford).

Sandwiched between the Rome and Tokyo Olympics were the 1962 Commonwealth Games at Perth, Australia. Kenya was now entering athletes in a wider range of events than ever before, from 100 yards to six miles and from the 440 hurdles to the triple jump. From a Kenyan perspective the Perth Games witnessed the first Kenyan Commonwealth gold medals, not from a distance runner but from the sprinter Antao who won both the 100 and 220 yards (Figure 1.3). Kimaru Songok won a silver medal in the 440 hurdles. Maiyoro's distinguished running career had come to an end but it was at Perth that the first really 'global' Kenyan athlete made his initial major appearance. Buried in the results of the heats of the mile, and finishing well down the field in the three

Figure 1.3. Seraphino Antao (left) was the first Kenyan to win a Commonwealth gold medal. He is here seen running in Cardiff, Wales, in 1963 (courtesy of Jan Agertz).

miles, was a Nandi runner called Kipchoge Keino. Like Maiyoro at the White City, he opened up a huge lead over the rest of the field only to be caught on the last lap and finish eleventh. Three years later he was to be described as 'the world's most exciting athlete'[16] and, over the ensuing years, he proceeded to win two Olympic gold medals and break many world records (Figure 1.4).

The first Olympic medal to be won by a Kenyan, however, was in the 1964 Tokyo games when Wilson Kiprugut won the bronze in the 800 metres, a year after his nation's independence (Figure 1.5). Kiprugut surprised the world experts since his form was virtually unknown. Kenya's first Olympic medal had been won in an event between the sprints and the middle distances; the country was still not labelled a nation of distance runners. It had taken ten years from Chepkwony's appearance at the White City to Kiprugut's medal-winning run at the Olympics.

It was at the next Olympics, held at Mexico City in 1968, that Kenyan athletics really arrived as an international force and obtained a much higher level of visibility than hitherto in the global sports arena. In Mexico, Kenyan track athletes won 11 medals in 6 events ranging from the 4 × 400 metres relay to the 10,000 metres. Gold medals were won by

Amos Biwott in the steeplechase (though he had failed to win the Kenyan secondary schools' championship earlier in the year), Kipchoge Keino in the 1,500 metres and Naftali Temu in the 10,000 metres. Kiprugut won a silver in the 800 metres while in both the 5,000 metres and the steeplechase Kenyans achieved two places in the first three.

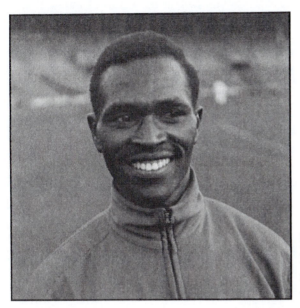

Figure 1.4. Kipchoge Keino, the first truly world-famous Kenyan runner (courtesy of Jan-Erik Karlberg).

Until 1968, little if any reference had been made to the 'altitude factor' in relation to Kenyan running. We have already noted that, in the 1950s, attitudes in the athletics press towards Kenyan running had been more concerned with exposing the myth of the black long distance runner; journalists appeared more interested in 'ethnicity' than altitude. With successes of the Kenyans (and, to a lesser extent, Ethiopians) in Mexico an excuse had to be made: they could succeed at long distances because they had been competing at a high altitude, similar to the physical environment of their homeland. The elevation of Mexico City (7,300 feet or 2,300 metres) had affected the Europeans negatively but was seen as being a marked advantage for the Kenyans from the highlands of east Africa. One journalist described the Games as the 'unfair Olympics' because of the results of the long distance races; another described the steeplechase as 'humiliating to a lover of distance running' because of the unsophisticated way in which Biwott had won.[17] Yet the 5,000 metres was won by an athlete from a low altitude country, as was the longest event of all, the 50 kilometre walk. The *benefit* of altitude was not invoked to call into question the 'fairness' of world record performances of the American long jump or British 400 metres hurdles champions. Nor had the enormous *economic* and *cultural* advantages which the Europeans and north Americans traditionally had over the Africans in previous Olympics ever been cited as unfair. Racist attacks and interpretations have littered the history of Kenyan running.

Figure 1.5. The 800-metre runner Wilson Kiprugut (number 19) was the first Kenyan Olympic medalist, winning a bronze at Tokyo in 1964 and a silver in Mexico City in 1968. He is seen here racing against the Canadian, Bill Crothers in Stockholm in 1965.

However, just as *Athletics Weekly* had respected Maiyoro's breakthrough, the self-styled 'Bible of the sport', *Track and Field News*, addressed the altitude factor in more sober terms. It noted correctly that it was 'a gross oversimplification to credit altitude completely' for the Kenyan victories.[18] And Allen Guttmann, in *The Olympics*, approvingly quotes the defence by Avery Brundage of the International Olympic Committee's choice of Mexico City: 'The Olympic Games belong to all the world, not the part of it at sea level'.[19] Kenyans were to show that they could perform with equal, and indeed greater, success at sea level as events of subsequent years would prove. This is not to say, however, that the debate about the apparent association between athletic performance and altitude has come to an end and we return to this question in Chapter 6.

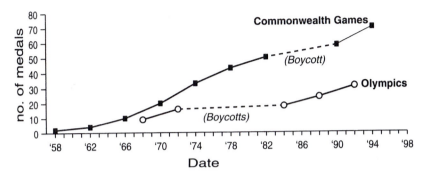

Figure 1.6. Cumulative frequency graphs of numbers of medals won by Kenyan athletes at the Commonwealth and Olympic Games.

Since 1968, Kenya's rapid emergence as an athletic power has become legendary (Figure 1.6). A highly partial list of the great names of Kenyan track running includes Kipchoge Keino, Ben Jipcho, Benjamin Kogo, Naftali Temu, Henry Rono, Mike Boit, Wilson Waigwa, Paul Ereng, John Ngugi, Julius Kariuki, Julius Korir, Billy Konchellah, Moses Kiptanui, Yobes Ondieki, Douglas Wakihuri, Ismael Kirui and William Sigei; but there are many, many more. We should make explicit, however, the fact that the overwhelming majority of Kenya's great athletes have been men. No Kenyan woman has ever held a world record or won a major track championship. The nearest that Kenyan women have come to winning such a title have been the World Championship bronze medals won by Susan Sirma (3,000 metres in 1991), Sally Barsosio (10,000 metres in 1993) and Tecla Lorupe in the world 10,000 metres in 1995 (Figure 1.7). Several world junior women's cross-country victories have been achieved by Kenyans but it was only in 1994 that Helen Chepng'eno became the first Kenyan woman to win the world women's senior cross-country championship.

Kenya, a country of about 27 million people, is today an athletic nation to be reckoned with, its runners criss-crossing the globe in order to compete in the track, road and cross country competitions to which they are lured. Since the mid-1960s Kenya has been near the top of every medal table in all international track and field meetings in which it has participated. In the 1995 World Athletics Championships, Kenyan athletes won seven medals; British athletes, from a country twice the size of Kenya, won five. Kenya can be said to dominate the middle- and long-distance track races (Table 1.1) to an extent only previously known by the legendary runners from Finland in the 1930s. In addition to the exploits of track athletes, Kenyan teams won the 1995 senior and junior men's and women's world cross-country championships. In the 1994 championships Kenyans won all of the four individual titles. The country's athletes also excel at road racing, particularly in distances between ten kilometres and the half-marathon. Kenya is today widely perceived as a nation of middle and long distance runners – world beaters at events from 800 metres upwards.

Figure 1.7. Tecla Lorupe, seen in the stadium at Gothenburg, Sweden, shortly after gaining a bronze medal in the World 10,000 metres championship, 1995. Note the uneasy alliance between 'Kenya' and 'Snickers' on the runner's chest (courtesy of Ismael Kirui).

TABLE 1.1.
Number of Kenyan runners in annual world top 20, 1964–94 at ten-year intervals.

Event	1964	1974	1984	1994
800 metres	1	4	2	8
1,500 metres	1	2	1	4
5,000 metres	0	1	2	6
10,000 metres	0	2	3	4
steeplechase	0	2	2	11

This brief overview of the 'development' of Kenyan athletics represents, to a large extent, a traditional way of looking at sports. The records and performances which we have quoted – which these days are always measured to the nearest hundredth of a second – reflect the statistical nature of the sport itself. Sports, and track and field in particular, are, like notions of economic development, measured in numbers. Quantification and recording are central to sport and are also often central to its historiography. Much writing on sport is, like sport itself, a record of statistical achievements.[20] Our problem with this approach is that it runs the risk of 'reducing knowledge of societies and human beings to teams and individuals with their "measurable" results on one narrow dimension'.[21] We will not avoid statistical coverage of sport in this book but we will limit our use of such an approach.

Kenyan running did not start in 1954 at London's White City Stadium. Its roots lay in pre-sportised running in the mountains and plains of east Africa. Neither did Kenyan racing start in 1954. Organised, timed races had been held in Kenya since before the 1920s and other kinds of racing had taken place much earlier than that. What the events at the White City and Vancouver, Cardiff, Rome, Perth, Tokyo and Mexico City did was to propel the image of the Kenyan athlete onto a world stage. No longer would black athletes be stereotyped as sprinters and no longer would an awareness of black distance running be confined to travellers' tales or within the boundaries of Kenya itself.

Notes and references

1. The world ranking lists are compiled and produced annually by the Association of Track and Field Statisticians (ATFS). These have been published since 1951 (relating to the 1950 season) in various formats and by various publishers.
2. Jokl, *Medical Sociology and Cultural Anthropology of Sport and Physical Education*, p. 70.

3. Throughout this book we will use the terms 'athletics' and 'track and field' synonymously.
4. Taylor, *Political Geography*, p. 117.
5. The recent history of this stereotype, set in a north American context, is described in Wiggins, 'Great speed but little stamina'.
6. Quoted in *Athletics World*, 1 (3), 1952, p. 1. In 1955 one of the Nigerian jumpers, Julius Chigbolu, was to establish a new British Commonwealth and Empire record. Comments which infer that black athletes succeed through 'raw talent' are racist because they attribute special qualities to particular 'races'.
7. *Manchester Guardian* (9 July 1954), p. 3.
8. *The Times* (9 July 1954), p. 6.
9. *Athletics Weekly*, 8 (29) (1954), p. 12.
10. *Manchester Guardian* (12 July 1954), p. 8.
11. *The Times* (12 July 1954) p. 3. Such stereotypical attitudes are also reflected in more recent television commentaries. When Ethiopian runners exchanged the lead in the Moscow Olympics it was described as 'naive' in contrast to the 'disciplined' running of the Finns: see Whannel, *Fields of Vision*, p. 129.
12. *Athletics Weekly*, 8 (29) (1954), p. 3.
13. *The Times* (12 July 1954), p. 3.
14. *Athletics World*, 2 (8) (1954), p. 61. We wonder if this comment 'satisfied the traditional [European] demand for someone to play the role of the ... African buffoon': Spurr, *The Rhetoric of Empire*, p. 46.
15. *Athletics World*, 2 (12) (1954), p. 103.
16. Watman, 'Keino: the world's most exciting athlete', p. 16; see Noronha, *Kipchoge of Kenya*, for a biography.
17. Bank, 'Dick Bank's Mexico reflections'.
18. Drake and Henderson, 'Blacks of Africa, US prevail in Mexican extravaganza', p. 3.
19. Guttmann, *The Olympics*, p. 133.
20. Eichberg, 'Stronger, funnier, deadlier . . .', p. 130. Standard works of this statistical genre include Quercetani's *A World History of Track and Field Athletics*, and his *Athletics: a History of Modern Track and Field*.
21. Galtung, 'The sport system as a metaphor for the world system'.

2

The Significance of Kenyan Running

A child who practises a sport is no longer playing but is
taking his place in a world of serious matters.

JEAN-MARIE BROHM, *Sport: a Prison of Measured Time.*

Sport is important to many countries of the world for at least two
reasons. Externally it provides a means of projecting a national image to
an international public, and internally it has the potential to bond the
nation's various social and political groups together. Boosting and
bonding can only be achieved if the country has something with which
it, and the outside world, can easily identify. Wars readily serve the
purposes of projecting a country's strength and, at the same time, of
binding its diffuse social or ethnic groups together in a common cause.
In the absence of war it is arguably sport that performs these functions
better than any other cultural phenomenon.

Sport *per se* is not enough, however. Unless *success* is achieved in
sport, international visibility is unlikely to be obtained. Success in sport
can only be achieved in most of the modern world by a particular kind
of sporting culture. Running can mean different things to different
cultures and in this chapter we therefore feel that there is a need to
describe what kind of movement culture we are talking about when we
describe athletics in modern Kenya. There is also a need to establish
what is meant by 'success' in sport. We will explore this question by first
locating Kenya's athletic situation in a continental and global context.
We will then proceed to examine the boosting and bonding functions of
Kenyan athletics.

What kind of running?

International sporting competition, like international political and
economic competition, is founded on deep ideological bases. These have
been identified collectively by Galtung as an isomorph of the world

system, carried by the notion of national teams.[1] Western attitudes towards conceptions of space and time, knowledge, relations to nature, and interpersonal relations are encapsulated in sport.[2] Sport (as we are using the term) is seen as an essentially Western phenomenon, radiating outwards from the European core which gave it to the rest of the world – a centre-periphery conception of global space. In addition, time is viewed as linear, as progress, climaxing at the 'big event'. Sports knowledge is atomised, 'operationalised exactly as in physics'.[3] Mental and spiritual dimensions are discounted. At root, sport could be regarded as anti nature with concrete and synthetic stadiums replacing grass, trees and soil. Finally, sport is eminently hierarchical with its ranking lists, winners and losers – little less than an athletics arms race. These basic observations make up a configuration which carries the message of Western sports cosmology. Indeed, it has been further noted that 'in contemporary sport it often seems as if it is more important to look good on the scoreboard than to be a good athlete, or a good person'.[4] The widespread practice of cheating in sport supports this view.

Olympic sport as we know it would not exist if it were not for the achievement orientation of those who take part. The promotion of achievement in sport is, as we noted above, explicitly related to the nation state, even in what are sometimes called 'poorer' countries such as many of those in Africa. At the same time, however, achievement sport can be used for personal gain – either in terms of status, or financial advancement, or both. For the athlete projected to the status of an Olympic medalist, financial gains via the Grand Prix circuit invariably follow. International sport is, therefore, a serious business; so serious that, apart from the rather ersatz opening and closing ceremonies, it is not obvious that there is much fun left at the Olympics.

Achievement sport is only one possible version of what has been called 'body culture' or 'movement culture'. By this is meant the culture of the body (including, of course, body movement), rather than the body as simply a matter of biology. Movement culture as a paradigm for the study of sport places sport firmly in the context of culture.[5] This is not to say that culture stops at the surface of the body. With each cultural configuration of sport there is a different biology: there is no one biological view of the body in movement culture.

It is possible to conceive of what Henning Eichberg calls a 'trialectic' of movement cultural configurations which we can illustrate by the example of running.[6] These differing configurations not only relate to the body of the runner but also the landscape on which the runner performs, body and landscape each being a response to a particular *culture* of running. This idea is illustrated in Figure 2.1. Each element within the trialectic is socially produced and reproduced: none should be regarded as 'natural'. Indeed, social anthropologists tend to take the view that what is 'natural' is culturally specific. The arrows between each part of the trialectic in Figure 2.1 are included to indicate a degree of possible fluidity between them. It is possible, for example, that running as 'keep fit' could become partly sportised; indeed, one can see this in the gradual organisation and achievement orientation of 'fun running'. Likewise, achievement sport could have hygienic elements within it though it is often injurious to health as 'over training' and drug abuse testify. Achievement sport may also have elements of fun in it but this seems to be rather untypical these days, given the seriousness with which it is taken.

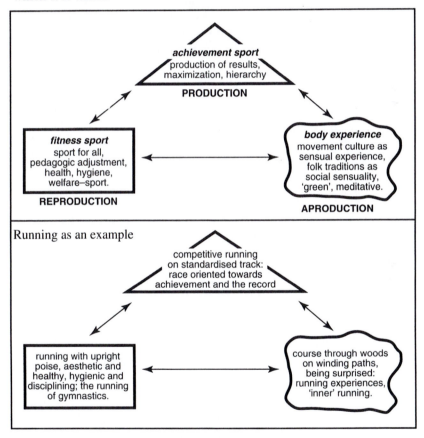

Figure 2.1. A trialectic of modern running cultures (after Eichberg, 1989).

Achievement sport is essentially synonymous with modern sport which is only a couple of centuries old. The sport-like activities which preceded it are sometimes called 'traditional sports' but may possess some characteristics of modern sport (Kenyan examples of these are examined in the following chapter). Sports as we know them today have certain features which are not found in other forms of contemporary movement culture. Eichberg, elaborating implicitly on the ideas of Galtung (noted earlier), suggests seven basic characteristics, each of which apply to the configuration of modern Kenyan (and all other achievement-oriented) running. These are:

i)   competition which often leads to aggression and can be compared with the competition found in capitalism;
ii) the production of results and their subsequent improvement, making the joy of human movement a subordinate activity, likened to the capitalist and state monopolist focus on the growth of production;
iii) the quantification of results, paralleled by the quantification of intelligence (IQ tests), educational achievement and gross national product, for example.
iv) the production of élites and hierarchies – artificial inequality instead of democratic solidarity;
v)   the parcelling of space in sport with its monocultural sites, standardised facilities, the separation of sport from non-sport activities and of men from women;
vi) the related fragmentation of time in sport accompanying the separation of work from play;
vii) discrimination against women and their subjugation to male patterns of sport, parallel to the male patterns of industrial exploitation.[7]

The form of running which best subscribes to these conditions is known as racing. The only equivalent word used to apply to such conditions in throwing and jumping is 'competition'. Physical education and leisure may embrace running, throwing and jumping but neither the bodies nor the landscapes of physical education and leisure are configured in the same ways as Olympic bodies and landscapes. Physical education does not require racing, with times taken to one-hundredth of a second. It may, however, include running for fitness and the subsequent examination and ranking of performances in physical education. In this sense it does resemble running as achievement sport. Sport could also be frolicsome and fun; a Zen of running could exist in which sensuousness and bodily experience could be more important than performance and the record.[8] In the case of running as play, none of Eichberg's Olympic configurations would apply. Of course, the body and the landscape required for frolic would differ from that required for Olympism. There is some evidence that in early modern sports, the achievement orientation, as illustrated in the configuration of the human body and the cultural landscape, was not as great as it is today. There are also some signs that less serious forms of body culture are experiencing a revival in many countries of the world, typified to some extent by the so-called jogging revolution – although sometimes this can be taken almost as seriously as achievement sport.

Although sport does not have to be as serious as it currently seems to be, it is difficult to resist the pressures which are made explicit in the Olympic code – higher, stronger, faster – with its emphasis on centimetre, gram and second. In our modern society there are no prizes for slow running; there are no prizes for style, and results are often regarded as being more important than performance.[9] National success in sport is not unlike success in the national economy. In both a key word is 'development'; another is 'growth'. As Eichberg notes: 'show me how you are running and I can see in what society you are living'.[10]

Measuring success in Olympic track and field

How successful has Kenya really been in track and field athletics? To what extent is Kenya an 'athletic giant'? Using the norms of achievement sport the rest of this chapter sets out, first, to measure and analyse Kenya's success, development and growth in track and field athletics, assuming that success in sport is to be taken as a serious objective. It then elaborates on why athletic success, as generally interpreted, is so important in the modern nation state.

In much of this book we will be using metaphors borrowed from the realms of economics and industry – terms like 'athletic *production*', 'national athletic *output*' and the '*export*' and '*packaging*' of athletes. We are fully aware of the ideological bases of this kind of language and the connotations that it carries. It is used basically because we feel that global track and field really does approximate to a multi-national enterprise. Hence, athletes do appear to be 'developed', 'processed' and 'marketed'. At the same time they are encouraged to attain the highest levels of 'output' or 'record' production. On the one hand such language sounds rather brutal but it also seems appropriate when, in many ways, human beings do seem to be reduced to inanimate objects, lacking freedom to decide when and where they compete and being subject to rigid and sometimes dehumanising training schedules.

Geographical variations in athletic 'output' can be measured in various ways. Such measurements can hardly avoid being subjective and all indices are inevitably influenced by ethnocentricism. They are often devised by Western experts and the norms adopted tend to be those of an affluent society. We have few measures of 'success' which can be applied to pre-modern movement cultures and all we can measure is the performances of athletes mimicking skills and sports of our own cultural systems. The measures we adopt usually serve to underestimate the achievements of athletes from what is often derogatorily known as the 'Third World'. That such norms are not the only possible norms and that other societies or other times have accepted totally different criteria of excellence is invariably overlooked.[11]

Although international comparisons of sporting success or 'output' are somewhat spurious, we recognise that if nations really are serious about comparing themselves athletically, those who compare them should at least be aware of the problems inherent in the methods they are using. We feel that the most widespread method (the Olympic medal count) is seriously flawed; we also feel that few, if any, alternatives are very much better. We will nevertheless use some approaches to highlight Kenya's position in the world of track and field, but acknowledge the shortcomings of our statistics.

Let us first consider the use of data generated by the Olympics as a means of comparing national variations in athletic status. Three basic inadequacies immediately come to mind. First of all, not all élite athletes compete in Olympic track and field because each country is restricted to a maximum of three athletes per event. Kenya, for example, would probably appear more dominant in the steeplechase than it already is if more than three of its runners could take part. Secondly, not all countries take part in the Olympics. Such partial participation sometimes results from political decisions to boycott the Games, as has happened in recent years in Montreal, Moscow and Los Angeles. Without all countries being present the Games do not provide a meaningful basis for comparison. Thirdly, not all athletic events are included in the Olympics. Those which are included tend to be overwhelmingly Western in origin and all use quantitative measures as the criteria for success. It is rarely recognised that striving for athletic betterment over a neighbouring state could be anathema to certain ideologies; indeed, the cases of Maoist China and present-day Libya, to some extent, illustrate such ideological positions. Nor is it recognised that merit could be based on performance rather than results.[12]

The Olympics as a database for national comparisons can also be criticised because the prime criterion for inclusion of a nation in the overall rankings is the aforementioned medal table. The most obvious point to consider here is the arbitrariness of only selecting three athletes in each event in arriving at a total score. The fourth (non-medal-winning athlete) could have achieved an identical time or distance to that of the third finisher – or even to the winner – yet is excluded from the data being used to define 'success'. Other studies, subject to exactly the same criticism, have explored success in the Olympics by allocating points to each of (usually) the first six finishers in each event.[13]

A more 'scientific' approach to measuring national differences at the Olympics was undertaken by Jokl, using the massive amount of quantitative data generated by the 1952 Games.[14] He recognised the inadequacy of utilising only the first three (or six) finishers in each event as a meaningful basis for comparison and instead calculated the number of points each country gained by taking into account the number of participants in each event. He argued against giving the same number of points to each winner (gold medalist) since this introduced an element of 'comparative equalization ... in that all winners obtain the same point allocation, irrespective of the nature of the event'.[15] Winners gain the same number of points on the Olympic medal table if they are in events with six finishers or if their event has 96 finishers. Arguing that it is more difficult to beat 96 athletes than it is to beat six, Jokl allocated points on the overall rank of each competitor in each event, the winner being awarded 100 points and the athlete ranked last being awarded 0 points. The point distance between the winner and the athletes placed second, third, etc. depends on the total number of athletes in the event.[16] In his analysis Jokl identified a number of important variables. These are shown in Table 2.1.

TABLE 2.1.
Variables in determining 'Olympic Success' (Source: Jokl, 1964)

participations	the number of participations from each country.
point share	the number of points collected by a country.
participation rate	the number of participations per million inhabitants.
point rate	the number of points per million inhabitants.
point level	the average number of points per participation.

The absolute number of points achieved by each nation in the Olympics – what Jokl termed the point share – fails to take into account a number of other important variables. For example, all other things being equal, countries with large populations would be expected to obtain a higher point share than small countries. For this reason Jokl added a number of other indicators based on a per capita approach.

Though Kenya did not compete in these particular Games it is of interest to the theme of this book that Jokl, while not focussing on track and field *per se*, drew attention to the performance of black athletes in the Olympics. Although scoring relatively low on most measures, he pointed out that the average *point level* of black athletes was 37.3, compared with 25.0 for whites. In other words, although only a relatively small number of black athletes took part, those who did achieved high rankings. This led to his prediction that, as more African nations came to take part in the Olympics, black athletes would come to feature prominently. For those interested in analysing the Olympics statistically we feel that Jokl's approach has much to commend it. Yet it has not been repeated since his studies of the 1952 Games.

A second group of studies tries to build 'models' which will predict Olympic success. The details of these studies have been reviewed elsewhere and need not detain us here.[17] They are not concerned with track and field athletics as such and basically conclude that success in the Olympics is related to gross national product and a socialist economy (these studies were undertaken before the break-up of the Soviet empire). It is worth noting, however, that in one such study it was observed that there was always a possibility of correlations existing between the various socio-economic, political and military variables hence leading to spurious relationships being established. It was therefore suggested that *partial* correlations should be compared, recognising that the factors which influence Olympic Games success are different for different *groups* of countries.[18] When 'Third World' countries were studied in isolation it was found that the best predictors of Olympic success were population, gross national product (GNP), military expenditure and the number of Olympic sports taught in schools.

We do not wish to dwell on these kinds of studies except to note that the 'scientific' approach adopted by them is consistent with the scientific approach to sport itself, particularly track and field athletics. There remains, however, the question of how the athletic *production* of a nation can be measured and it is to this subject that we now turn.

Measuring athletic output

The approaches described above seek to identify factors which can be used to measure and predict Olympic success. This is not surprising, given the perceived importance of the Olympic Games. It is not the same, however, as measuring the national 'production' of superior athletes simply because only a tiny proportion of each nation's athletic 'output' actually competes in the Olympics. Measuring 'output' can be done in three simple ways. First, we can simply count the number of athletes in each nation who achieved a particular level of performance in a given year. This would represent the absolute level of superior output (equivalent to Jokl's 'participations'). We use the term 'superior output' because most countries of the world, despite the high level of surveillance in sports, do not maintain records of *all* participating athletes. We have to rely, therefore, on the annual data produced by the Association of Track and Field Statisticians (ATFS). In the early editions of the ATFS annuals, the top 50 or more athletes in the world in each event for a given year were included; in more recent years the top 100, at least, have been included. Totalling all athletes from each country included in the top 100 for each of the standard Olympic events in a given year represents absolute superior output (that is, all superior athletes in the world). In 1992 there were over 3,500 such athletes (Table 2.2). In addition to the world lists, continental or sub-regional and national lists have also been produced, including annual data sets for Africa.

Because performances have been improving over time, however, comparative use of these annual data involves the use of a variable threshold as the criterion for inclusion. For example, in 1988 the 100th best 1,500 metre runner in the world was ten seconds faster than the equivalent in 1958. We are here reminded of a conversation between Paavo Nurmi (the great Finnish runner from the 1930s) and his son. Father Nurmi told son Matti that he would never be a great runner to which the son replied, 'I'll beat your times though!'[19]

A problem with the absolute measure of output is that it fails to take into account the population base of each country. Ultimately, athletic performances emerge from the total number of human bodies making up a nation's population. This is why the Olympic medal table is such a meaningless set of statistics; the population base of each country – the raw material which provides the seed corn of Olympic success – is excluded. A second way of approaching the problem of how to measure national athletic output is, therefore, to adopt a per capita approach (equivalent to Jokl's 'participation rate'). The overall per capita level of athletic production can be presented as an index of 1.00, against which national differences can be readily gauged. Hence, if a country had an index of 5.00, it would be producing at five times the global per capita norm. If, on the other hand, a country had an index of 0.5 it would be

producing at half the world norm.[20] In order to illustrate this approach
consider Table 2.2. In 1992, continental per capita output figures ranged
from 6.53 for Oceania to 0.20 for Asia, though indices for men and
women displayed some marked differences from the overall figures.

TABLE 2.2.
Continental variations in the production of world class athletes, 1992
(Data courtesy of Heikki Herva)

Continent	Absolute output			Per capita indices		
	Overall	Men	Women	Overall	Men	Women
Oceania	85	42	43	6.53	6.00	7.16
Europe	1,851	945	906	3.59	3.52	3.79
America	1,027	618	409	2.47	2.80	2.21
Africa	303	218	95	1.06	1.52	0.84
Asia	297	117	180	0.20	0.14	0.28
World	3,563	1,940	1,623	1.00	1.00	1.00

The per capita approach graphically demonstrates the considerable
geographical variations which exist in the 'production' of superior
athletes. It is reasonable to assume, however, that most countries would
ideally prefer a diversified group of superior athletes rather than have all
their successes in one or two events. It is necessary, therefore, to include
a measure of the specialisation of output in order to complement the per
capita index. Again, there are several ways of doing this but one simple
method is to compute a score of 100 for a nation having all its athletic
output in a single track and field event; the lower the score, the more
diversified the output.[21]

These statistical approaches, which we apply at a variety of
geographic scales in this and later chapters, mirror the 'scientific' basis
of achievement sport itself and of much of its academic study. However,
such approaches are not without flaws and some of their limitations need
to be outlined. First of all, we need to be aware that the data, tables and
maps included in this chapter provide a 'commanding view' of the world
of athletics. The panoramic vista of sport so obtained offers not simply
aesthetic pleasure – from the maps which follow, for example; it also
offers information and authority, a symbolic sense of mastery over the
previously unknown and unmapped.[22] Those observed and recorded are
all too easily reduced to mere numbers; people are seen as statistics,
national populations as indices. Human beings, with feelings and
experiences, are regarded as 'things' to be recorded and ranked.

Other problems – of a technical nature – exist. Population figures may not be accurate for many nations of the world; in some cases they may be little more than 'guesstimates'. This is, of course, a common problem with all studies involving the use of global population data. Nor can we be absolutely certain that the ATFS data are comprehensive. A number of logistical problems may have existed in actually putting the data together, especially in the early years of their compilation. Difficulties may have existed in tracing performances by emigrant athletes, some performances by politically incorrect athletes may have been obliterated, and phantom performances may have been invented.[23] However, the ATFS, while carrying no official status, has achieved a large measure of recognition from the IAAF (in that recent statistics handbooks published in connection with major championships have been compiled largely by members of the ATFS). In addition, while many of those supplying the data are amateur collectors of athletic information, many also hold official positions in national governing bodies or collaborate in the production of yearbooks for national federations. It is generally recognised, therefore, that high levels of accuracy are achieved by this organisation, the result of its global network of members who are involved in carefully monitoring athletes' performances. Thirdly, in using this approach we are guilty of 'comparative equalisation' – the athlete ranked first in the world is given the same weighting as the one ranked 100th. Comparative equalisation is practised, however, in numerous other national comparisons, for example, literacy rates and car ownership. It is the number of literate people and the number of those who own cars who are being measured, not the quality of their literacy or of their cars. In this respect, therefore, the data used in the per capita approach are similar those used in the 'most official' of United Nations publications.

Kenya in an African context

The significance of Kenyan track and field in a continental context can now be explored using the approaches outlined above. Let us first consider African track and field production as it stood in 1993. Although the figures for individual countries do vary from season to season, 1993 is broadly typical of Kenya's position during the last decade. The productivity of the nations of Africa in 1993 is illustrated in Table 2.3 and Figures 2.2–2.5 which show national variations in the output of 'superior' athletes. 'Superior' is, of course, a relative term and in this context is defined as those athletes of 'African class' (that is, those

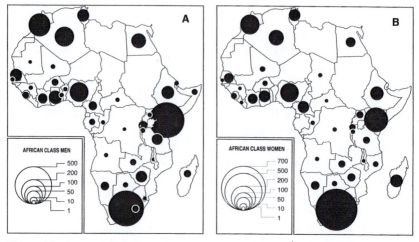

Figure 2.2. Geographic variations in the 'production' of African class athletes, 1993.

included in the African – *not* the world – ranking lists).[24] Contrary to what many observers believe, Kenya is *not* the major athletic 'producer' in Africa. In 1993 South Africa, produced 31.7 per cent of African 'output' compared with Kenya's 18.6 per cent (Figure 2.2). Using the per capita approach, which compares a nation's productivity with the continental norm of 1.0, South Africa was still the continental leader with an index of 5.72 (Figure 2.3). The index for Kenya was 4.65. No other countries had indices of more than 4. Several nations producing rather large numbers of athletes in absolute terms do not appear in Table 2.3 because of their low per capita scores. For example, Nigeria produced 222 athletes but has an overall index of only 0.39, the result of its very large national population.

TABLE 2.3.
Major national producers of 'African class' athletes, 1993 (countries with overall per capita indices of more than 1.4 times the African norm).

| Nation | Number of rankings | Per capita indices (Africa = 1.00) | | |
		Overall	Men	Women
South Africa	1,071	5.72	4.57	7.28
Kenya	628	4.65	5.94	3.10
Namibia	34	3.62	3.34	3.94
Morocco	285	2.14	2.29	1.93
Djibouti	4	1.85	3.41	0
Senegal	68	1.75	2.05	1.41
Tunisia	75	1.74	1.71	1.77
Algeria	192	1.46	1.71	1.13

The output of 'African class' athletes is, however, highly gendered. It is clear from Table 2.3 that among the major athletic nations of Africa, only in the case of South Africa is the per capita index for women significantly greater than that for men. Although producing about the same number of male athletes as Kenya, South Africa produced over three times as many African class women (Figure 2.2 [B]). It is also clear that Kenya is the major male producer with 5.94 times the continental average number of superior male athletes. The geographical patterns of relative 'production' are shown in Figures 2.3, 2.4 and 2.5. It can be seen that in relation to the continental per capita norm of 1.0 most countries of Africa produce few athletes of African class – that is, most produce athletes at well below the continental average.

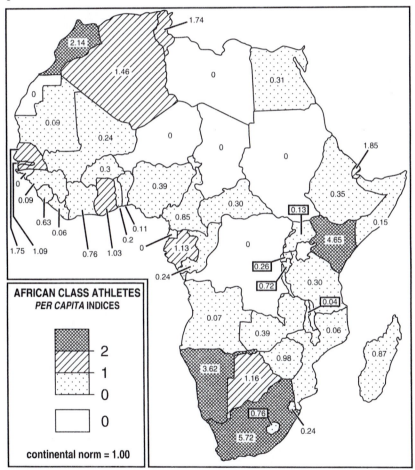

Figure 2.3. Per capita variations in output of African-class athletes, 1993.

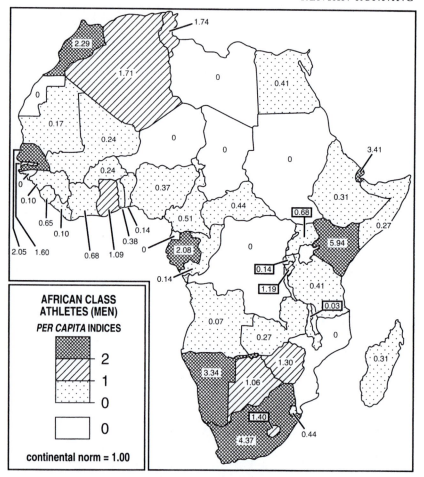

Figure 2.4. Per capita variations in output of African-class male athletes, 1993.

Kenya is well represented in all the event groups which make up the total repertoire of track and field, as shown in Table 2.4. Kenya is prominent among the African leaders in each event group except the women's jumping events. But even in that case the country is still producing athletes at well above the continental norm. The one event group in which Kenya really does dominate the African scene at this level of performance is men's distance running. In this case the stereotype is confirmed by the statistics.

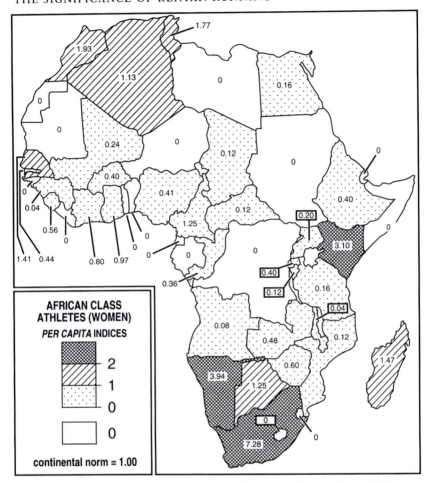

Figure 2.5. Per capita variations in output of African-class female athletes, 1993.

In the list of top nations in African men's distance running it may appear surprising that Ethiopia is not included (Table 2.4 [b]). Ethiopia has produced a number of excellent distance runners and is often perceived as a rival to Kenya's African hegemony in the long distance events. When national differences in population are taken into account, however, Kenya is seen to have produced African-class distance runners at nearly ten times the continental per capita average whereas Ethiopia produced at only about three-quarters the African norm (index of 0.73).

TABLE 2.4.
Top African nations in terms of African-class athletes by event group, 1993.

(a) Men's sprints:

1	2	3
Gabon	6.59	6
Gambia	5.96	4
Namibia	5.07	7
Kenya	**4.69**	**94**
S. Africa	4.31	118
Senegal	4.06	23

(b) Men's distances:

1	2	3
Kenya	**9.87**	**237**
Morocco	3.53	85
Djibouti	3.41	4
Burundi	3.31	17
S. Africa	2.70	90
Tunisia	1.77	14
Lesotho	1.77	3

(c) Men's jumps:

1	2	3
S. Africa	5.73	127
Namibia	5.41	6
Kenya	**4.69**	**50**
Senegal	2.37	34
Algeria	2.07	34
Tunisia	2.07	11

(d) Men's throws:

1	2	3
S.Africa	5.62	108
Kenya	**3.81**	**53**
Namibia	3.08	3
Algeria	1.81	26
Algeria	1.81	26
Marocco	1.63	23
Senegal	1.63	7

(e) Women's sprints:

1	2	3
S. Africa	7.34	203
Senegal	2.40	14
Kenya	**2.02**	**41**
Cameroon	1.90	18
Morocco	1.39	27
Zimbabwe	1.39	2
Namibia	1.39	2

(f) Women's distances:

1	2	3
S. Africa	6.67	170
Kenya	**5.04**	**93**
Morocco	2.72	49
Tunisia	1.63	9
Namibia	1.50	2
Zimbabwe	1.36	10
Rwanda	1.36	7

(g) Women's jumps:

1	2	3
Namibia	12.75	10
S. Africa	7.15	112
Tunisia	4.56	11
Botswana	6.93	4
Tunisia	2.68	10
Senegal	2.46	8
Gambia	2.46	1
Kenya	**2.23**	**25**
Cameroon	2.23	12

(h) Women's throws:

1	2	3
S. Africa	7.99	143
Tunisia	3.51	15
Namibia	3.31	3
Kenya	**2.73**	**35**
Morocco	2.34	30
Ghana	0.97	8
Madagascar	0.97	6
Cameroon	0.97	6

1: Country; 2: Per capita index (African norm = 1.00); 3: Absolute 'output', i.e. number of rankings.

Kenya in the global arena

Rather than look at 'African-class' athletes, what is Kenya's position in Africa if 'world-class' athletes (that is, those in the top 100 in the world in any of the Olympic events) are considered? And how does Kenya rate in a global context? Table 2.2 showed that, in 1992, Africa as a whole produced world-class athletes at about the world per capita norm, the African per capita index being 1.06.[25] By comparison the index for Kenya was 6.03. Only five other African nations produced world-class athletes at above the global average and none of those began to reach the level of output achieved by Kenya (Figure 2.6). The next highest producer was South Africa with an index of 2.54. While South Africa outproduced Kenya in the production of African-class athletes, the situation was reversed when world-class athletes were considered. As noted earlier, however, African athletic output was highly gendered. The African per capita index for men was 1.52 while that for women was only 0.84. For Kenya, output of male athletes was 9.79 times the global per capita norm while the respective index for women athletes was only 1.52 (Figures 2.7 and 2.8). Indeed, South Africa was the major African per capita producer of superior women athletes with an index of 2.84.

African athletic regions

At this stage we make a minor digression. It should be clear from Figures 2.3–2.8 that the distribution of national producers of athletic talent is not randomly distributed across the African continent. Although the number of countries with world-class athletes is markedly less than that with athletes of African class, the broad distribution is basically the same. There appears to be a regional pattern, best illustrated perhaps in Figure 2.6. Regions may be defined as contiguous areas (in this case nations) which share a particular distinguishing feature, in this case the presence of world class athletes. It is clear that there are three 'regions' of athletic productivity in Africa. First, the three north African countries of Algeria, Morocco and Tunisia, though the latter is an extremely modest producer; secondly, a semi-contiguous string of west African coastal states, dominated by Senegal; and thirdly and most clearly, a large block of eastern and southern African states stretching unbroken from Ethiopia to South Africa and Namibia. Although each of the countries in this block produces some world class athletes, the region is clearly dominated by Kenya and South Africa. We note this east African bloc because it presents Kenya as part of what appears to be an 'athletics region' and not an isolated giant of athletic productivity among a sea of non-producers. Indeed, we should reiterate that Kenya is not the major continental 'producer' of either African- or world-class women athletes.

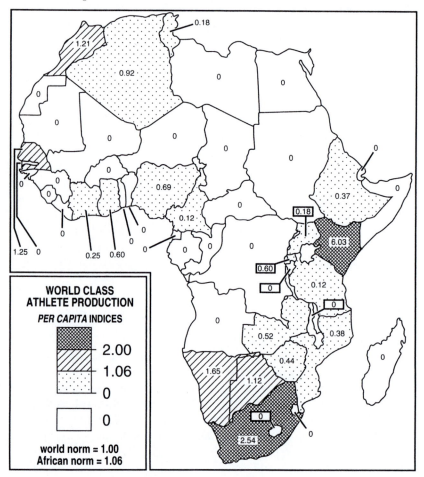

Figure 2.6. Per capita variations in output of world-class athletes, 1992.

Kenya in a world of sport

We should not become too impressed by Kenya's level of athletic productivity. In order to place these African statistics in some kind of intercontinental perspective it might be worth noting that, at the peak of its international success, the former East Germany was producing superior athletes at 22.04 times the global average. Many countries continue to have a much higher level of per capita output than Kenya, with its index of 6.03 (see below). So Kenya *is* an impressive producer of world class athletes – especially male athletes – but its production needs to be seen in its correct perspective.

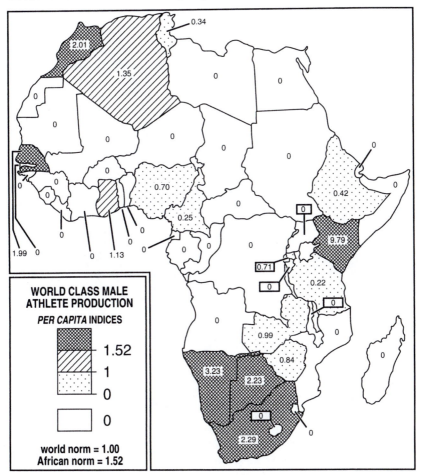

Figure 2.7. Per capita variations in output of world-class male athletes, 1992.

The world map of overall superior athletic production is shown as Figure 2.9. This is a cartogram in which the countries are drawn in proportion to the number of world class athletes they produced in 1992; the shading of each country indicates its per capita output. A comparison with a conventional map will show that some of the world's largest

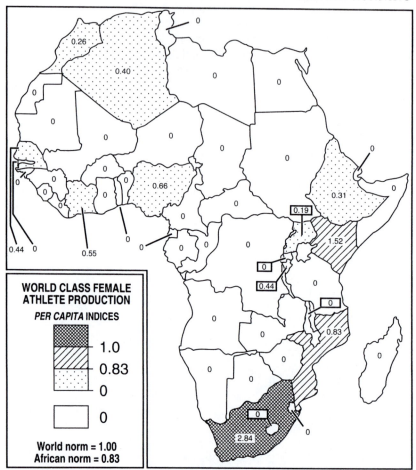

Figure 2.8. Per capita variations in output of world-class female athletes, 1992.

countries are insignificant or even absent in 'track and field space'. The
imbalance in global production is immediately apparent. Latin America is
a minor appendage of its northern neighbour; India is a tiny 'athletic
space' to the south-east of China; Pakistan, Indonesia and Egypt, three of
the world's largest countries, are absent from the map altogether. The
world of 'track and field space' appears top-heavy; it is almost a surrogate
of the more conventional economic 'north–south divide'. Although
several of the major producers are small countries (for example, Iceland
with a per capita index of 48.26, Bermuda with 50.60, and Bahamas with
83.82), small nation status does not guarantee a high index. Many small
states, like several of the giant nations, are absent from our map. Of

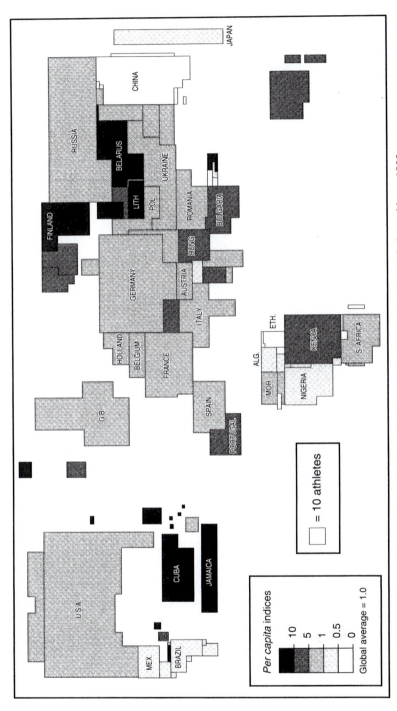

Figure 2.9. Kenya in world track and field space. A world map of the 'production' of world-class athletes, 1992.

countries with over 5 million people, the highest per capita producers of world class athletes in 1992 were Finland (21.81), Belarus (12.03) and Cuba (10.41) although each of these forms a part of broader regions of high per capita production. Equally apparent, however, is the contribution that Kenya makes to the athletic map of Africa.

Kenyan athletic output may be diversified by African standards but appears specialised by world standards. If superior athletes of world, rather than African, class are considered, Kenya's emphasis on running, at the expense of the jumping and throwing events, becomes immediately obvious. In recent decades Kenya has not produced any world-class field event athletes. In 1988 72 per cent of Kenya's world-class athletes were distance runners but in Cuba's case (for example) the talent was distributed among the throws (34 per cent), the sprints (34 per cent), and the jumps (31 per cent). Kenya's 1992 specialisation index for male output was 42.23; for women athletes the respective figure was 60.09. Easily the most diversified nation in Africa was South Africa with respective indices of 33.25 and 30.43. We should avoid any environmental or economic determinism in explaining Kenya's high level of specialisation. Other so-called 'Third World' countries, particularly Cuba, as noted above, have shown that it is possible to create a diversified squad of world class athletes, spread across the range of track and field events. In 1992 Cuba's specialisation indices were 34.89 (men) and 33.53 (women). The Kenyan, South African and Cuban indices should, however, be compared with those of France (26.45 and 28.20) and USA (26.43 and 27.27) in order to put their respective specialisation scores in perspective. Having said this, there can be little doubt that Kenyan athletes are highly visible at Olympic Games and world championship events. The purpose served by such visibility is the subject of the following sections.

(Re)presenting the nation

We have now established Kenya's place in the world of track and field, using the methods of sport itself, that is, numbers and statistics. But does Kenyan athletics have implications for the people of Kenya beyond the realm of sport? Is the relative prominence of Kenyan track and field of political relevance?

Sport and place bonding

A representational sport 'is one in which the athlete realizes he [sic] represents his town, state, or country, and the spectators feel that the athlete is representing them against another group'.[26] It can be argued that, apart from war, no other form of bonding serves to unite a nation better than representational sports and nowhere is the sport-place bond more graphically illustrated than in the Olympic Games.

It is widely felt that, through representational sport, psychic income can accrue to individuals and the nation as a whole. People feel good when 'their' athletes win; they feel proud to be associated with them through shared nationhood. Place bonding through sports is, of course, tutored by business, politicians, the Olympic movement, and governments and is therefore ideological. By 'ideology' we mean 'partial or "biased" truth'.[27] It is often thought of as a 'taken for granted' view. It may, nevertheless, facilitate the pursuit of particular interests.

Bonding disparate groups through allegiance to a national team occurs by placing an emphasis on national pride, 'national identity' or nationalism – that is, a feeling of belonging to a nation. This is particularly important in 'states' possessing various 'nations' or in countries which are not ethnically homogeneous. Kenya is a good example of a heterogeneous state, various ethnic groups existing in its boundaries (Figure 2.10). In terms of population the main ethnic groups, as shown in the 1989 census, were the Kikuyu (20.8 per cent), the Luhya (14.3 per cent), the Luo (12.3 per cent), and the Kamba and the Kalenjin (each 11.4 per cent). No other group had more than 10 per cent of the total population.[28] Various tribal groups have been well-publicised in various media. For example, the Kikuyu were the first tribe to become politically aware of the potential for national independence and gained much press publicity in the 1950s through their role in the political fight for Kenyan self-government. The Maasai, on the other hand, have been among the most conservative and among the least integrated into 'Western' ways of life. Despite their relatively small numbers (1.5 per cent of the population) they seem to have been disproportionately attractive to American and European media and are close to being stereotypical Kenyans. They are widely cited in school textbooks and 'popular' works on Kenya as examples of pastoralists and nomads, photographed and trivialised wearing exotic styles of dress in magazines such as the *National Geographic*.[29] In history books the Nandi (less than 2 per cent of the population) are known as the tribe which resisted imperial rule with the greatest ferocity, their resistance only being brought to an end following the assassination of their leader in 1905.[30] Nevertheless, inter-tribal tensions have long been present in Kenya and continue to exist. Antagonism towards the once politically dominant Kikuyu has resulted in much inter-tribal hostility, especially between the

Kikuyu and the Luo,[31] and currently the Kalenjin and Kikuyu. Indeed, it has been suggested that in Kenya 'there is really no concept of a nation. One is always a Kikuyu, a Luo, a Nandi, an Asian or a European'.[32]

It is, nevertheless, felt by many people, particularly those politicians wary of tribal assertiveness, that when 'Kenya' does well in what is arguably the most visible of popular cultural forms (namely sport), tribal differences temporarily disappear. President Arap Moi himself recognised this when, in a 1987 speech he noted that 'sport is one factor that unifies all people regardless of their race, tribe, ethnicity or denomination'.[33] This was hardly surprising in a one-party state where political opposition had been banned and where inter-tribal tensions existed and continue to be potentially divisive. When athletes from different tribal backgrounds each compete with the word 'Kenya' on their chests, a diffuse collection of ethnic groups becomes, for a time and for some people, an 'imagined community'.[34] This is not to ignore the fact that sport, as a demonstration of some kind of national expression, may be declining in significance as its homogenisation and internationalisation proceeds into the twenty-first century. We return to this theme in the final chapter.

Media coverage of national sports success assists the establishment of national identity. The nation is held together, therefore, 'by people's strong united desires, hopes and expressions of delight' in their country's success in sports. The same thing happens in 'defeat which awakens the lust for revenge'.[35] At the same time, however, sport can serve to bond and enforce attachment to units other than the national. The local and tribal connections can be strengthened by the very medium which also serves to bond the nation. Among the Nandi tribe (one member of which is Kipchoge Keino), songs which praise courage and bravery are sung during initiation ceremonies. Traditional and newly composed songs are included. Consider for example, the following which was sung in the late 1960s and early 1970s:

> *Laleyo laleyo laleyo laleyo*
> See Kipchoge the man
> Who runs for his country Kenya.
> Kipchoge, the man Kipchoge,
> Who runs for Kenya ...
> [repeated continuously].[36]

Keino is seen as a symbol, of *Nandi*, as well as of Kenyan manhood. The contents of the song reflect not only the Nandi acceptance of change (modern track running) but also what it means to be Nandi. The song's

Figure 2.10. Provincial boundaries and ethnic groups in Kenya (after Ochieng, 1990, p.i).

contents also show how allusions to modern sports can feed into traditional cultures.

International success in sport may not only create national pride and 'psychic income' but may also be used to show people at home and abroad that a Kenyan model of athletic development is working successfully. Jomo Kenyatta drew the parallel between many forms of self help (*Harambee*) in the economic and social world with self help in athletics. He observed that 'we want to show that our model of Harambee can be applied to sport, that people of all creeds and colours can pull together. We want Kenya to be an example to the rest of the world'.[37] The extent to which the Kenyan model, if it can be so called, has worked can be inferred from our quantitative analyses earlier in this chapter and will be reconsidered in Chapter 7.

Place boosting and sport

Athletes do not represent themselves in major sporting festivals such as the Olympics; they are officially selected by national committees and parade in national colours and other means of national identification. If they achieve the status of an Olympic medalist, their national flags and (for gold medalists) and national anthems are projected to the rest of the world. Here, national symbolism is 'over explicit'.[38] Countries vie with each other for a position on the unofficial Olympic medal table. These international festivals are not random events; they are regular and periodised, hence providing the opportunity to plan for the 'production' of results at preordained times and places. International sports success projects a nation to the world beyond its boundaries. The historian of sport, Richard Mandell, has gone so far as to suggest that the prowess of Kenya's élite runners has generally strengthened black self-confidence the world over. In addition they have 'boosted their country's international prestige, diplomatic standing, and very likely its political stability as well'.[39] It has also been noted that during its short history as an independent nation state 'international athletic competition has thrust this young country into the world limelight more than any other single factor'.[40] This latter view perhaps verges on hyperbole but the significance of sport in the projection of positive national images should not be underestimated.

The images which African countries have in the occidental world is generally communicated through their most visible representatives. For most countries these representatives are politicians – Qadaffi from Libya, or Mandela from South Africa, for example. In Kenya's case its most visible representatives in the global arena tend to be athletes, not politicians. Though football is more important than athletics in Kenya, it is through Kenya's runners that the country is most well known overseas. The fact that they are athletes rather than politicians may benefit Kenya if it is true that we assign characteristics to foreign people as reflected by the acts of their representatives.[41] Kenyan athletes have a clean image. They are not, to any significant extent, associated with drug scandals and are rarely the focus of interviews by the English language media. Their running speaks for them.

International visibility is especially important in nations for whom prominence in events of global newsworthiness are few and far between. In the global media the countries of Africa are all too often associated with negative images – drought, war, disease, famine, natural disasters. National success in sport can create a more positive image and is therefore highly prized. Images can contribute to attitudes and behaviour in relation to a country. Placed in the context of the Olympic or Commonwealth Games, the communication of national icons such as flags, uniforms and anthems is a major slice of free advertising.

But good publicity is not inevitably the outcome of athletic success. The visibility afforded to Kenyan athletes may be contrasted with that afforded, for example, to the former German Democratic Republic. In the case of the latter, success and media visibility did not necessarily lead to a positive response from consumers of the world media. Instead, metaphors such as the East German sports 'machine' communicated an image of cynical, drug-induced and state-controlled automatons. In contrast, the Kenyan image often appears to be 'naturalised' and 'eternalised'. By this we mean that the images of Kenya's athletes, tutored of course by the media (see Chapter 1), are similar to Africans in other sports, tending to be projected as possessing 'natural' characteristics of the mythologised African – in this case, uninhibited, naive, impetuous. Such characteristics are the 'eternal' or 'typical personality' of the African; 'running wild', 'out of Africa' – attributes 'whose existence works to obliterate material conditions and material change'.[42]

How visible internationally is Kenyan athletics? We can begin to answer this question by considering the results of two (rather unscientific) surveys. The first was administered in Finland in 1994 and included 25 students of sport who were asked to write down the words that came into their heads when Kenya was mentioned. Sixty-seven per cent mentioned 'running', easily the most frequently mentioned word associated with the country. This was slightly more than the percentage identifying Brazil with football and twice as many as that associating Sweden with ice hockey. The second survey involved 33 British geography students. Of these, only 9 per cent associated Kenya with running, though 45 per cent linked Brazil with football. We tentatively conclude, therefore, that Kenya is highly visible as an athletics nation among those members of the public with a serious interest in sports but not so among the broader public. For them Brazil has a much stronger image of football while Kenya's running image is rather weak.

Nor should we overstate the significance of athletics to Kenyans themselves. In the mid-1970s field work by Dirk Berg-Schlosser revealed that 'social and economic achievements' (which would, we assume, include sporting achievements) by Kenyans were mentioned by only 21 per cent of Kenyan respondents to his survey of what made them feel proud of Kenya; 27 per cent responded 'nothing'.[43] And let us remember that athletics is by no means the most popular sport in Kenya. In this respect it is far outstripped by football with team games being strongly favoured by students in the nation's schools.[44]

Conclusion

In this chapter we have explored three broad themes which form the basis of the rest of this book. First, we considered what sort of running, throwing and jumping we are focusing on but stressed that achievement sport was not the only possible form of such movement cultures in modernity. Second, we considered ways in which the national athletic 'success' or 'output' of different nations could be quantified. Of course, quantitative measures are not the only ways of assessing competitive sport but by using the most 'objective' indicators available we identified Kenya as the foremost African nation in terms of its ability to produce world-class (though not African-class) athletes. Performance may be as valid a criterion as results but in the modern age the latter are generally given prominence. Finally, we considered the way in which track and field is important for the status of Kenya on the continental and global athletic stage and outlined the importance of such status in terms of intra-national bonding on the one hand and international visibility on the other. Having cleared this empirical and conceptual ground it is now appropriate to spend the next three chapters tracing the emergence of Kenyan athletics.

Notes and references

1. Galtung, 'Sport as a carrier of deep culture and structure'.
2. Ibid, p. 14.
3. Ibid.
4. Gibson, *Performance Versus Results: a Critique of Values in Contemporary Sport.*
5. Eichberg, 'Body culture as paradigm: the Danish sociology of sport'. For an excellent overview of body culture also see Brownell, *Training the Body for China*, pp. 8–21.
6. Eichberg, 'Body culture as paradigm: the Danish sociology of sport'. A temporal

dimension is added to the trialectic, in a Tanzanian context, in Larsen and Gormsen, *Bodyculture*. Other important papers by Eichberg which focus mainly on running include 'Stronger, funnier, deadlier' and 'Forward race and the laughter of pygmies'.

7. Eichberg, 'Olympic sport – neo colonialism and alternatives'.
8. Rohé, *The Zen of Running*.
9. Gibson, *Performance Versus Results: a Critique of Values in Contemporary Sport*.
10. Eichberg, 'The societal construction of time and space as sociology's way home to philosophy. Sport as paradigm'.
11. Buchanan, *Reflections on Education in the Third World*.
12. Gibson, *Performance versus Results: a Critique of Values in Contemporary Sport*.
13. For a review of these approaches see Bale, 'Towards a geography of international sport'.
14. Jokl, *Medical Sociology and Cultural Anthropology of Sport and Physical Education*.
15. Ibid.
16. Ibid. The formula used in calculating the points for a given nation is:

$$P = 100(1 - \log x/\log n)$$

where P is the number of points, x is the placing of an athlete or team, and n is the number of contestants in an event.
17. See Bale, 'Towards a geography of international sport'.
18. Shaw and Pooley, 'National success at the Olympics: an explanation'.
19. Quoted in *Track and Field News*, 10 (7) (1957), p. 2.
20. This approach was adopted in the seminal sports-geographic study by Rooney, *A Geography of American Sport*. The formula used here, and repeated in many other studies, is:

$$I = (N/P) \times (A/1)$$

where N is the number of athletes from a given country, P is the population of that country, and A is the total number of people per athlete in the overall area (world, continent, etc.) being considered.
21. The formula used for the index of specialisation is:

$$I = \sqrt{a^2 + b^2 + c^2 + \ldots n^2}$$

where a, b, c, ... n are the percentages of a nation's athletes in each track and field event. The highest value is always 100, indicating maximum specialisation (in other words, all athletes in one event). The lowest value, indicating the maximum diversification, depends on the number of events. In track and field athletics a nation with an index of less than 30 can be regarded as very diversified.
22. Spurr, *The Rhetoric of Empire*, pp. 35–6.
23. Magnusson, 'Rätt och fel'. From a statistical point of view it could be suggested that the ATFS lists, being ranked data, are not normally distributed. However, it has been argued that they do fall within the definition of a random variable and that they do constitute 'a representative sample of a population of top class athletes': see Furlong and Szreter, 'The trend of the performance differential between leading men and women athletes' (we are grateful to Andrew Huxtable for this reference).
24. By 'African class' we mean those athletes who achieve a performance capable of

inclusion in the 'African top 100' in any event in a given year (in some events the number of athletes ranked is less than 100). The African data are similar to those published by the ATFS: see Abmayr and Pinaud, *L'Athlétisme Africain '94*. For a map of the situation in 1984 see Bale and Sang, 'Out of Africa'.

25. The respective index for the United Kingdom was 4.62: Heikki Herva, unpublished data, Department of Social Science of Sports, University of Jyväskylä, 1994.
26. Gibson, *Performance Versus Results*, p. 37.
27. Peet, *Global Capitalism*, p. 9. On sport as an 'ideological state apparatus' see Brohm, *Sport: A Prison of Measured Time*, especially pp. 138–62.
28. We are grateful to Anders Närman (University of Gothenburg) for this information.
29. Lutz and Collins, *Reading National Geographic*. Note also Rothenberg, 'Voyeurs of Imperialism', and Spurr, *The Rhetoric of Empire*, pp. 49–52.
30. Meinertzhagen, *Kenya Diary*.
31. Monnington, 'The politics of black African sport'.
32. Thiong'o, *Homecoming*, p. 23.
33. Quoted in Godia, 'Sport in Kenya'.
34. Anderson, *Imagined Communities*.
35. Ehn, 'National feeling in sport'. We are grateful to Niels Kayser Nielsen (University of Odense) for this reference.
36. Langley, *The Nandi of Kenya: Life Crisis in a Period of Change*, p. 51.
37. Quoted in Noronha, *Kipchoge of Kenya*, p. 47.
38. Ehn, 'National feeling in sport'.
39. Mandell, *Sport: A Cultural History*, p. 269.
40. Hall, *The Role of Physical Education and Sport in the Nation Building of Kenya*, p. 224.
41. Buchanan and Cantril, *How Nations See Each Other*.
42. Blain, Boyle and O'Donnell, *Sport and National Identity in the European Media*, p. 11; note also pp. 71–6 for a brilliant analysis of European press coverage of African footballers.
43. Berg-Schlosser, *Tradition and Change in Kenya*, p. 204.
44. Mählmann, 'Perception of sport in Kenya', p. 128.

3

Antecedents of Kenyan Sport

There is a crucial difference between the primitive who carves
out an existence on the wind-swept plains and the athlete who
tests himself on the artificial surface of the stadium.

JOHN HOBERMAN, *Mortal Engines*

In the following three chapters we trace the changes which have taken
place in the character of movement culture in Kenya, from the traditions
of tribal folk activities to those of globalised modern sport. We start with
a view of the kind of movement cultures which characterised the region
of Africa which is today Kenya in what might loosely be called the pre-
modern period – that is, prior to European invasion and colonisation.

What configurations were found in the movement cultures of
running, jumping and throwing – the basic bodily movements which
today make up the repertoire of track and field events – before the
introduction of modern sport? No written records exist of movement
culture in Kenya from the pre-European period. We must, therefore,
assume that the forms observed by the early twentieth century
imperialists and travel writers were similar to those of earlier times. On
the basis of their observations, two or three basic types can be
recognised. First, some body cultures would have been associated with
the world of work. Running and throwing would have been required for
hunting, fighting and defence; that is, utilitarian uses of the body (Figure
3.1). In addition, such bodily activities would have been associated with
certain rituals such as rites of passage and their related initiation
ceremonies. In such cases running and jumping were often integrated in
the form of dance. Thirdly, a wide variety of physical games existed
which involved throwing, jumping and running. While these would have
been performed in a spirit of play, joy and adventure, they would also
have implicitly assisted in training for fighting and self-defence and
hence could be regarded as partly utilitarian.

The movement cultures of pre-modern Kenya (sometimes called
'traditional sports') can be viewed as being fundamentally different
from modern sports in a number of important respects. First of all, they

were not bureaucratised in the way that modern sports are. They were also not standardised with various groups practising different forms of the same basic bodily movements (namely running and jumping); and they did not possess records or record orientation (in the modern sense, though anecdotes may have 'recorded' outstanding physical feats while point-scoring games involved the 'recording' of scores).[1] We have used the past tense with respect to these folk activities. Strictly speaking we are wrong to do so but where such activities remain today they have all too often been transformed into living museums or have adopted the values of modern sport.

Figure 3.1. Running and throwing were skills which came together in the activities of the Maasai soldier. This image from *Through Masai Land*, by the geographer and traveller Joseph Thomson, emphasises the individual warrior rather than an organised group of soldiers. Its original caption read 'On the war path in Masai land' (source: Thomson, 1885).

It is sometimes believed that, in tribal societies such as those found in Kenya, competitive physical games were absent before the coming of the imperialists and that cooperation was more significant than competition. Such a view is supported in the case of some African societies such as the !Kung San of the Kalahari.[2] Here physical games were present but the competitive element was virtually non-existent.

In the case of pre-modern Kenya, it is impossible to be so adamant about the absence of 'sport-like' activities. This is in spite of the fact that while studying the Kamba, south of Mount Kenya in 1910–12, the Swedish visitor Gerhard Lindblom noted that despite the presence of various dances and competitive games there were 'no real sports' found there.[3] Likewise, twenty years after Lindblom had published his report, the sports scientist Ernst Jokl noted that 'it is a peculiar fact that primitive people [sic], e.g. the numerous aboriginal races of the African continent, do not indulge in athletic exercises such as hurdling, high jump, long jump, pole vault, shot put and javelin throwing'.[4] In each case we observe the familiar rhetorical strategy of traditional colonialist writing, that of negation – the occident conceiving the other as absence or nothingness. It is a projection onto athletics of the vast 'emptiness' of Africa itself.[5]

We are charitable enough to interpret Jokl's use of the word 'peculiar' as meaning 'particular' rather than 'odd' but, whatever attribution we give, his statement is simply incorrect. Of course, such events, in their European sportised form, would hardly have existed in Africa, just as African movement cultures would not have been found in Britain or Germany. Observers such as Lindblom and Jokl (and many other Europeans mentioned in subsequent pages) failed to recognise the values of the societies at which they were looking. They imposed a Western thought process on the African body and, as we will show, reflected the modernist need to impose order on the African's physicality.

In fact, pre-modern Kenya did possess many forms of movement culture which *were* physical and competitive – and some were not so different from those in Jokl's list. Indeed, skills in hunting (running and spear throwing) have been interpreted as 'an early version of competition and of a quest for glory' in many African societies.[6] In some Kenyan tribal societies titles were given to portray a person's particular physical skill. For example, *Barng'etuny* was the name given to skilled members of the Nandi tribe who had succeeded in killing a lion. For some physical games, measurements were made and victory was given considerable significance. Prizes were awarded, high performances were demanded, and, to an extent, planned physical training was required.[7]

Pre-colonial Kenya possessed many folk-games which included events analogous to today's sports. While not lacking in physical competitiveness they did possess different ideological bases from those found underpinning modern athletics. Did these indigenous movement cultures provide the athletic soil into which the seeds of British sports

would be later planted? Or was the adoption of modern sport unrelatèd
to pre-existing customs? Here we are faced with the traditional historical
problem – that of continuity or change. This question cannot be
categorically answered here, but in the pages which follow we will show
that the idea of a pre-modern inheritance, from which success in modern
sport has been derived, cannot be taken for granted.

Running and the colonial image

In volume 13 of his monumental *The Universal Geography*, the
nineteenth-century French geographer, Elisée Reclus, noted that 'the
men of pure Masai blood average six feet high, and generally have slim,
wiry figures, admirable for running'.[8] The linking of the Maasai with
running was commonly found in travel writing about east Africa during
the early decades of the twentieth century. Other observers commented,
in a typically self-effacing way, that 'the whole race [*sic*] is proficient in
speedy and long distance running'[9] while in a description of a Maasai
shepherd it was noted that 'his gait, as he strides, is an example of what
human carriage can be at its best'.[10] Another observer noted that the
Maasai 'are extraordinarily fleet of foot, and can run without tiring for
incredible distances. Their usual pace is a long, sloping trot.'[11]
Sometimes an element of inter-racial homo-eroticism could barely be
disguised in descriptions of their grace and vitality. Hence 'the warriors,
burnished with grease and scantily draped in the skins of animals, have,
almost to a man, the graceful carriage of athletes'.[12]

To these lyrical, idealised, and sentimental judgments can be added the
European desire to objectify, quantify and compare performance, reflected
in its most simple form in an observation from 1912: 'the Maasai runner
thinks no more of carrying a message sixty miles a day than we should a
three mile stroll'.[13] It is not clear whether the 'sixty miles' should be taken
literally or whether it is a reflection of nineteenth-century Darwinism
which romanticised 'human potential while tracing its sources to a
primeval vitality which the white race cannot hope to match'.[14]

Among the most detailed descriptions of Maasai running is that
found in Ernest Hemingway's *Green Hills of Africa* which is mainly
concerned with his big-game hunting exploits in Kenya in the early
1930s. He describes how on one occasion he stopped his car at a Maasai
village and was immediately surrounded by

> long-legged, brown, smooth-moving men ... They were the tallest,
> best-built, handsomest people I had ever seen. ... Finally, when we
> were moving, they started to run beside the car smiling and

laughing and showing how easily they could run and then, as the going was better, up the smooth valley of a stream, it became a contest and one after another dropped out of the running, waving and smiling as they left until there were only two still running with us, the finest runners of the lot, who kept pace easily with the car as they moved long-legged smoothly, loosely, and with pride. They were running too, *at the pace of a fast miler*, and carrying their spears as well. ... [A]s we slowed, climbing in first gear, the whole pack came up again, laughing and trying not to seem winded. We went through a little knot of bush and a small rabbit started out, zigzagging wildly and all the Masai behind now in a mad sprint. They caught the rabbit and the tallest runner came up with him to the car and handed him to me.[15]

Although the distance run was not specified, and Hemingway's view of what a 'fast miler' was cannot be ascertained, the stamina and speed of the Maasai runners obviously impressed him. This was written when sportised running was beginning to become established in Kenya, as the next chapter will show. Clearly overlapping with it, however, was the pre-sportised running which Hemingway describes.

It appears that many European writers were particularly fascinated by the Maasai who seem to have been paid a disproportionate amount of attention, given their relatively small percentage of the total Kenyan population. Running as a Maasai phenomenon seems to have been highlighted by a sufficiently large number of observers to indicate that it was beyond the ordinary. This may have accurately reflected the athletic presence of the Maasai athlete; but it may also have been part of a wider submission of Europeans to what was termed 'Maasai-itis'. Some officials became so enamoured by the Arcadian ways of Maasai life that they lost their effectiveness as administrators.[16] We cannot begin to speculate about how many European officials 'went native' and participated in the African athleticism and physicality that they apparently so admired.

Although it may have been the Maasai's 'cult of physique' which made them so well known throughout the world,[17] allusions to the stamina of other tribes are far from absent and the Maasai, therefore, should not be singled out. A District Commissioner, St John Orde Browne, undertook work among the Meru in 1909–16 and recorded that as runners, though not particularly fast, the Meru were capable of travelling 'enormous distances'. The district commissioners used runners as messengers and on one occasion it was recorded (again in basic quantitative form) that Orde Browne's 'favourite runner' left with a message at 6 p.m. and arrived back with a reply at 10 o'clock the following night having covered a distance of 92 miles including fairly hilly country, darkness, and risk from wild animals.[18] Even assuming that some rest period was taken, this seems a perfectly plausible claim. In 1919 it was again recorded that the African – this time the Turkana ('a well-made race, and capable of great exertion') – 'thinks nothing of walking fifty or sixty miles in one day'.[19] According to A.T. Matson the Nandi had a tradition of being 'agile, athletic, and able to travel long distances without fatigue: when marching, hunting and raiding, they exhibit considerable powers of endurance and great reserves of strength'. Yet such comments do not seem consistent with his additional observation that they lacked 'stamina for sustained work' and showed 'no pronounced muscular development', lacking 'the physical strength for heavy manual labour'.[20] It seems, therefore, that the European eulogy of the African's running capabilities may have been not only exaggerated but also ambivalent.

The emphasis on the quality of the African's running (and, as we will show, jumping and throwing) seems to reflect a propensity to elevate the black man's athletic stamina and prowess, in much the same way as the Europeans had exaggerated his 'sensual staying power'.[21] All this amounts to what might be called 'Africanism'. This is analogous to Edward Said's notion of 'orientalism' and may be defined as a style of thought based on a distinction made between the 'African' and the 'occidental'.[22] It can also be seen as a Western way of dominating, restructuring and having authority over the African – by speaking for the African. In our context it produces the undifferentiated type called 'Kenyan'. Put another way, what we encounter here is what is known (notably in post-colonial studies) as 'othering'. This is an 'I–not-I' dualism which invariably creates a hierarchy and a power relationship. It is described by Mary Louise Pratt as follows:

> The people to be 'othered' are homogenized into a collective 'they', which is distilled further into an iconic 'he' (the standardized adult male specimen). This abstracted 'he'/'they' is the subject of verbs in a timeless present tense, which characterizes anything 'he' is or does not as a particular historical event but as an instance of a pregiven custom or trait.[23]

We have noted the centrality of the *athletic body* in much colonial writing about Kenya. In early twentieth-century travel writing, but also in more modern histories of sports, Africans, Kenyans, Maasai or Kalenjin are homogenised (or 'averaged'), often depicted as having fantastic strength and/or stamina. The 'eternal African' is normalised as a super athlete, though often in terms of 'brute strength'.

Such views were, however, often accompanied by a more ambivalent and overlapping perspective, exemplified in Matson's reference (above) to both the presence of athleticism and the absence of physical strength in the Nandi. This typifies a broader and more general colonial ambivalence towards the African *per se*. Seen as part of nature, the African body has been treated in the same way as much colonial writing treated nature: that is, imbued with different values depending on the particular function of colonial discourse. As David Spurr notes, 'the concept of nature must be available as a term that shifts in meaning, for example, by idealizing or degrading the savage, according as the need arises at differing moments in the colonial situation.'[24] Although much early twentieth-century travel writing tended to eulogise the Kenyan's impressive physicality, the negative side was reflected in the views of many missionaries and, later, those of athletic coaches and other observers of the athletics scene. We have noted that the African's running and stamina were often praised, but it was also widely believed, for example, that the 'negro' was incapable of success at long-distance running (see Chapter 6).

Various forms of running and racing did exist in pre-modern Kenya prior to the colonialists' use of natives as messengers. Such exercise acted as a basis for stamina building and physical exercise. In the case of several ethnic groups, the Kalenjin and the Maasai for example, running also served a utilitarian function; it was needed for herding as well for warriors carrying out cattle raids which required travelling over long distances. Traditions of cattle rustling formed an important part of the culture of tribes such as the Maasai, Kalenjin, Turkana and Kuria, being a major element of the tribal economy. But it was more than that; commenting in 1959, a Provincial Commissioner noted that 'stock theft is the traditional sport of the young men of many tribes'.[25] In the case of the Nandi, raiding was not regarded as theft (unless it was from a member of the same tribe) but a routine occupation which was part of their everyday lives. At the same time no warrior was worthy of the name unless he distinguished himself in one of the raids. 'Distance and natural barriers' were not insuperable difficulties, for it did 'not take the Nandi long to travel twenty miles'.[26] However, the raids may have involved travelling about one hundred miles; if so, physical fitness was obviously essential.[27] In the case of the Nandi the main reasons for fighting were cattle and sport. The group being raided was not disrupted; the acquisition of human beings was not an objective. It has been noted that for the Nandi 'war was a form of sport, the only kind on a large scale that they understood, which gave them something real and exciting to live for, and underlay the other reasons for warfare'.[28] In the case of the

Maasai, an aggressive pastoral tribe, war, sport and cattle were inseparable parts of political and economic life. Physical fitness for pastoral people did not generally require special training although in times of war restrictions on drinking beer may have been enforced.[29]

A highly competitive form of running was found among the Kikuyu. During initiation ceremonies related to the circumcision of teenage boys, a competitive race was held over a distance of about two miles (3,200 metres). This served the purpose of selecting a leader of the age group being initiated. In referring to ceremonies during the 1920s and 1930s, Jomo Kenyatta noted that:

> at the start of the race a ceremonial horn is blown ... The boys start running ... it is really considered a sort of fight between the spirit of childhood and that of adulthood ... the one who reaches the tree first and throws the wooden spear over the tree is elected ... as the leader and spokesman of the age group for life.[30]

Notice how a tree, a natural feature of the landscape, was integral to this race, in contrast to the synthetic, and/or accurately measured landscapes and prescribed time periods over which modern foot racing invariably occurs. Notice also the seriousness attached to this running event; to see it as part of a culture of laughter (something sometimes inferred as a characteristic of pre-modern movement cultures) would be clearly erroneous.

Status enhancement was the principal outcome of such a race and had much symbolic value to Kikuyu society. Any competitor falling over during the race was rendered ceremonially unclean and had to be symbolically purified before he could take part in the circumcision operation. Such competitions acted as a means of establishing status within the society and creating stability as a result of peers not having to fight among themselves to find a leader.

Among other racing activities, Kamba boys competed in walking on their hands as far as possible.[31] Meru children, on the other hand, took part in a game called *Kururania Kavuno* which involved a considerable amount of running. This was similar to the Embu *Kugwatania Kavuno* and was a popular sport-like activity played in the evenings. Its aim was for players to outwit each other by speed and agility, by making sure that they were not touched by another player. It involved two players at a time and the one who was touched last during an evening's game carried what was termed the 'laziness' over to the following day.[32] The game symbolised the fact that the community did not like laziness and hence had to get rid of it.

Most emphasis has been given here to long distance running. This is not to say that sprinting was absent from Kenyan body culture. It was, however, most usually integrated into dances which often involved much fast running. In a Kikuyu dance, for example, a 'course was cleared, and the performance began by two performers running at full speed down its length', to be followed by leaping and jumping of various kinds. The *kibuiyu* dance was a 'rough and tumble affair'. Taking between two and ten minutes, two competitors raced around a square and back to their original positions. Each athlete had to prevent his opponent from doing so by almost any means within his power.[33]

The forms of running which have been described above probably had their counterparts in many tribal groups the world over. It would therefore be unwise to suggest that such running customs have placed present-day Kenyans at any particular advantage over athletes from other countries with similar pre-modern traditions. Indeed the tribal group which seemed, through European eyes at least, to have had the best reputation for running, (that is, the Maasai) has not been especially prominent in 'producing' world class runners in modern times. The Nandi, on the other hand, also mentioned above, have been renowned for a long line of great distance runners, a subject to which we shall return in Chapter 6.

Throwing

Games which involved throwing at a target reflected a society in which hunting and military activities were of central importance. Throwing activities were used to train marksmanship in a number of ethnic groups. Among the Kikuyu and Meru, teams of boys divided themselves into groups and armed themselves with an apparatus for 'shooting'. This device was a long, thin stick which was either forked or sharpened at one end. The object of the game was for opposing teams to try to 'shoot' down a ring which had been thrown, with considerable force, into the air. If the member of one team failed to hit the ring with three throws he had to join the other team. Such participants were known as 'brides'. The whole team could therefore be defeated by losing all its members as 'brides' to the other team. If a team had not lost all its members, the game was restarted when the ring was thrown into the air. The team whose members had been captured then had to try to snatch the ring before it was 'shot'. If they succeeded, this freed the 'brides' to run back to their original team. Once they started running, however, each team gave chase. It has been suggested that such a chase could take up to ten miles or even two days.[34] In this situation we observe a typical characteristic of pre-modern movement culture, that is, the lack of specialisation within a particular activity. Was this a throwing or running event? It was, of course, both; it was more like the modern biathlon than either modern running or throwing. It demonstrably eschewed the modern fetish of specialisation.

Figure 3.2. A 1920s view of Maasai *moran* apparently throwing for accuracy rather than distance. Note the low trajectory of the flight of the spear. What appears to be a posed representation reflects the ability of the photographer to organise and capture the scene, including the centrality of the cultural symbol of the straw-thatched hut (source: Geilinger, 1930).

Spear and club throwing was much more clearly defined. Throwing skills again provided a basis for hunting and warfare. Among the Keiyo, spear-throwing was undertaken in the form of competitions. This was done in pairs, every loser having to retire as the victor continued to challenge others until he lost. The Maasai (Figure 3.2) and the Turkana had spears of between six and ten feet long (between 1.85 metres and 3 metres compared with the modern men's javelin which is between 2.6 metres and 2.7 metres) with wooden shafts which were iron shod (see Figure 3.1). Again the European desire to *measure* and *record* performance is reflected in Juxon Barton's assessment that such Turkana spears could be thrown 210 feet (64 metres).[35] Although the spear was of an unrecorded weight this would appear to be a very creditable performance by the standards of 1920, even though it was probably measured by pacing out the distance. This was not the same, however, as throwing a modern javelin (see below).

Club-throwing was also a traditional activity and was practised until relatively recently. It was employed originally for hunting and warfare. The German adventurer, Ludwig Krapf, noted that among the Wakaufi and the Maasai a club could be hurled 'with the greatest precision'; 'at a distance of from fifty to seventy paces they can dash out the brain of an enemy'.[36] Although the degree of precision may have been exaggerated there is no doubt that strength as well as accuracy was required in reaching such a target. In the case of the Nandi, club throwing was integrated with running. One boy would throw the club as far as possible and the others would scramble and run to retrieve it. The boys always tried to outrun each other in getting the club back to the thrower. The game was still played by Nandi boys in the school holidays in the 1960s and gold medalist in the 1968 Olympic steeplechase, Amos Biwott, recalls playing it while looking after cattle in the early 1960s. Today, however, the game is virtually extinct.[37]

Throwing events are today viewed as 'strength' events. Tribal activities of a day-to-day nature involved much use of physical strength. It was the women as much as the men whose strength was regularly displayed. Allusions to the 'astonishing weight carrying feats' of women is exemplified by the case of an old woman observed to have walked 11 miles with a load of wood weighing 115 lbs.[38] Again the European desire to quantify physical performance systematically is evident, in this case both the weight and the distance covered. But the extent to which the throwing activities of pre-European Kenya can be described as 'strength events' in the modern sense is not clear. In general, however, it would seem that among the variety of throwing activities that were practised, accuracy was as important as distance.

A game involving hitting rather than throwing illustrates the 'sport-like' nature of pre-modern games. The Kamba played a competitive game using an old pot which was set up as a goal in a cleared space. This was guarded by a 'goalkeeper' with a stick. With this he tried to prevent the goal being reached by a peg which another boy struck with a stick. When the goalkeeper hit the projectile back, the distance to the position where it fell was paced out and for every ten full paces he obtained a point. When the goal was hit he had to change places with his opponent.[39] Here we see forms of measurement and point scoring (recording) being used, each of which are often regarded as eminently 'modern' characteristics. Yet in describing the games as precisely as they do, it is the difference between the African and the occidental that is emphasised.

Jumping

Jumping is integral to much traditional Kenyan dancing and has always formed an element of African movement culture. Among the Kikuyu, war and initiation dances were used in order to display physical prowess and adroitness at handling spears and shields. The routines of the dance involved proving one's ability to perform high and long jumps while handling both implements. These exercises were alleged to make the Kikuyu fit and become good runners as much as good jumpers. According to Kenyatta:

> Through these exercises, Gikuyu men become good runners and some of them can run many miles without stopping. This is important for a community which has no mechanical aid in travelling and it becomes useful in times of pursuing an enemy or dangerous animals.[40]

Among the Kamba, regarded by some as the best dancers in Africa,[41] dance took the form of gymnastics and acrobatics, dancers having to jump, somersault and balance themselves while performing. It was a form of art and entertainment and the inclusion of an element of restraint provided Kamba dancing with an aesthetic quality. Dances of a number of tribes involved much high jumping, for example in age-set meetings involving Maasai warriors (*moran*). A sport-like dimension to jumping was noted by Kenyatta when he observed that different age-sets among the Kikuyu '*competed* in dances ... as well as high and long jumps', though no further details are given.[42] Accompanying chanting and singing were often integral to such events which were held on sites which had been cleared of minor objects which would otherwise create hazards for the performers.

The implications of indigenous east African dance styles for modern high jumping have been hypothesised by Blacking. He suggests that a connection – a 'submerged continuity' – may exist between dance styles and an ability in sportised high jumping, citing the early successes of the Ugandan (and, we might add, Kenyan) high jumpers in 1950s Empire Games competitions.[43] This is an interesting hypothesis but no attempt is made to outline how the specific forms of (and skills used in) Ugandan or Kenyan dance styles make them particularly appropriate for high jumping. It is possible, however, that studies of the Kikuyu in the early years of this century shed some light on this hypothesis. They reveal that tribal dances contained two elements central to modern high jumping technique. These involved springing into the air from one foot while running at speed, and springing vertically upwards from a standing position from one foot.[44] However, we do not know if these dances survived long enough for the successful Kenyan high jumpers of the 1950s to have had any experience of them.

There is certainly no shortage of evidence of early high jumping prowess, as opposed to high jumping as an integral part of dancing, in east Africa. From the turn of the century, if not before, Europeans had known of the love of high jumping by boys of the Ankole in what is present day Uganda.[45] F. A. M. Webster (later to become a well known coach and writer on athletics) noted that while serving with the King's African Rifles in the 1910s he 'saw any number of untutored, barefooted natives who could jump anything between 6 feet [1.829 metres] and 6 feet 5 inches [1.956 metres] with the greatest ease'.[46] That such athletes could have been tutored in the skills of *some form of high jumping* does not appear to have crossed Webster's mind. It seems unlikely that the skill and coordination needed to jump 1.95 metres could have been totally natural. If this was the case, this example suggests that the transition from indigenous traditions to modern sports may have been a smooth one.

Even more renowned were the feats of the Watussi (today known as the Tutsi), an ethnic group found mainly in what is now Rwanda and Burundi. The area of these two countries was formerly part of German East Africa which bordered on British East Africa, part of which is today Kenya. Before that, the lines dividing country from country simply did not exist in eastern Africa. Tutsi high jumping is very well documented and we include the earliest photographic evidence of this form of movement culture as Figure 3.3. Photographed by Adolf Friedrich, Duke of Mecklenburg, while expeditioning across east Africa in 1907, it shows an anonymous Tutsi athlete taking part in some kind of high jump event. The Duke described it thus:

> A line, which could be raised or lowered at will, was stretched between two slender trees, standing on an incline. The athletes had to run up to this and jump from a small termite heap a foot in height. Despite these unfavourable conditions, *exhibitions* were given which would place all European efforts in the shade. The best jumpers, slender, but splendid figures, with an almost Indian profile, attained the incredible height of 2.50 metres, and young boys made the, relatively, no less wonderful performance of 1.50 to 1.60 metres.[47]

The actual height cleared was less than this because the take-off was raised and it has been suggested that, under modern conditions, the Watussi would be able to clear no higher than 1.80 metres (6 feet 1 inch).[48]

At the time of Mecklenburg's observations the men's world record stood
at 1.97 metres; at the time of writing (mid-1995) it is 2.45 metres. The
performances of the Tutsi were unknown in Europe before his return from
Africa in 1908 and the scene in Figure 3.3, and other photographs of Tutsi
high jumping taken on the Duke's travels, aroused great interest in
Germany. Although the view that '*long before* the emergence of the
modern sports movement' the Tutsi had been known to be excellent high
jumpers has been contested,[49] it seems highly unlikely that such jumping
skills could have been achieved by novices and performed without any
previous experience.[50] Ndejuru avers that Tutsi high jumping symbolised
the passing over from youth to manhood and the transcending of evil; in
other words, it was a rite of passage.[51] In one of the more detailed English
language descriptions of Watussi high jumping, however, it is suggested
that skill in high jumping *competitions* had traditionally been a quality
aspired to by would-be members of the corps of the King's pages while it
is also noted that high jumping over the head of a visitor was a special
greeting to honour guests to the royal estate.[52] This seems to have been the
purpose of the event photographed by Mecklenburg.

Figure 3.3. Watussi high jumping in 1907 (source: Mecklenburg, 1910, p.60).

The 'event' shown in Figure 3.3 is clearly not sport as it is known
today. The uprights are made of untreated wood from local trees. A

length of hemp rope with weighted ends takes the place of the modern rigid crossbar (in other, later, photographs it is replaced by a more rigid reed). Notches have clearly been cut into the uprights to permit the rope to be placed at increasing heights but it is not clear how or by whom these had been calibrated (they are absent in several other, later, photographs). A natural feature, the termite mound, forms an integral part of the event, distancing it from the smooth plane of the artificial, modern take-off apron. Spectators are crowding around the jumper and, even if they have been arranged by the photographer, there is minimal, if any, separation of performer from spectators. We have no real idea of what sort of 'event' is taking place. Are the spectators local people or some of the 500 porters Mecklenburg had with him? Is it a demonstration or a competition? Has the jump been undertaken voluntarily or under pressure from the German visitors? Adolf Friedrich does not describe the event as a competition but as 'sports and athletic exercises'. Is the intention of the photographer to illustrate the jumper's native prowess or how easily the Tutsi could adapt to Westernised forms of body culture? Whatever the answers to these questions may be, the physical ability of the athlete concerned cannot be in doubt, even if on this occasion he is failing to clear the height at which the rope has been placed. This style of jumping was not restricted to one or two élite performers and appeared to be commonplace among male Watussi in villages in Rwanda and Burundi visited by British, American and German 'explorers', at least into the 1940s. Such performances were again illustrated by photographic evidence which reveals only the most modest of refinements in the high jumping equipment and the continued use of the mound for purposes of take-off.[53]

To our knowledge this precise form of high jumping has never been attributed to the territory which is today called Kenya. It is possible, however, that Kenyan tribes may have matched the performances of neighbouring peoples whose achievements were so spectacularly communicated to the voyeurs of an increasingly visible *fin de siècle* Africa, as suggested by Webster's comments, noted earlier. Indeed, the style of the Tutsi jumpers does not appear to be significantly different from that of the 1950s Maasai shown in Figure 4.4. It has also been suggested that the dances of the Tutsi 'differed in no material respect in their character' from those of the Maasai and that both Tutsi and Maasai may have shared common geographical origins, prior to migrating southwards to their present locations.[54]

What is of interest, however, is whether the pre-modern athletes of east Africa – be they runners, throwers or jumpers – were aware of their levels of achievement and how good they were. Ndejuru's research reveals that the best Tutsi high jumpers were not anonymous and that their feats as superior athletes were recalled by subsequent generations, their names recorded in the collective memory.[55] This suggests that they certainly were aware of the significance of their physical achievements, although being outside the emerging performance cult of modern sport. We can only speculate that the same might have been the case for Webster's Kenyan novice high jumper, bringing his African skills to the English high jump. However, only diligent anthropological and historical research will be able to tell us for certain how widespread east African pre-modern high jumping was and how different it was from its modern sportised equivalent.

Folk-games today

Although traditional dances were disliked by the colonialists and banned by the missionaries, folk-games continued into the 1960s. They played a sufficiently important role in some parts of Kenya for them to be retained in the school curriculum. At the Jeanes School at Kabete between the 1920s and the mid-1950s, the school's programme included African cultural forms ranging from games to folk-songs and drama. The Jeanes School had been formed by American philanthropists who sought to experiment with traditional forms of education and hence prevent the destruction of African culture, a philosophy quite different from the public school system. In 1950 Jeanes School became the home of Kenyan athletics and is the place most associated with its development.

Modern track and field athletics gradually replaced the folk versions of running, throwing and jumping. The hypothesis that the basic folk activities we have described in this chapter provided a basis for, and a smooth transition to, analogous modern sports is, however, a risky one. The existence of indigenous traditions of 'sport-like' body culture in certain regions did not guarantee that they would be replaced by, or lead to, national sports systems which would 'produce' world class athletes in cognate modern sports events; far from it. Neither the Tutsi nor the Ankole high jumpers, for example, were followed by a line of world class high jumpers in modern Rwanda, Burundi and Uganda. No high jumpers from any of these countries appeared among the top 100 Africans in 1993, though 11 Kenyans did. The world class athletes from war-torn Rwanda and Burundi have been Tutsi middle-distance runners. Neither the Turkana nor the Maasai have produced any world class javelin throwers (the best Kenyan throwers have tended to be Kalenjin and Gusii)[56] and, as we will show, the conservatism of the Maasai means that their much-heralded runners are today significantly outnumbered by those from other ethnic groups in Kenya. Webster (an English national javelin champion) found that 'using a spear of the weight and length of approximately the Olympic javelin I could beat any native I ever took on, whereas with their own light casting spears they could always beat me by yards.'[57] This neatly sums up our view that pre-modern Kenyan body culture has little to do with modern athletics. The latter was not neatly bolted onto the former; nor was the Kenyan's adaptability to modern sport in some way 'natural'. African and European running, jumping and throwing were, each in their own way, cultural not natural. It was not so much a case of continuity but one of change. This is not to deny that the adoption of particular sports by particular tribal groups may not have been made easier by pre-existing cultural traits (see Chapter 6). Indeed, it has been suggested that improved performance and competition – two of the basic ideologies of modern sport – were part of the consciousness of traditional Kenyan societies. What was novel was the striving for records with the new concepts of time and the standardisation of space.[58] Yet there remain the relatively good performances of the Kenyan high jumpers and javelin throwers in the early days of international competition described in Chapter 1, only to have been subsequently retarded by modern technological constraints (see Chapter 7). Our conclusions about change rather than continuity must be cautious and not too dogmatic.

Political independence for Kenya did not involve a decolonisation of the body and little has been done to revive the nation's traditional folk-games. School students today perceive traditional dances to be less attractive than modern sports.[59] 'In Kenya, in our own country', wrote Ngugi wa Thiong'o, 'isn't it strange that the call to ape foreigners and be satisfied with paths already trodden by our erstwhile British masters comes from some Kenyans?'[60] Running was common in traditional Kenyan society and much of it made practical sense. But the subsequent adoption of a *particular kind* of running made 'an entirely different kind of sense',[61] even if it did share some of the characteristics of pre-modern forms of movement culture. This cultural shift can be interpreted in various ways. One is through the idea of 'invented traditions' which would see modern Kenyan running having an important symbolic function, the nature of which will be elaborated in subsequent chapters.

Although the centimetre-gram-second model of Olympic sport was readily adopted in Kenya it does not mean that folk-games have totally disappeared. But they have tended to become museumised or, in exceptional cases, quasi-sportised. For example, an Ajua (a traditional chess-like game) Association of Kenya is affiliated to the Kenya National Sports Council showing how a folk game can become a sport. It is integrated into a Western value system without having significantly changed its style and organisation. The game is not well supported, however, and is in decline. Other traditional movement cultures also exist, particularly those of dance, but in museumised form. They are live museum pieces and represent a fossilised culture, having degenerated into a form of folklore, acquainting present-day Kenyans and tourists with the country's past.[62] This is not an atypical situation in countries of Africa which have taken the Western route to 'development'. The decline of folk games is, of course, a classic example of cultural imperialism and the erosion of regional cultures. At the African Games, Western sports now dominate the competitions while traditional African dances precede the athletic contests.[63] Although (or because) Kenyans now beat the Europeans, Western sport as an institution will continue to stand in the way of more indigenous pursuits.[64]

Such a situation is similar to that of theatre in Kenya; Western theatrical forms flourish while indigenous forms flounder and are actively discouraged by the neo-colonial élite.[65] We might reasonably assume that Ngugi would oppose the suppression of Kenyan folk-games – the 'people's sports' – as much as he would that of people's theatre and dances. Oddly, however, athletics – the most internationally well-known performance genre of modern Kenya – is not even mentioned in his powerful pleas for opposing the cultural priorities of the neo-colonials currently ruling the country.[66] Instead, in what is perhaps the nearest thing we have to an African voice on sport and imperialism, he focuses on the sporting activities of the contemporary Kenyan élite who have copied the settler who 'played golf and polo, went to horse-races or on the royal hunt in red-coats and riding breeches, a herd of yapping or growling hounds on the chase. The black pupils now do the same, only with greater zeal: golf and horses have become "national" institutions'.[67] Would Ngugi regard another imitation, that of the adoption by the Kenyan masses of another form of Western body culture – modern athletics – any less invidious?

The decline in Kenyan folk-games overlapped with the emergence of modern sports. This period of overlap extended from the end of the nineteenth century to the mid-1960s. By then Kenya was not only becoming highly visible on the world stage of achievement sport but was also being exposed to some of its excesses.

Notes and references

1. The distinctions between folk-games and modern sports have been excellently reviewed by Guttmann, *From Ritual to Record*; see also his *A Whole New Ball Game*. In addition, note the view that 'the main characteristics of modern sports are their organization on national and international levels and their accompanying standardization. These are the main differences between modern sports and traditional sport-like pastimes': Stovkis, 'Sports and civilization', p. 122. The question of how 'modern' the pre-modern 'sports' were is addressed in several of the essays in Carter and Krüger (eds), *Ritual and Record*, notably by Decker, 'The record and the ritual', in which it is suggested that the 'sports records' of the Eighteenth Dynasty of ancient Egypt were first recorded in Africa.
2. Marshall, *The !Kung of Nyae Nyae*.
3. Lindblom, *The Akamba of British East Africa*, p. 425.
4. Jokl, 'High jump technique of the Central African Watussis'.
5. Spurr, The *Rhetoric of Empire*, pp. 92–3.
6. Mazrui, *The Africans*, p. 63.
7. Mählmann, 'The role of sport in the process of modernisation: the Kenyan case'.
8. Reclus, *The Universal Geography*, p. 364. We have used 'Maasai', the accepted and preferred spelling, throughout this book.
9. Hinde and Hinde, *The Last of the Masai*.
10. Ross, *Kenya from Within*, p. 130.
11. Hinde and Hinde, *The Last of the Masai*, p. 38.
12. Leys, *Kenya*, p. 87. Note the use of the term 'warriors'; the term 'soldier' is rarely used in such contexts. Yet 'African warriors were not simply acting as individuals or in hordes, but operated in organized fashion and in some cases formed armies': Pieterse, *White on Black*, p. 79.
13. Boyes, *King of the Wa-Kikuyu*, p. 61.
14. Hoberman, *Mortal Engines*, p. 56.
15. Hemingway, *Green Hills of Africa*, pp. 213–14 (emphasis added). We are very grateful to Bob Phillips for drawing our attention to Hemingway's description.
16. Schneider, 'Pakot resistance to change', p. 163. The attraction of such tribes as the Maasai was, in part, likely to result from their perceived qualities of 'manliness' but such attraction was not always without qualification: see Cairns, *Prelude to Imperialism*, p. 114.
17. Shorter, *East African Societies*, p. 37.
18. Brown, *The Vanishing Tribes of Kenya*, p. 47. Runners were widely employed as messengers by white farmers and other settlers. See, for example, Dinesen, *Out of Africa*.
19. Barton, 'Notes on the Turkana tribe of British East Africa'; Rayne, 'Turkana'.
20. Matson, *Nandi Resistance to British Rule*, p. 9.
21. Hyam, *Empire and Sexuality*, pp. 204–5. On exaggerated images of African women see Gilman, 'Black bodies, white bodies'.
22. Said, *Orientalism*, pp. 2–3.
23. Pratt, 'Scratching on the face of the country', p. 139.
24. Spurr, *The Rhetoric of Empire*, p. 168. Note also Young, *Colonial Desire*, p. 104. The ambivalent attitudes of nineteenth-century British travellers to central Africa are excellently reviewed in Cairns, *Prelude to Imperialism*.
25. Quoted in Anderson, 'Stock theft and moral economy in colonial Kenya', pp. 399–416.

26. Huntingford, *The Nandi of Kenya*, p. 83.
27. Matson, 'Nandi traditions of raiding'.
28. Huntingford, *The Nandi of Kenya*, p. 77.
29. Ibid. p. 81.
30. Kenyatta, *Facing Mount Kenya*, p. 140. For a more detailed treatment see Leakey, *The Southern Kikuyu*, pp. 615–16.
31. Lindblom, *The Akamba*, p. 425.
32. Mwaniki, *The Living History of the Embu and Mbeere*, p. 74.
33. Routledge and Routledge, *With a Prehistoric People*; Leakey, *The Southern Kikuyu*, pp. 403-4. Regrettably we have been unable to find any photographic illustration of early Kenyan running such as that described in this section. This may be because few photographs could be taken, given photographic technology at the time. In the early twentieth century shutter speeds were still very slow.
34. Mwaniki, *The Living History of the Embu and Mbeere*, p. 73. The Kikuyu version of this game is well described in Leakey, *The Southern Kikuyu*, pp. 577–8.
35. Barton, 'Notes on the Turkana', pp. 113–14.
36. Krapf, *Travels, Researches and Missionary Labours During an Eighteen Years' Residence in Eastern Africa*.
37. Okroth, 'The Amos Biwott Story', p. 29.
38. Browne, *Vanishing Tribes*, p. 48.
39. Lindblom, *The Akamba*, p. 425.
40. Kenyatta, *Facing Mount Kenya*, p. 97.
41. Middleton, *The Kikuyu and Kamba of Kenya, 1953*, pp. 97–8.
42. Kenyatta, *Facing Mount Kenya*. 'An age-set is composed of all men who have been circumcised in youth during a specified period of time, and a new one is generally formed every 12 to 14 years': Spencer, *The Samburi*, p. 80.
43. Blacking, 'Games and sport in pre-colonial African societies', p. 8. Surprisingly, Blacking does not mention Tutsi high jumping. Either he was unaware of its existence, which seems unlikely given its extensive academic and popular coverage, or he assumed that it was not a pre-colonial form of movement culture. The term 'submerged continuity' is taken from Burton, 'Cricket, carnival and street culture in the Caribbean'. In this paper Burton suggests, without any evidence, that 'possible continuities' may exist between nineteenth-century Caribbean stick-fighting (*calanda*) – of African origin – and the modern champion cricketer.
44. Routledge and Routledge, *With a Prehistoric People*, p. 178.
45. Roscoe, *The Northern Bantu*, p. 141.
46. Webster, *Why? The Science of Athletics*, p. 384. We are very grateful to David Terry for access to this work from his personal athletics library.
47. Mecklenburg, *In the Heart of Africa*, p. 59, italics added. The jumps of 1.50–1.60 metres were made by 10–12-year-old boys according to Ndejuru, *Studien zur Rolle der Leibesübungen in der traditionellen Geselleshaft Rwandas*, p. 186. We are grateful to Roland Renson (University of Leuven) for alerting us to Ndejuru's important dissertation, to Wolfgang Decker (University of Cologne) for making a copy of it available to us, and to Ruth Bale for translating sections of it from the German.
48. Abmayr, *Africa: Track and Field*. At the time of writing (1995) the national records for Burundi are 2.05 metres (men) and 1.55 metres (women). These were established in 1986 and 1987 respectively. Those for Rwanda are of inferior quality. We are grateful to Andrew Huxtable for this information.
49. Jokl, *Physiology of Exercise*, p. 125 (italics added).

50. Mecklenburg seems somewhat ambivalent about his part in this high jump event. Ndejuru suggests that King Musiaga of the Tutsi provided the athletic displays to please his German visitors but Mecklenburg has implied that the event was set up under the direction of his adjutant. Later, Mecklenburg stated that they organised the high jump because the Tutsi obviously enjoyed it so much: see Ndejuru, *Studien zur Rolle der Leibesübungen*, pp. 129-32.

51. Ibid, p. 184-7.

52. Gatti, *South of the Sahara*, p. 169; Birnbaum, 'Reception in Rwanda'. It is elsewhere suggested that Tutsi high jumping was 'a spectacle rather than a contest': Cotlow, *In Search of the Primitive*, p. 25.

53. It could be argued that, after dance and wrestling, Tutsi high jumping is the most photographed form of pre-modern African body culture. The most well-known photograph of such jumping (taken on the same occasion as Figure 3.2) is also included in Mecklenburg, *In the Heart of Africa*, opposite p. 58. It has been reproduced many times. See, for example, Ndejuru, *Studien zur Rolle der Leibesübungen*; Hilderbrand, 'The geography of games'; Jokl, 'High jump technique', p. 146 and *Physiology of Exercise*, p. 125; Bernett, *Leichtathletik in Historischen Bilddokumenten*, p. 105; and, most recently, Guttmann, *Games and Empires*. In this photograph the visiting dignitaries, the Duke of Mecklenburg and his adjutant are pictured standing between the uprights while the jumper easily clears the rope above their heads. In many ways this photograph was typical of those included in the *National Geographic* with its juxtaposition of images of imperialism and the 'raw native'. It is, perhaps, significant that the picture invariably reproduced from Mecklenburg's 1910 publication is that of the jumper successfully clearing the rope, not the one included here of the athlete failing. The latter might have carried all the wrong messages. Many other allusions and photographs, apparently unknown to Ndejuru, are found in various English language sources. For example, a photograph published in 1937 shows a Tutsi jumper clearing about 1.93 metres (6 feet 4 inches) with Patrick Balfour, a British traveller, standing between the uprights. The take-off mound was said to be 'a few inches' high and the run up about 15 metres. Several athletes were claimed to have 'soared over with ease'. There are slightly more conventional high jump uprights and bar. In other respects, the scene is pre-modern with the termite mound still being used for take-off, crowds around the athlete and no evidence of a prepared run-up or jumping pit: see Balfour, *Lords of the Equator*, pp. 241–2 (photograph opposite p. 258). Also from the same period, for photographs showing a jumper clearing an allegedly measured 8 feet $3^1/_8$ inches (2.52 metres), including an ant hill take-off said to be $2^1/_8$ inches (0.06 metres) high, see Gatti, *South of the Sahara*, p. 192. In the late 1930s it was noted that the take-off mound was *constructed* by the jumpers, 'two or three inches high to mark the point from which they leap': see Birnbaum, 'Reception in Rwanda', p. 307. It seems that sometimes a stone was used for take-off, 'more as a grip for the bare foot than as a rising lever'. It was also noted (with yet another photograph) that jumpers often tended to take off from generally rising ground: Roome, *Tramping through Africa*, pp. 102–3. A publication from the 1940s includes a photograph showing the same style of jumping. The caption notes that with their special jumping talent Tutsi (men) are able to jump their own height without any training and that it would therefore be easy to introduce European sports to the region (see Berenatzik, *Afrika*, pp. 896–7). A photograph from a colonial travel guide of the 1950s shows a Tutsi clearing about 1.90 metres with modern high jump uprights but the take-off mound still in evidence (Tourist Bureau for the Belgian Congo and Rwanda-Urundi, *Traveller's Guide to the*

Belgian Congo, p. 405). 'The Watussi can hold their own with our best athletes', the guide noted, though we can find no evidence that they ever competed in Belgian championships. The scene, and those from the 1930s, are good examples of body culture 'between' folk-games and modern sport (see Chapter 4). For a technical description of Tutsi high jumping see Jokl, 'High jumping technique' and *Physiology of Exercise*, pp. 124–8. Noting the high jumping feats of the Tutsi and shorter 'plantation negroes' in the 1920s, a German physician asked, 'What, then, will be left of our world records?' (quoted in Hoberman, *Mortal Engines*, p. 46). The answer is that they were certainly not affected by the Tutsi, despite an abortive suggestion from Jokl to the King of the Tutsi in 1959 that a team of high jumpers be entered for the Olympic Games (Jokl, *Physiology of Exercise*, p. 128). Since then the state of high jumping in Rwanda and Burundi is reflected in a colonial publication of 1960, intended to provide information about Rwanda-Burundi, which noted that athletics was practiced 'on a very small scale' with no mention at all of Tutsi high jumping traditions: see Belgian Congo and Rwanda Urundi Information and Public Relations Office, *Rwanda-Urundi: Social Achievements* (trans. Goldie Blankoff-Scarr), Brussels, 1960, p. 62.

54. Mecklenburg, *In the Heart of Africa*, p. 60.
55. Ndejuru, *Studien zur Rolle der Leibesübungen*, p. 187.
56. Ndoo, 'The Kenyan success', p. 51.
57. Webster, *Why? The Science of Athletics*, p. 384.
58. Mählmann, 'The role of sport', p. 128.
59. Mählmann, 'Perception of sport in Kenya', p. 134.
60. Thiong'o, *Detained*, p. 190.
61. Hobsbawm, 'Introduction: inventing traditions', p. 3.
62. Were, 'Cultural renaissance and national development'.
63. Uwechue, 'Nation building and sport in Africa'.
64. Galtung, 'Sport as a carrier of deep culture', p. 13.
65. Osotis, 'The theatre in independent Kenya'.
66. Thiong'o, *Barrel of a Pen*.
67. Thiong'o, *Detained*, p. 58.

4

Between Folk-Games and Modern Sport

> The rise of sport as a distinct and celebrated type of
> performance may be related to the technologizing of other
> physical accomplishments, such as geographical exploration ...
>
> JOHN HOBERMAN, *Mortal Engines*

The (English) Amateur Athletic Association (AAA) was founded in 1880. It was the sport's first national governing bureaucracy. The global equivalent, the International Amateur Athletic Federation (IAAF) followed in 1912. The Kenyan AAA was formed in 1951. Kenya's acceptance of achievement oriented track and field athletics meant that modern sport had formally replaced the traditional folk-games of tribal Kenyan society. This constituted the beginnings of the modernisation – and the globalisation – of Kenyan athletics. This chapter takes us up to the early 1950s and explores the period between the dominance of folk body cultures and the primacy of modern sports.

In the history of Kenyan track and field, much of the first half of the twentieth century represented what Victor Turner might call a 'liminal period', that is, one of ambiguity and discontinuity, 'neither here nor there, betwixt and between'.[1] In the Kenyan case, athletics in the inter-war years displayed characteristics of both its folk antecedents and those of modern sport at the same time, having a limited number of the attributes of both its past and future state. It exhibited local as well as increasingly global characteristics. This 'in-between' period will form the focus of much of this chapter. But first we will explore the reasons for the introduction (innovation or imposition would be words used by observers of varying ideological positions) of sportised athletics into Kenya and the evidence for it being an explicit form of social control. The chapter ends with the institutionalisation of athletics as a new form of movement culture possessing all the characteristics of a modern sport.

Europeans had ventured into the interior of what was to become Kenya in the mid-nineteenth century but British hegemony only really commenced in 1888 through the activities of the British East Africa Company which acquired a royal charter to administer Uganda and

Kenya. It was in 1895 that the British crown took over the Company and established the East Africa Protectorate. The first white settlers began to arrive in the first years of the new century. Europeans brought their sports with them but initially they were practised by the Western settler communities themselves and were socially distanced from indigenous Africans. It can be inferred that most of the early European settlers were not especially well disposed towards athletic achievement. 'Sport' was often interpreted by the white population as big game hunting and safari rather than football and athletics. This is not to say that the white colonialists lacked opportunities for competitive – although non-serious – sports. The English settlers in the 'White Highlands' of the Rift Valley had polo grounds, race courses and gymkhanas. These helped to relieve boredom and to cement social bonding. In Nairobi the East African Turf Club was founded as early as 1900 while the first golf club followed in 1902. Kisumu had a similar club by 1908. Early Kenyan golf courses were examples of culture uneasily allied with nature; it was not unknown for players to be mauled by lions. Cricket of a relatively high standard was played widely, on matting wickets, often in connection with such salubrious organisations as the Gymkhana Club in Mombasa. Lawn tennis and polo were popular, yachting was practised, and in 1907 the first association football match in Kenya took place between the Rift Valley Sports Club and a Nairobi XI.[2] At the Muthaiga Country Club in Nairobi there existed a golf course, squash courts, and croquet lawns. By 1931 Nairobi had a race course, a polo ground, two golf courses and many facilities for cricket.[3] The formal layout of the new sports landscapes contrasted, of course, with the less geometric and more natural pattern of the African cultural milieu. They were also segregated spaces with facilities strictly reserved, primarily for the recreational sporting pastimes of the white settler community.

Recreation of a flamboyant nature characterised the idea of one of the early settlers, A.S. Cooper, who in 1900 started what became known as 'race weeks'.[4] The double meaning of the word 'race' is not without irony. It involved a kind of 'tribal' gathering, not unlike the *nagmaal* among Afrikaners in South Africa. According to James Fox, the race weeks of the 1920s were more like a bacchanalian orgy than anything resembling any form of modern sport.[5] Settlers attended the festivities and various Western games were played in an atmosphere of informality, fun and recklessness. The African population was expected to simply observe the action while 'waiting' on visitors for whom the meetings often represented gatherings of old friends. The central focus was horse racing but cricket, tennis and golf were also part and parcel of these events. Games were often arranged spontaneously and were not taken very seriously. Although practised by the white élite, like the African folk-games, they were not seriously sportised (Figure 4.1).

Figure 4.1. White settlers at play in 1910s Kenya (source: Hinde Collection, Royal Commonwealth Society Library, Cambridge).

Information being provided for potential British emigrés (as in Henry Owen Weller's *Kenya Without Prejudice*) made no mention at all of track and field athletics.[6] In the early years of the century, running, which was undertaken by the colonialist class, was mainly what would today be called jogging. Sir Percy Girouard, Governor of British East Africa from 1910 to 1912, was a great believer in keeping fit. He was not alone in taking pre-breakfast runs around the outskirts of Nairobi dressed in shorts and sweater,[7] but running as serious racing did not seem to attract the settler class. It may have been too much of a young man's sport, or perhaps the excessive display of the human body would have accumulated the wrong kind of cultural capital.

From running to racing

We are certainly not in a position to say precisely who introduced track and field athletics to Kenya, nor in which year. Such uncertainty remains part of the broader problem of operationalising the concept of national 'adoption' of athletics as part of its geographical diffusion in Africa. Only hazy information exists about the introduction to Kenya of athletics in its modern form but it seems safe to say that the missions and schools, the armed services and, most notably, the colonial administration through the work of district officials, were the most important agencies. It is to these agents of change that we now turn.

Missionary and military: the germs of modern athletics

While missionaries had been instrumental in abolishing slavery in Kenya from the 1840s to the 1880s, they also paved the way for the enslavement of Kenyans to Western culture. They preached assimilation, hence leading to the undermining of African culture. Churches, hospitals and schools were all established but they too were crucial agents in introducing the African to the ways of the Western world. The notion of cultural relativism was anathema to missionaries. Urch notes that

> as the leading exponent of the western way of life the missionary ... was often antagonistic toward African culture, for it was accepted by him that western culture was superior to the indigenous traditional society. The African was considered to lack the attribute of civilisation and the diffusion of European culture through education together with the propagation of the gospel was considered necessary for the benefit of Africans.[8]

Among the many means of subjugating Africans in aiding and abetting the maintenance of imperial rule was athletics. This formed part of the early twentieth century ethos of 'muscular Christianity' through which sports were introduced to the African population by the work of mission schools. Although African children were not compelled to go to school, once they were there they were certainly coerced into the discipline of physical education. Physical training, games, and drill were central aspects of the curriculum (Figure 4.2). Such 'taught' movement culture emphasised the straight body in straight lines with no room for individual expression. It exemplified the hygienist mode of body culture which contrasted with the more sensuous and fluid movement culture of the indigenous peoples described in Chapter 3. Such 'welfare sport', however, possessed some of the characteristics of achievement sport which was to parallel its development. As Eichberg notes, 'the values of fitness, health and social discipline .... are not alien to the world of sport'.[9] Likewise, the recording of performance is central to many forms of physical education as well as to modern sports. The kind of physical training shown in Figure 4.2 was, however, to remain separate from achievement sport as a form of movement culture; it became 'drill' – a routinised form of physical training. It only became sportised by competition and the ranking of performance.

Figure 4.2. Straight backs in straight lines. Physical training at a Maasai school at Narok in the mid-1920s (source: Ross, 1927, p. 144).

The missions had held 'sports days' at least as early as 1906. They featured rather light-hearted events such as climbing the greasy pole, obstacle and sack races, and the tug-of-war.[10] On the face of it they appeared more illustrative of a culture of laughter than of the world of seriousness which would typify modern track and field athletics. In this sense they were similar to the disport of the 'race' weeks noted above, though obviously serving a different purpose. Such laughter was, however, constructed on a deadly serious ideological base and by the early 1920s the missions were organising more formal and more serious-looking events. Although not yet under the aegis of any regional or national governing body, the events were very well attended and carefully supervised. At these events the body management of the colonialist was clearly differentiated from that of the African. This, and the hierarchical ordering of sports space, is clearly shown in the photograph of the high jump competition in Figure 4.3. Here the photographer has centrally framed the European in his tropical outfit;

Figure 4.3. In 1922 the sports day at the Church Missionary Society at Butere attracted a substantial crowd of spectators (source: photograph collection of E.O. Ashton, Rhodes House Library, Oxford).

though seated, he clearly dominates the African officials and the competitor. The camera's gaze seems to want to capture the evidence of colonial control (the well-trained African assistants and the orderly environment) as much as the athletic performance. While many of the trappings of a modern sports milieu were still lacking, evidence of organisation, seriousness and effort were clearly present. Events for girls were included as well as events for boys. Whether it was 'drill' or sport, images such as those in Figures 4.2 and 4.3 emphasise the missionary's power to 'civilise' the African.

At the turn of the new century the germs of sportised athletics were also present in the activities of the military. The King's African Rifles (KAR), constituted as a regiment in 1902, played an important role in developing athletics.[11] An attempt to teach the African to race was made as early as 1902 by Captain Richard Meinertzhagen, soldier, ornithologist, racist and alumnus of Harrow School (an élite private institution in England). While on duty in Kenya, at festivities for the coronation of King Edward VII, he organised sports for his KAR company at Muranga. These were not regarded as a success, however, 'as the winner had to fight the rest afterwards'. Nevertheless, latent achievement- and record-orientation is reflected in the fact that Meinertzhagen recorded that the winner of a race of 2.25 miles (3.6 kilometres) covered the course in 'exactly 14 minutes'.[12] The performance was unexceptional but this was almost certainly the first timed foot race in Kenyan history.

Before the end of the second decade of the new century the KAR had begun to hold their own athletics championships. In the 1919 championships, held at Nairobi, F.A.M. Webster recorded that he 'was beaten into third place in the 100 yards championship ... by two men who had been at that station for months'.[13] His observation that his two conquerors had benefited from their longer residence at high altitude prefigured arguments used 60 years later in relation to the middle- and long-distance events. It seems unlikely, however, that the KAR meeting involved multi-ethnic competition if the segregationist traditions of the British army athletics matches in India were replicated in Africa.[14]

The athletic ethic and social control

The missionaries and the military were not unimportant as agents of body-cultural change but it was the colonial administrative officers who were to provide the ideology. Kenya was a public (that is, private) schoolboys' colony *par excellence*. Indeed, Lord Cranworth urged public schoolboys to go to Kenya, their leadership qualities and love of sport making them ideally suited to life in East Africa.[15] An interest in sport was often an explicit criterion in the selection of officers for colonial service but evidence from selection procedures suggests that while rugby, football, cricket and fives were often mentioned, athletics seldom seemed to be of any significance.[16] Perhaps track and field was insufficiently redolent of 'team games' through which the ethos of team work could be infused.

We feel that it is important to briefly sketch the characteristics of the men involved at the top of a chain of agents involved in the diffusion of track and field athletics to the African population. The kind of person the Colonial Office was looking for as an administrative officer was not an intellectual. Rather, he would reflect a kind of Baden-Powellism, possessing 'modest intellectual achievement, *athletic prowess, a taste for outdoor life*' and, implicitly, unquestioned acceptance of the 'aristocratic' ethos of the rules and ideals of imperialism.[17] The Kenyan administrative officers were imbued with a sense of imperialism and 'manliness', born of their élitist background. Of 216 officers in Kenya during the period 1890 and 1959 for whom data are available, 164 out of 216 (76 per cent) had attended private schools; 293 out of 382 (77 per cent) had attended the universities of Oxford or Cambridge.[18] The colonial administration would set the tone for the work of the school teachers, district commissioners, and the physical education instructors in the army and prison service.

The Europeanisation of African movement culture has been viewed by many observers as a form of social control – that is, behaviour of individuals regulated by groups in dominant positions. The military and the missionary both recognised this. They may not have explicated the fact that sport was the ideal form of social control but it can be argued that it was. Drill was an obvious type of spatial constraint – an 'iron cage' of bodily discipline with no illusions of freedom. Track and field athletics, on the other hand, may have provided the impression of free, less rigid, movement but a neo-marxist reading of its rule-bound disciplines, within the quantified confines of the athletic arena, shows its release from the world of work to be an illusion.

Sport was to be used by the administration as an alternative to tribal dancing which was deemed sexually explicit, lascivious and hence undesirable.[19] The adoption of the white man's customs would also provide the African with a diversion from political discontent; sport would provide a safety valve for excessive anti-imperialist feeling and would assist in the creation of a fit workforce. These perspectives were encapsulated in the philosophy of Dr John W. Arthur, an athlete and graduate of Glasgow University. An enthusiastic opponent of clitoridectomy, Arthur arrived at Thogoto in 1907 and took charge of physical education and games at the Church of Scotland's Mission. He believed in spreading the values of the British 'public school' to the Kikuyu and saw sport as a necessary part of the African curriculum. He believed that

> the game of football played in the afternoon, was played for moral benefit as much as recreational relief, ... to stiffen the backbone of these boys by teaching them manliness, good temper and unselfishness – qualities amongst others which have done so much to make a Britisher.[20]

The ethos of muscular Christianity, as applied here to football, could, of course, be applied equally to all sports.

One observer of the Kenyan scene was quite explicit about the social control function of English sports, noting that missionaries and others 'seek to divert the minds of people from politics by giving them such innocent delights as football, boy scouts, Boys' Brigade and so forth'.[21] Likewise, a provincial commissioner stated in 1923 that he had introduced football among the Kamba in order 'to allay discontent and premature political agitation'.[22] While missionaries were not always interested in teaching athletics they were, nevertheless, urged to recognise that the spirit of play, traditionally satisfied by native dancing, could be replaced by sports. Whenever the spirit of play is denied, wrote Norman Leys, 'the thwarted emotions find vent in secret vices and smug hypocrisy'.[23]

Track and field was weakly organised, if it was organised at all, and was sporadic both in location and over time, and it was only in the 1920s that the sport became more common in schools and in the police, army, and prison services. The bureaucratisation of Kenyan athletics was initiated by the colony's first Director of Education, James Orr. In early 1924 he suggested that an African native sports association be formed and in July of the same year a working party made up of prominent European members of the police, army, schools and the church met in Nairobi. The result was the formation of the Arab and African Sports Association (AASA). Although the East African Protectorate had become the Colony of Kenya in 1920, a national sports federation, in the form assumed in many European countries by this date, did not appear to be appropriate. The AASA was not intended to accommodate white settlers and the customary (but lacking a legal basis) colour bar remained enforced. It was agreed that a national sports meeting should be held annually and that local committees should arrange local events from which competitors would be drawn to compete in the national meeting. Enshrined in the first national association, therefore, was the ideology of an athletic hierarchy, based on the principle of athletic performance.

The first formal athletics meeting for non-Europeans to be held in Kenya under the auspices of the AASA took place on 7 February 1925 at the race course in Nairobi. Restricted to Africans, the competitors represented districts and it was not until the 1930s that provinces became the main representational unit. From their early days the model for these events was European, explicated through the use of the term 'African *Olympics*'. The place-bonding function of representational sport was stressed, albeit with more than a hint of hyperbole: the 'first sense of tribal unity rather than dislike of people over the river came from District and Provincial athletic rivalries', noted one optimistic observer.[24] Local sports meetings were attractive entertainments for the settler class as well as the native Africans. By 1929 Maasai sports days were considered important enough to be visited by senior officials from Nairobi, including the governor or his representative.[25]

Although not representing the whole of the Kenyan population, the AASA was, *de facto*, the first national governing body for the sport in Kenya. It signalled the formal adoption of athletics and a bureaucracy to govern it (even though the *de jure* Kenya AAA was not established until 1951). The Kenyan example clearly illustrates the danger of depending on the date of formation of the *national* governing body as the date of a sport's adoption when researching that sport's continental pattern of diffusion.[26] To rely on the date of formation of the *de jure* national association is to record a much later date of adoption than was often the case.

Among the principal agents involved in encouraging athletics among the African population were the army and police. The need for a fit force in both sectors was facilitated through training in athletics. The arrival of R.G.B. Spicer as Commissioner of Police in 1925 stimulated the development of the police force as a major factor in the growth of Kenyan athletics. He had 'played a good game of golf, played an excellent game of cricket, was a horse-lover, a keen and good polo player, and an amateur jockey on the flat or steeplechase'.[27] Spicer placed considerable emphasis on the 'games ethic' and included physical fitness in the force's regular curriculum. During his time in the Kenyan police he strongly supported athletics, among other sports. As a result, the police gained a high sporting reputation. The police team, allowed to compete in the 'African Olympics', was dominant in this event for several years. The team was mainly stocked with Kikuyu athletes, resulting perhaps from the fact that they were the largest group numerically and they were located in the central region of Kenya around the capital, Nairobi; it was upon this group that British influence was initially most strongly felt. Nevertheless, Spicer's fundamentally racist views of the African's capabilities reflected the prevailing colonialists' ideology. He thought it necessary to push the abject Africans hard, noting that physical training needed to be emphasised in the Kenya Police 'in order that the comatose mind of the raw native may be awakened'.[28]

The involvement of the armed forces in the spread of athletics to schools is exemplified by the role of the District Commissioner of West Suk (now West Pokot), P.J. de Bromhead, who suggested that an army physical training instructor should be attached to all Rift Valley schools.[29] Suk games and songs were encouraged alongside English sports. Military influence was also present in the first athletic meeting involving the whole of the Maasai Reserve in 1936. The meeting, held in a newly constructed 'stadium', was presided over by the Commanding Officer of the Northern Brigade of the KAR as well as the Commanding Officer of the Royal Air Force (RAF). Maasai from throughout the reserve took part in events 'honoured' by a performance of the KAR band and the presence of the power and majesty of aircraft from the RAF.[30] If these displays of military presence at athletic meetings were not enough, the social control function of athletics was again made explicit:

> there is no doubt that if the Maasai warriors can be given an opportunity of frequently displaying their physical prowess by means of sports and games, this will become an important factor in civilizing the Maasai youth and in replacing the feats of physical endurance and daring indulged in stock raiding in the past.[31]

Commercial organisations, as well as the armed forces, encouraged the growth of athletics. Plantation owners arranged races of up to ten miles for their workers. In 1933 Kipchoge Keino's father took part in (and won) a six mile race, organised by the owner of the tea plantation where he worked. His prize was two 4 gallon tins of oil.[32]

From the late 1920s schools began to play an increasing role in Kenyan athletics. In 1929 the Colonial Secretary, Henry Moore (later to be Governor from 1940–44) again emphasised the significance of sport as a form of social control. He noted that

> the government attaches great importance to African athletics and to the encouragement of a spirit of local emulation, if for no other reason than because such pursuits provide not only a substitute for

political intrigue but also a legitimate channel into which may be diverted inherent instincts which otherwise lead to raiding and stock-thieving. They are in fact a not unimportant part of the African's education.[33]

Mission stations, with their schools periodically visited by a missionary, were not the most important of agencies leading to the more widespread adoption of athletics but, as we have already noted, they were not unimportant at the local level. For example, a report published by the Catholic Mission of the Consolata Fathers noted that the best place the Kikuyu could find true morality was through the mission stations, not only because of the availability of Holy Communion and confessions but also because they provided 'smart drill ... with uniform and banner: where frequent sport competitions take place with prizes and cups, certain as we are that physical training is of great importance'. The Bible followed the starting pistol as well as the gun. At the sports day at Nyeri in May 1932, on the occasion of the consecration of the Right Reverend C. Re, it was reported that 'each mission station competed with its team, and the show offered by that *disciplined* multitude of black boys is an unforgettable thing for those who had the good fortune to attend it'.[34]

As was common throughout the British Empire, it was British teachers who were most frequently recruited to staff the new secondary schools for the African population, often modelled on élite English institutions such as Eton and Harrow. The imperial power hoped that the élite African students of such schools would, upon graduating, spread 'Western' enlightenment (part of which would be Western movement culture) to the mass of the population by a process of 'downward diffusion'.

One of the most famous of such Kenyan schools, Alliance High School, Kikuyu (known as the Eton of Kenyan schools for Africans), was established in 1926. One teacher at Alliance was Frederick Crittenden. Educated at Whitgift Grammar School, Croydon, and Oriel College, Oxford, he had been a keen sprinter while at school and was able to renew his enthusiasm for athletics at Alliance. In line with the somewhat fascistic trait of favouring brawn over brain outlined earlier, he believed that the kind of man required for the development of sport among the native people

> should have a good degree and must be a competent teacher. Life adaptability and readiness to help were needed and more important than academic distinction, but work has to be sound and thorough and there is plenty of scope for the use of any powers which a man possesses. He must be a willing member of a team (Black and

white) and be prepared to throw himself vigorously into out-of-class activities, valuable lines such as games.[35]

With this ideology permeating the consciousness of teachers and, gradually, students, the seeds of athletic endeavour were firmly implanted.

In 1940, Alliance High School welcomed a new and influential headmaster named Edward Carey Francis who was transferred from Maseno school where he had been since 1928 (Figure 4.4). Carey Francis was arguably the most influential educationist in Kenya's modern history. He was equally important as a propagator of the athletic ethic. At Maseno he had established his credentials as a 'muscular Christian'. A product of William Ellis School, London, Francis had been head boy and captain of football, cricket and tennis. He attended Trinity College, Cambridge, where he further developed his football skills. During the late 1920s he became a lecturer in mathematics at Peterhouse College, Cambridge, where he also coached a team of choir boys at football.[36] But why should he have given up the arcane world of university life at Cambridge and gone to Africa? In the strong traditions of Baden-Powellism Francis answered, 'I suppose I felt that Africans had few guides into the new life which was forced upon them willy-nilly. I believed I knew some things that would help them ... I wanted to share all that I had that was good. I thought educating Africans would be something like running Christian scouts ...'[37]

Figure 4.4. Carey Francis, an advocate of 'muscular Christianity', with his dogs, mother and two Maseno schoolboys, 1934 (source: Greaves, 1969).

Carey Francis was a committed Christian and a strong believer in the traditions of the English private school. 'A devout Evangelist and an unrelenting paternalist',[38] he continued his serious interest in physical fitness. While he did not recommend formal Western clothing to the élite African students at Alliance, he was certainly a great advocate of Western sports. At Maseno he had coached nine football XIs. He organised swimming competitions, wrote a book on hygiene, personally trained the boy instructors who were to coach Alliance to eight years of successive victories in an 'inter school physical training competition', and was elected to the council of the Arab and African Sports Association. He contributed hugely to Alliance's success, building on the apparent athletic ability of his students. Major Selwood, a sports master at the school, had earlier noted the ability of Alliance students in spear-throwing and archery[39] but in the 1950s it was a half-mile performance of 1 minute 57.8 seconds by Luka Njeru which most caught Francis's eye. 'A two minute half-mile at a school like this is in some sense comparable to a 4-minute mile in the great world outside', he observed.[40]

It was Alliance which established something of a breakthrough in race relations in 1949 when it took part in a competition against the whites-only Prince of Wales School. Two years later a triangular match occurred between these two schools and the Indian High School. This was, in effect, the first multi-racial athletics meeting to be held in Kenya. Alliance was, nevertheless, 'a colonial school in a colonial world'; its aim was 'to produce leaders who of course, had the necessary character and knowledge to faithfully but intelligently serve King and Empire'. It was a school of cold showers, raising the Union Jack, parades, boy scouts, mountain climbing, Shakespeare, Biggles – and sports.[41]

Carey Francis, while being of undoubted significance in the history of Kenyan sport, could not fail to betray what Eichberg has termed a 'Pygmalion mentality'.[42] His values were well intentioned, to be sure, but his efforts were essentially undertaken in order to make the African more like the European and less with the interests of the mass of the African population in mind. In an odd mix of Eurocentricism, negation and progressiveness, Francis noted that Kenyan

> boys have a poor background in things of European civilization: they know nothing of wireless and motor bicycles ... yet they are essentially the same as English boys. They would bear comparison with those of European schools in this country, in intelligence, in athletic prowess, in industry, courage and trustworthiness, and as gentlemen.[43]

It is English schools and European boys, of course, against which and whom the Kenyan should be measured. The English were the norm, the

African the 'other'. It is ironic, therefore, that when Francis died in the mid-1960s he was given what amounted to a state funeral by the many leaders of the new Kenya who had been educated under him.

All this is not to say that Alliance was unchallenged at athletics. The most notable opposition came from Jeanes School at Kabete. Founded in 1925 by the government, with the funding of the Carnegie Corporation in New York, it had an educational programme geared towards improving community life. The school's name came from the Jeanes movement in the United States, led by a philanthropic Quaker who supported the development of African-American education in the American south. In addition to health and agriculture, sports formed an important part of the curriculum. An objective was to train rural teachers who, by virtue of their profession, would become leaders of public opinion and disseminate their skills in the villages and reserves. The significance of sport in this dissemination process was recognised in a 1931 guide for visiting teachers which noted that 'daily drill and games will appear later in every bush school they visit'.[44]

Schools such as the Government African School (GAS) at Kapsabet, which had been established in 1926, also played a major part in the development of the sport. A new headmaster, previously at Jeanes, was appointed to GAS Kapsabet in 1940. Arthur Selwood Walford – known popularly to the Nandi as *Chepsungulgei* (indicating a proud, strutting, peacock-like posture) – was to make an important mark on Kenyan athletics too, working with African teachers to take athletics into the villages. In the early 1950s this school had the only accurately measured running track in Nandi district, the lanes inscribed in old engine oil which killed off the grass. A landmark was established in the 1950s when the first permanent track, made of sun-baked compacted earth, was constructed in Nandi, a district which in later years would provide Kenya with most of its best athletes. It was built by local prisoners using shovels and wheelbarrows, being seen by the District Commissioner as a worthy use of their labour.

These schools aped the wide range of trappings common in the traditional English private schools, which were also subsequently copied by the British grammar schools. Cups were regularly awarded for the *victor ludorum*, for example, and inter-district shields were contested. Teams in the Dagoretti district competed for the Goodman Cup. Such prizes served to acculturate Kenyan boys into the English athletic model. It was not so different in the Kikuyu Independent Schools Association and the Karinga Schools Association which had become established in 1929 in opposition to the mission schools. The latter refused to admit any circumcised Kikuyu. With missionary opposition to the circumcision of women, the Kikuyu felt that the missions were encroaching on their cultural rights. The Kikuyu did not oppose Western sport however. On the contrary, they borrowed several aspects of Western culture which did not threaten their own cultural traditions. Annual sports competitions were held, reinforcing further the spread of athletics in Kenya.

The fact that the secondary schools were established for boarders rather than day students would seem to be a central factor in the successful adoption of athletics. Boarding schools provided so much time for things to be done; the pupils were a captive audience and there was no shortage of time for extracurricular athletic training and events. Athletic events were sometimes scheduled to coincide with the birthday of King George V, hence relating Kenyans to Britain by honouring their symbolic ruler. These schools' competitions were, therefore, far from being leisurely entertainments or a means of keeping fit; they were, as Tony Mangan points out, 'a significant instrument of moral training', inculcating the spirit of 'fair play' in the context of athletic competition.[45] The establishment of such facilities as running tracks and the awarding of medals and titles were also, in their own small ways, a local index of the 'physical transformation of the imperial realm'; part of cultural hegemony by persuasive means, rather than through physical force.[46] Indeed, the sports field could be said to have become a metaphor for the Empire. At different levels of scale, each were sites of 'unbreakable laws'; each involved the conquest of space; each was 'many-dimensional, discontinuous, and spatial'.[47]

Betwixt and between folk and modern sport

It is difficult to recreate and represent in words the character of Kenyan athletics between the 1920s and the 1950s. There were clear signs of 'sportisation', evidenced, of course, by the formation of a *de facto* national bureaucracy to govern athletics in the form of the Arab and African Sports Association. But in the composition of athletic events, the modern, sportised versions co-existed with more traditional forms. The flavour of such local sports meetings is caught in the contemporary comments of a European visitor to a Maasai sports event in 1929. Daphne Moore, the wife of the future Governor of Kenya, wrote:

> We trooped off to the sports ground after lunch and spent the afternoon there, till after dark, watching the Maasai doing the high and long jumps, 100 yards, bolster bar, etc. For each event there

was a junior and an open entry, the junior competitors being the boys of the Maasai Government school ... and the senior warriors from every part of the Maasai reserve. ... The audience watched the proceedings with enormous interest and much display of partisanship, but mishaps on the part of the competitors raised far more applause than exhibitions of athletic skill. The two most popular and most interesting events were spear-throwing and the tug-of-war. The spears were about six or seven feet long, the blade being three feet of soft metal and the shaft a few inches of wood, joined to another three feet of pointed iron. .... The target was a lion skin stretched out on sticks and the men had to throw from a distance of thirty yards. It is a beautiful action, like a drawing on a Greek vase.[48]

The 'sports ground' where these events took place was an open expanse of grassland edged by bushes with the athletes competing in native clothing. The pre-sportised world of the spectators' laughter at the antics of the athletes overlapped the world of achievement sport with its accurately measured and deadly serious 100 yards sprint. The indigenous form of spear throwing coexisted with the modern high jump, graphically revealing the limen between pre-modern and modern sport. Similar events, often held in conjunction with cattle sales, attracted huge crowds and continued into the early 1950s.

In the early 1930s an 'obstacle race' was included in the 'African Olympics', again reminiscent of a more fun-oriented athletics than is found today. While inspecting GAS Kapsabet in 1933, a government inspector found folk games being played with much enthusiasm. They had been integrated into the school's 'drill' lessons – an example of physical education through the use of a form of body culture to which the students could relate. These periods of drill would be followed, however, by some hard running around the quarter mile track. A more traditional form of body culture was also evidenced by the widespread presence of the 'spear throwing' event, often at a target, rather than as in the modern javelin throw for distance. The absence of a standardised javelin and the use of a traditional spear reflected a residual folk-tradition and a sporting environment that was not yet fully modernised.

At Alliance High School in the 1930s, spear throwing and archery were encouraged alongside the more standardised athletic events. At the Maasai School at Kajaido, Maasai movement culture such as 'hares and hounds' and 'lions and warriors' were practised. Major Clarence Buxton, an energetic district officer in Maasai district, held athletics meetings in conjunction with lion hunts.[49] The lion hunts were perceived as a prerequisite for Maasai participation in athletics. The programme for the Tambach district sports meeting in December 1939 included a number of traditional forms of entertainment such as club (*rungut*) throwing and archery, alongside the usual running and jumping events. The fact that over 100 bowmen turned out to show their skills indicated the continued popularity of the folk traditions at that time. Sometimes sports events dispensed with the track and field syllabus altogether and concentrated on more traditional folk cultures, attracting, as they did, larger crowds. A local sports event at Marakwet in 1941, for example, included a 'cross country' race down the escarpment as well as archery and club throwing.

Despite these continuing folk legacies, athletic events were gradually being recorded and quantified. More precise indicators of achievement were replacing the anecdotes of many of the travellers' tales. For example, in the 1935 'Olympic Sports', Bartion'y Arap Chemoron won the high jump with a performance measured at 5 feet 7 inches (1.702 metres). Later that year he was to break the Kenyan record with a leap of 5 feet 10 inches (1.778 metres). For most secondary schools, however, records did not start to be kept until the late 1940s. Even in the 1950s many track and field meetings were a world of both the traditional and the modern – without conflict but arguably in an uneasy alliance. The 'landscape' in Figure 4.5, showing a Maasai runner and high jumper taking part in a 'sports meeting' at Narosura, is neither wholly African nor European. The photographs make up part of a much larger portfolio taken during the 1940s and 1950s by the Africanist Joy Adamson. For some Europeans, at least, the enemy was now a spectacle.

Adamson's reading of Maasai athletic performance included the claim that 'one exceptionally good looking and very tall young *moran*, Sijey Auge, beat the world record for a high jump with such ease that wherever he went the cheering never stopped'.[50] She did not, however, provide us with a recorded height (a somewhat uncharacteristic omission in view of the European propensity to quantify African performance) and we have no knowledge of the extent of her familiarity with world athletics. At the time the world high jump record was 6 feet 11 inches (2.108 metres). This kind of alleged performance is certainly consistent with the traditional praise for the African's physicality. It also accords with the Maasai–Tutsi link, noted earlier, although the exceptional performances claimed (and apparently authenticated through photographs) for the Tutsi were never claimed for the Maasai in earlier travel writing. We are, therefore, reluctantly forced to conclude that her claim is almost certainly unfounded.

Figure 4.5. Between disport and sport. (Above) Maasai runner taking part in a 'long distance race'; (below) Maasai high jumper. The date of the event at which these pictures were taken is uncertain. They probably depict scenes in the late 1940s or early 1950s (source: Adamson, 1967, p.232).

In Figure 4.5 the anonymous runner's body management and the apparent absence of a specialised track for the 'long distance race' reflect an African tradition rather than a European tradition. In the case of the high jumper, the specially produced high jump equipment (in contrast to that in Figure 3.2) and the pith-helmeted official stand in contrast to the grass take-off, the barefoot jumper and his native headdress. The closeness of the spectators can also be contrasted with the modern, more detached and distanced crowd; and, like the distance race, no special site appears to have been prepared for the event. But despite the apparent 'Africanness' of these images, it could be argued that (like many of those of traditional African 'sports' taken earlier in the century) they display power, confined and arranged. The crowd is presented as orderly and controlled. The athletes providing the spectacle are certified as the 'other' by their native clothing or their nudity, by their exotic style, and by the invisibility of their agriculture; but they are domesticated by the photographic capture, by the British-imposed order on their sport.[51]

As with Figure 3.2, however, it is not clear what kind of 'event' is taking place. The high jump and the 'distance race' could be competitions (and Adamson suggests that they are) but they could equally be posed demonstrations. We are not sure what images are being sought by the photographer. They could be pictures of 'progress' with the African engaging in 'organised' sport under the colonial official's supervision (unobtrusive in the way the photograph is framed); or they could be representations of 'raw natives' demonstrating their natural physical ability. Through the camera's gaze the photographer certainly seeks to encourage our interest in the runner in nature rather than in culture, and in the native jumper rather than in the occidental official. What is going through the minds of each of them? And through the minds of the spectators? In these ambiguous pictures it is not clear whether they are faithful portraits or whether they reflect a concern for the photographer's own society.[52]

Although the performances of the winners in track events were timed to one tenth of a second (times of non-winning athletes were rarely, if ever, recorded), it was clear that the measurement of the tracks or, more likely, the distances run, were sometimes inaccurate. The number of laps run by each runner could easily become confused with large numbers of athletes taking part. In the 'African Olympics' in 1947, for example, the winners of the three miles and six miles, Leting and Tarus respectively, were timed at 13 minutes 13.7 seconds and 28 minutes 33.6 seconds. The respective world records at that time were 13 minutes and 42.4 seconds, and 28 minutes 55.6 seconds. The excited spectators thought

Figure 4.6. The 1949 Kenyan championships at Nakuru, showing the long jump competition in progress (source: Colonial Office, *Report on the Colony and Protectorate of Kenya*, 1951, p. 72).

that world records had been broken until it was realised that the races had been run over incorrect distances.

The colony championships were traditionally held at Nairobi and later at Kisumu, Nakuru and Nyeri. The 1949 event at Nakuru certainly had a decidedly 'modern' look about it – yet another symbol of the European appropriation of the African landscape. Figure 4.6 shows an impressive arena with the crowd segregated from the area of performance, and a very well supported event with white officials overseeing African competitors. Yet some of the times recorded in the long distance races in the 1948 and 1949 championships must also be regarded with suspicion, even if this may appear to adopt a Eurocentric attitude toward African performances. In 1948 the time recorded for the 3 miles was 13 minutes 15.4 seconds which would also have been a world record, and in 1949 the 6 mile event was recorded at 30 minutes 12 seconds, a time which would have been the second fastest in the world that year. Some of the performances recorded at the 1946 event appear more plausible: for example, 22.5 seconds for the 220 yards by Kimutai, 51.5 for the 440 by Kipsuge, 15 minutes 15 seconds for the 3 miles by Noah Leting and 31 minutes 29.6 seconds for the six miles by Tarus.

It is now appropriate to return to one of the themes of the previous chapter, namely the possibility of a carry-over or a continuity from folk-games to modern sports. Sometimes the link between tradition and change appeared easy. In 1950s Kenya, for example, it was noted that

> at a national championships meeting a member of a warrior and hunting tribe was competing in throwing the javelin. He presented himself at the assembly point in his tribal dress and with his spear. No amount of persuasion could get him to change into athletic dress and only by dint of much argument could he be prevailed upon to use the javelin. The net result was a throw of 194 feet 5 inches (about 59.28 metres) made from well behind the throwing line.[53]

How might we evaluate such a performance? It was certainly very good by prevailing African standards and good by British standards. However, like those from the 1946 championships noted above, and those of the high jumpers from the 1930s noted earlier, it was modest by world standards. The world record stood 60 feet (18.30 metres) further. The performances we have described do not seem earth-shattering enough to support the implicit view of 'the "primitive" as an idealized male type, an athletic version of the "noble savage"'.[54] They were the kinds of performances which would be expected of talented newcomers to the sport anywhere, as much (but no more) 'natural' as 'cultural' but supporting the notion that the fabulous athleticism of the Kenyans was 'the progeny of fable rather than measurement'.[55] When maths replaced myths or when the norms of modern sport were applied to the early post-war Kenyan athletes, they generally appear to be the promising novices that they were.

As noted in the last chapter, however, there is a need for caution here. After all, we have no idea of how hard the athletes were trying or how well their lifestyles had prepared them to perform in the white man's sports. It is plausible that the notion of 'maximum effort' was unknown to many Kenyans at that time. Early Kenyan track and field measurements were not weighted for the athletes' degree of motivation.

By 1949, athletics was spreading throughout the country but especially in the central and western districts. Football was the most popular sport in Nyanza but the Rift Valley was very clearly the dominant athletics province.[56] The social control function remained clearly explicated, however. Commenting on the growth in the number of sports grounds, the District Commissioner for Elgeyo-Marakwet, for example, noted that

> a good deal of energy was evinced, if not much skill, and attendances were quite good, particularly at Tot and Kamarin. It is

felt that the promotion of sports is worth a great deal of attention. It provides recreation, entertainment and diversion and is an antidote to those local channels of youthful activity such as stock-theft and beer drinking.[57]

Such writing reflected not only the appropriation of native resources for the construction of sports grounds but also the appropriation of the native point of view. The District Commissioner spoke *for* the African.[58]

While athletics was being adopted at many locations throughout the colony, as noted above it would be wrong to assume that the sport was evenly spread among the tribes and regions. In the Rift Valley, the Kalenjin, especially the Nandi, had, between the mid-1930s and the late 1940s, already established a degree of dominance which marked them out from other tribes. In Nandi district the administration showed considerable pride in the performance of the athletics team. The local Native Council, of its own accord, requested that each taxpayer in the district should contribute 10 cents to a Nandi Sports Fund. The effort raised 1,000 shillings which would be used for the development of sport and the purchase of sports equipment. This type of initiative pointed the way to involvement in cultural importation as a self-sustaining activity on the part of Kenyans themselves.

A small, but nevertheless significant index of the extent to which running had become part of Nandi life by the late 1940s is revealed in the contents of a little reading book for upper primary school students, written by the English educationist, J.M. Popkin, while serving as a teacher in Kapsabet between 1948 and 1950. Written in Nandi, three of its 36 sections are devoted to an imaginary account of a boy runner (Kipserem) who progressed from his local sports all the way to the inter-territorial meeting, using the organisational framework of athletics in Kenya (see below) to introduce pupils to regional geography.[59]

In contrast to the Nandi, the Maasai were much more reluctant to participate in athletics (and in European culture in general), despite the popular images of their athletic prowess which had been communicated by the European media. In 1930 a disillusioned district officer remarked that Massai '*moran* are not really keen on sports but submit to them as an easy method of pleasing District Officers'.[60] They suspected that encouraging them to take part in sports was simply another way of recruiting them into the KAR.[61] Nor did they necessarily adopt the gentlemanly conduct desired by their white tutors. At athletics meetings and football matches a man who lost an event or made a poor showing on the field was 'treated with withering contempt by his fellows' noted one European observer in the early 1950s.[62]

Despite the Maasai's apparent lack of interest in athletics, the administration's decision to concentrate its attention on field events involving jumping and throwing led to the imperial influence prevailing, to some extent. For example, Jonathan Lenemuria – who was noted at London's White City Stadium in 1954 (see Chapter 1) – was a member of the Samburu, regarded by many as related to the Maasai. His achievements reflected the success of the colonial coaxing of such athletes into competition when he broke the Kenyan high jump record with a leap of 6 feet 2 inches (1.88 metres) in 1948. A year later two *moran* won second and third places in the spear-throwing competition and also showed some modest success in distance running. Even so, the Maasai resisted the incorporation of Western culture more than other tribes in Kenya. Difficulty in encouraging Maasai children to go to school has persisted until recently.[63]

The District Officer at the coastal town of Malindi also found it difficult and frustrating to teach Western forms of movement culture. He 'found the Arabs generally very apathetic to physical exertion required in chasing a ball or running'. He added, hopefully, that 'when the Giryama of Malindi sub-district have come into closer contact with Europeans doubtless they will take more interest in athletics than at present'.[64] He was over-optimistic.

It should be noted that many Kenyans, in addition to those in the coastal areas, remained uninterested in track and field. The colonial schools could only take a small proportion of the total population. For women it was culturally unacceptable given the domestic traditions of their lives. And for those Kenyans who by now had been seduced to advancement within a colonial structure, schools were more often seen to mean economic, not athletic, advancement. As Mangan has put it, for many students 'schools were for school certificates, not for sport'; often the Kenyan's *toga virilis* was not the running vest but the graduate gown.[65]

Despite the uneven adoption of athletics in Kenya, its colonisation was unquestionably taking place. Yet Kenya did not yet have its own centralised governing body. This was to come with the formal adoption (that is, the national bureaucratisation) of the sport in the 1950s which was to bring Kenyan athletics closer to modernity.

On the brink of modern sport

As we have shown, the development of athletics in Kenya was encouraged by a variety of agencies. Among them was the Arab and

African Sports Association which, in 1949, requested the government to appoint a Colony Sports Officer who would be responsible for the development of sports throughout the colony. The successful appointee was A.E. (Archie) Evans who developed a well-organised system of athletic competitions, organised on a typically modern principle, that of a hierarchical arrangement of competitions at the local, divisional, district, provincial, national and inter-territorial levels. At the local (or 'locational') level, the meetings were run and organised by Africans. In the late 1940s the enthusiastic Kiptalam Keter organised and competed in locational sports while a pupil at GAS Kapsabet. In the early days no times were taken, selection for the higher level competitions being judged on rank order of finishing alone. Nor, at this level, were tracks accurately measured. Indeed, for the six miles race athletes ran on the road rather than track. At higher levels of competition, the meetings were organised and run by Europeans.[66]

It was Evans who was to initiate the formation of the Kenya AAA in 1951 and become its first secretary. The Alliance High School connection was maintained with one of its members, Charles O'Hagen, being the interim chairman. With a national governing body, competition could now take place between the Europeans, Asians, Africans and Arabs for the first time.

From the imperial perspective of the early 1950s, however, it could hardly be said that Kenya had developed any kind of 'image' of athletics. It was certainly not projected in contemporary colonialist literature. In the annual report on the colony by the Colonial Office in 1951 athletics was not even thought worthy of mention. The impression gained was that things were little different from the situation described in the promotional literature provided for the colonists of the 1910s. It was acknowledged in the report that every kind of sport could be enjoyed in Kenya but only the visits of a London University football team, a cricket team from Southern Rhodesia, a group of polo players from South Africa, and several of the world's leading golfers were considered worthy of mention.[67] Forty years later it would have been impossible to write in this way.

The first Kenya AAA championships were held at the Services Sports Ground in Nairobi on 6 October 1951. Unlike the earlier 'African Olympics', this was a multi-racial event despite the fact that a *de facto* colour-bar still operated in some parts of the country. Some aspects of the modernisation of Kenyan track and field were by now becoming evident. In 1949, for example, a regulation javelin replaced the traditional spear among the throwing events. Running tracks were increasing in number and more events were being recorded. The hierarchical system of athletic organisation in Kenya was typically modern, as was the notion of the further 'development' of Kenyan athletics. The Jeanes School had become the national focus for the sport. Courses in athletics for teachers and community development officers were organised there. The school had good training facilities and hosted various athletic teams when competitions were taking place in Nairobi. The school also acted as a residential camp for athletes selected for international competitions. During their period of residence they were coached by Evans. Community development assistants were involved in complementing the role of the district officers at the local level. They were expected to gain experience in organising sports meetings.

Among the most influential of the community officers of this period was Stanley Lockwood, an officer stationed at Mukureini in Nyeri who encouraged a large number of athletic meetings. Lockwood's programme of large scale athletic competition at the local level was subsequently adopted by other community development officers such as Edward (Ted) Harris who was based at Kapsabet in Nandi District. Nandi teachers were encouraged to assist in coaching and this move further contributed to the development of the sport.

Yet even in the early 1950s the flavour of earlier days remained. For example, on the occasion of the second Sikh Union athletic meeting at Eldoret in 1954 the times of the winners of the track events were not recorded. In addition, weight-lifting, tug-of-war, speed cycling, and 'slow cycling' were held in conjunction with the track events. Prizes for slowness were not to continue for very much longer. At the first inter-racial sports meeting of the African Railway Recreation Sports Club held a year earlier, also in Eldoret, the events were said to still provide 'much amusing entertainment'. They also continued to display considerable colonial patronage, evidenced by the report that a 'Mrs Mitchell, wife of the engineer in charge, cool and attractive in a sheer floral frock with white accessories, presented the prizes with grace and charm, the successful competitors receiving blankets, hurricane lamps, saucepans, *posho* etc.'[68] Getting the wife of a local dignitary to present the prizes was a popular part of the organisation of such ceremonies.

The seeds of the internationalisation of Kenyan athletic competition – a further index of its modernisation – can be said to have started following discussions between Kenyan and Ugandan delegates in 1934 when it was decided to initiate an inter-territorial athletics championship to be held annually between the two colonies. The first of these was held on a grass track at Kampala in Uganda in November, 1934. It involved eleven events with the throws being excluded. Alliance High School provided five students and two 'old boys' for the Kenyan team, one of the students reducing the Kenyan half-mile record to 1 minute 59.3 seconds. This was about ten seconds slower than the world record at the time, a further indication of the prevailing standards. Kenya won the first of these competitions and continued to dominate them in subsequent years. It was the Uganda-Kenya meeting which probably led the governing bodies of both nations to affiliate to the Amateur Athletic Association of England in 1936, another indication of the sport's growing international links.

In a somewhat inauspicious event held in 1952 two KAR soldiers became the first Kenyan athletes to win overseas titles. Competing respectively in the Malayan javelin and 3 mile championships in Ipoh, Chepkwony threw a distance of 55.39 metres and Kipsang registered a time of 15 minutes 3.4 seconds and became the Malayan record holder.[69] Later that year a Kenyan multi-ethnic team of 23 athletes was to make its first appearance in an international competition outside east Africa when it competed in the Indian Ocean Games in Madagascar. The event attracted a team of French Olympic athletes. While symbolically marking Kenya's entry into international competition it was rather ironic that it took place in a French-speaking part of Africa and not within the British Commonwealth. The Madagascan event was significant for the dramatic victory of Nyandika Maiyoro in the 3,000 metres. He only realised that the race had started when the field had run 100 metres down the track. Although still wearing his clothes and ordinary shoes, he entered the race, disrobing as he ran to the amusement of the crowd. After four laps he had caught the other runners and proceeded to win the race by 50 metres.

In August 1953 a Kenyan team of 22 Africans participated in an international meeting at Nkana in Zambia (then Northern Rhodesia) called the Central African Games, organised as part of the Rhodes centenary celebrations. Kenya demonstrated its dominance as the major athletic nation in British East Africa by winning the 'Copperbelt Trophy'. The best Kenyan performance was in the javelin where Tesot Maboria won with a throw of 198 feet 4 inches (60.45 metres).[70] The President of the national association observed that the Kenyan victories projected the nation's visibility in the world of African sport. The community development officer's report of these games implicitly recognised the subsequent internationalisation of athletics, though it failed to avoid both a degree of self-congratulation and allusion to Britain's imperial past:

> although the Central African territories were so out-classed, the points gained are of minor importance, for the first time Africans

from East and Central Africa have been able to meet socially and
engage in friendly rivalry on the sports field. This in itself is an
achievement and out of the games held in the centenary year of the
birth of Cecil Rhodes ... will come further tournaments of this
nature and sense to bring the African races of this vast continent
closer together.[71]

We have presented the inculcation of the 'games ethic', and hence
'Britishness' into the imperial realm as an efficient means of performing
a significant degree of social control, a function explicated by several
observers of the Kenyan scene in the first half of the twentieth century.
At the same time, we should not ignore the fact that an additional value,
that of 'manliness' has been central in our story so far.[72] 'Manliness' is
literal; women athletes have not been mentioned simply because they
were not significantly involved. Their invisibility in Kenyan running
reflected a form of 'double colonisation' – the patriarchy of men and of
colonial power. Indeed, it was not until 1956 that the first official
women's athletic competition was held in Kenya.[73] Women in Kenyan
society have traditionally assumed a domestic role – home-making,
child-rearing, cooking, cleaning and washing.[74] The inferior status of the
woman was also reflected in a number of traditional tribal rituals.[75]
Perhaps it is not surprising, therefore, that when international
competition for Kenyan women started in 1965 (by which time several
of the male athletes were of world class) a European-Kenyan was the
most prominent. When a Kenyan team participated in the first All-
African Games at Brazzaville in the Congo it was Diana Monks who
won the 80 metres hurdles, the first Kenyan woman athlete to make any
kind of international impact.

Interpretations and conclusions

The early history of Kenyan athletics clearly illustrates the role of
imperialists in spreading the athletic values of Victorian and Edwardian
England. It is fair to point out, however, that in the first third of the
century the colonial district officers cannot be said to have seen their job
as operating an athletic assembly line of Kenyan versions of Harold
Abrahams or Sydney Wooderson. 'Where such sporting demigods have
since arisen on the African scene, any seminal influence of the athletic
D.O. is hard to trace'.[76] Yet they did possess and transmit an ethos, an
atmosphere, an ideology. Sporting excellence for the colonial
'athletocracy' may have been a means to an end and not an end in itself;

it may have made the Briton a better administrator; but it also provided the milieu in which the Kenyan could become a better athlete, in the Western and modern sense of the word.[77] The principal agents in the diffusion of athletics were the foreign schoolmasters and district commissioners whose activities were to continue into the 1950s and early 1960s. Indeed, the role of European school teachers as agents involved in socialising young Kenyans into sports has continued to the present day, as the next chapter will show.

For several decades, athletics was a mixture of the African and the European. Fun was mixed with seriousness. It was, in a way, a kind of 'creole culture' belonging in its cultural mode to both the Kenyan and the Briton at the same time.[78] Unlike other forms of creolisation in popular culture, however, it could not last in athletics. Colonial contact through language and sex both produced hybrids (pidgin, creole and miscegenated children), leading to a 'pidgin' model, different from the simple dualism of colonialist and colonised.[79] In sport, however, it was (with the rare exception of Trobriand cricket)[80] all or nothing. No hybrid forms could be accommodated under the imperial measures (literally and metaphorically imposed) and the global rules and regulations which were to make sporting contests meaningful; the influence of fully sportised running, throwing and jumping made the culture of athletics monolithic. It was the end of a 'production line' which was based on the antithesis between the 'primitive' and the 'civilised'. This view had come over clearly in Lord Cranworth's book, *A Colony in the Making*, in which a photograph of a prospective member of the KAR in native dress was described as 'the raw material'; it was juxtaposed with an illustration of two impeccably uniformed members of the KAR dubbed 'the made article'.[81] Equally 'made' were the 'products' of the schools and missions who were to emerge in athletic uniforms and running shoes – examples of 'human material ... processed by the [colonial] machine', as Lord Cromer put it in his essay 'The government of subject races'.[82] This conversion of the 'natural' runner to the 'cultural' athlete can therefore be viewed as a human analogue of the systematising of nature and a part of 'a European discourse about non-European worlds'.[83]

We are here reminded of the possible application of the work of Michel Foucault to sport in the context of Kenyan athletics. Athletics can be viewed as what Foucault would call a 'disciplinary mechanism'. Modern running is clearly *a* discipline; it is also a tool with which *to* discipline others.[84] It is spatially contained and subject to considerable surveillance. But it could also be viewed, according to one's socio-political disposition, as an 'ideological state apparatus' or a form of 'hegemony'.[85]

The European values inculcated during this period were most visible in the changing cultural landscape. After all, the taking of land for the cultivation of another culture was a primary objective of colonialism. What was perceived as a primitive, unkempt landscape had created primitive people. By taming the wildness the British came to tame the primitive African; 'altering the landscape, in other words, asserts social control and advances imperialism'.[86] The schools, the army bases and the police stations had their sports fields and geometrically inscribed running tracks. Such landscape elements would have been totally absent forty years earlier in the 'chaotic glory' of the African ideal.[87] The running track, with its uniform plane and imperial measurements, was, in its own small way, an Imperial strategy involving the mastery of space. Whereas many traditional body cultures had taken place within the homestead or in places used for day-to-day activities, the sports field with its 440 yards track (reaching its apotheosis in the fully contained stadium) required a special space, separated from the day to day activities of the people and their social life. It was a typically modern, territorialised, space.[88] The 100 yards straight was a sporting analogue of the railway line from Mombasa to Nairobi; each was a colonial 'reaction to the winding African footpath'; each was a 'straight line, a man-made construct ... indicative of order and environmental control'.[89] It may be true, as Robert Young suggests, that 'a culture never repeats itself perfectly away from home'[90] yet the cultural landscape of sport does, of necessity (in order to produce meaningful and comparable performances), repeat itself from place to place, almost perfectly – and in doing so becomes placeless.

Such new 'formal ritual spaces',[91] and the practices which occurred on them, were secured by the central presence of the record and of recording (in other words, a system of surveillance). The record symbolically replaced the oral traditions of an earlier Kenyan society. As the African's spatiality was erased and place became more of an athletics space, so the pre-modern African became an athletic 'other', his movement culture being defined in terms of the imperialist.[92] The African view of such 'progress' may have been different from that of the colonialist, the imperialist, the schoolteacher and the athletics coach. For Ngugi wa Thiong'o, for example, the carefully prepared running track and the kind of running which took place on it might reflect, like the colonialist's carefully-tended garden, 'a well-finished application of sweat, ... [but with] so much energy and brains wasted'.[93]

The athletic body, as well as the cultural landscape, had changed. The relatively unrestricted and free movement of the pre-colonial period had been replaced by the corset of running as racing with its starting and finishing lines and its geometrically arranged lane markings. The bodies of the colonised athletic populace were 'captured' in these new spaces or landscapes of power. There was also the associated temporal tyranny of the stopwatch with races timed to a tenth of a second and a clear programme of hierarchical competitions neatly broken down into specialised events.

It can be argued, of course, that gains were obtained from these changes and we shall return to a sort of 'balance sheet' in relation to Kenyan athletics in our final chapter. Kenya was affiliated to the IAAF in 1954 and the Kenya Olympic Association was formed in 1955. The country hence became a *de jure* member of the global sporting community. 1954 witnessed the events at the White City and Vancouver. Cardiff and Rome were to follow, as were the achievements of Kipchoge Keino, Henry Rono, Moses Kiptanui and all the other great Kenyan runners. Nevertheless, in 1954 Kenyan running was still largely based in Kenya, east Africa, and the British Empire. The next chapter sees Kenyan athletes reaching out to modernity and globalisation.

Notes and references

1. Turner, *Dramas, Fields, and Metaphors*, p. 232.
2. Gale, *East Africa (British)*, p. 127; Huxley, *White Man's Country*, pp. 252–3; Cranworth, *Kenyan Chronicles*, pp. 86–7. Perhaps the best and most vivid descriptions of early colonialist and settler sports are found in Cranworth, *A Colony in the Making*.
3. Weller, *Kenya Without Prejudice*, p. 32. Note also Mählmann, 'Sport as a weapon of colonialism in Kenya', pp. 172–85. The new 'sports spaces' of Kenya were not restricted to such activities as recreational sports, however. In the 1910s and 1920s, the sports ground in Nairobi was equally well known for its political meetings. Not for nothing was it known as 'Kenya's Hyde Park Corner': Rosberg and Nottingham, *The Myth of the 'Mau Mau'*, p. 25.
4. Lewis and Foy, *The British in Africa*.
5. Fox, *White Mischief*, pp. 25–6.
6. Weller, *Kenya Without Prejudice*.
7. Huxley, *White Man's Country*, p. 239.
8. Urch, *The Africanization of the Curriculum in Kenya*, p. 103.
9. Eichberg, 'The societal construction of time and space'.
10. Letters of C.M. Dodds, held at Rhodes House Library, Oxford, MSS.Afr.S.504.
11. Moyse-Bartlett, *The Kings African Rifles*, p. 3.
12. Meinertzhagen, *Kenya Diary*, pp. 22–3.
13. Webster, *Why? The Science of Athletics*, p. 341.
14. We are grateful to David Terry for this observation. It is recorded that, in British East Africa in the 1900s, British officers did engage in tug-of-war competitions against native soldiers: see Younghusband, *Glimpses of East Africa and Zanzibar*, p. 306.
15. Kennedy, *Islands of White*, pp. 46–7.

16. Kirk-Greene, 'Imperial administration and the athletic imperative', pp. 81–113.
17. Berman, *Control and Crisis in Colonial Kenya*, p. 100 (italics added).
18. Ibid, p. 101.
19. Quoted in Kenya National Archives (hereafter KNA), ADM 21/2/342.
20. Quoted in Murray-Brown, *Kenyatta*, p. 47. Dr Arthur's battle against the circumcision of Kenyan women is described in Hyam, *Sexuality and Empire*, pp. 192–4.
21. Leys, *Kenya*, p. 329.
22. Hughes, *East Africa*, p. 109.
23. Leys, *Kenya*, p. 255.
24. Quoted in Clayton, 'Sport and African soldiers', p. 135.
25. Watkins, *Jomo's Jailor*, p. 54.
26. Bale, 'Sports history as innovation diffusion'.
27. Foran, *The Kenya Police*, p. 64.
28. R.G.B. Spicer, *Police Department Annual Reports*, 1925, p. 7.
29. KNA/PC/PVP 2/3/2. p. 6.
30. Hollis, 'The Maasai', p. 124. Note also Ranger, 'The invention of tradition in Africa', p. 235.
31. Ibid.
32. Noronha, *Kipchoge of Kenya*, p. 21.
33. Quoted in Jones, *Education in East Africa*, p. 32.
34. Cagnolo, *The Akikuyu*, pp. 282–3 (italics added).
35. Quoted in KNA, CMS 1/275.
36. Greaves, *Carey Francis of Kenya*.
37. Ibid, p. 17.
38. Throup, *Economic and Social Origins of Mau Mau*, p. 267.
39. Quoted in KNA, ED1/1023.
40. Greaves, *Carey Francis*, p. 136.
41. Thiong'o, *Moving the Centre*, p. 136.
42. Eichberg, 'Travelling, comparing, emigrating'.
43. Greaves, *Carey Francis*, p.140.
44. KNA, CMS 1/275.
45. Mangan, *The Games Ethic*, p. 191.
46. Said, *Culture and Imperialism*, p. 131.
47. Ibid.
48. Daphne Moore's papers, 1929, p. 24, quoted in Watkins, *Jomo's Jailor*, p. 57.
49. KNA, PC/SP 1/2/2.
50. Adamson, *The Peoples of Kenya*, pp. 230–3.
51. Faris, 'Photography, power and the southern Nuba', p. 214.
52. Jackson, 'Constructions of culture, representations of race', pp. 89–106; see also Scherer, 'The photographic document'. For an excellent insight into the variety of photographic gazes, see Lutz and Collins, *Reading National Geographic*, Chapter 7.
53. Millar and Cowley, *Athletics*, p. 11. We are grateful to David Terry for this reference.
54. Hoberman, *Mortal Engines*, p. 37.
55. Guttmann, *From Ritual to Record*, p. 51.
56. Colony and Protectorate of Kenya, African Affairs Department, *Annual Report, 1949* (Nairobi, Government Printer: 1951); quoted in KNA/PC/RVP 2/3/5.
57. Quoted in KNA, DC/KAJ 2/1/1.
58. Spurr, *The Rhetoric of Empire*, p. 34.
59. Popkin, *Kitabutab Bik che ng'ololi Nandi*. We are grateful to Michael Popkin for

drawing our attention to this everyday item, from which it is clear that in the late 1940s and early 1950s, running *meant* something to Nandi primary schoolboys.

60. Quoted in KNA, PC/RVP2/3/4 p. 31.
61. Quoted in KNA, ADM 21/2/342.
62. Stoneham, *Out of Barbarism*, pp. 37–8.
63. Knowles and Collet, 'Nature as myth'.
64. Quoted in KNA/PC/RVP 2/3/5.
65. Mangan, 'Tom Brown in Tropical Africa'.
66. We are grateful to Michael Popkin for much of the information in this paragraph.
67. Colonial Office, *Report on the Colony and Protectorate of Kenya*, p. 144.
68. Papers of G.J. Brindley, Rhodes House Library, Oxford: MSS.Afr.S.950. Posho is maize meal.
69. Quercetani and Regli, *International Athletics Annual, 1954*, p. 150. We are grateful to Tony Isaacs for the information on Chepkwony.
70. Ibid, p. 168. At the time the world record was 78.70 metres (258 feet $2^3/_8$ inches).
71. Quoted in CDO, 1953, p. 8.
72. Mangan, *The Games Ethic*.
73. Quoted in KNA PC/NKU 2/32/3.
74. Boit, 'Where are the Kenyan women runners?', pp. 22–7.
75. The situation and status of women in pre-modern Kenya is illustrated by a ritual preceding male circumcision. This involved bands of Kikuyu youths seeking a non-local woman with each youth raping her. 'In practice the ceremonial rape was ritually reduced, at least for most of the band, to a masturbatory ejaculation on the woman's body or in her presence' (Lambert, *Kikuyu Social and Political Institutions*, pp. 53–4). In addition, female circumcision had been common among many tribes until being abolished as late as 1982. It was only in 1985 that the preference laws favouring sons were abolished: see Boit, 'Where are the Kenyan women runners?'.
76. Kirk-Greene, 'Imperial administration', p. 108.
77. Ibid.
78. Hannerz, 'The world in creolisation', pp. 546–59.
79. Young, *Colonial Desire*, p. 5.
80. Trobriand cricket is illustrated in an anthropological film by J.W. Leach and Gary Kildea. See Guttmann, *Games and Empires*, pp. 185–6. Guttmann is surely wrong, however, to aver that this sport has become Trobriand cricket; rather it is a hybrid form, neither English nor Trobriand.
81. Cranworth, *A Colony*, p. 205.
82. Quoted in Young, *Colonial Desire*, p. 106.
83. Pratt, *Imperial Eyes*, pp. 34–5.
84. On Foucault and sport see Harvey and Sparks, 'The politics of the body in the context of modernity'; Andrews, 'Desperately seeking Michel'; Rail and Harvey, 'Body at work'; and Vigarello, 'The life of the body in *Discipline and Punish*'. From a spatial perspective, the open spaces of the sensuous African body culture and the contrast with the confined and regulated European athletics, with its surveillance and discipline, is certainly analogous to parts of Michel Foucault's *Discipline and Punish*.
85. These terms are associated with the work of Louis Althusser and Antonio Gramsci respectively. The application of their ideas to sport are outlined in Jarvie and Maguire, *Sport and Leisure in Social Thought*.
86. Binder and Burnett, 'Ngugi wa Thiong'o and the search for a populist landscape aesthetic', p. 51.

87. Ibid, p. 51.
88. Larsen and Gormsen, *Bodyculture*, p. 109.
89. Cairns, *Prelude to Imperialism*, p. 78. Note the allusion that 'no native path runs straight for more than a few yards': Stoneham, *Out of Barbarism*, p. 77.
90. Quoted in Young, *Colonial Desire*, p. 174.
91. Hobsbawm, 'Mass producing traditions', p. 304.
92. The gendered personal pronoun in this sentence is intended to be taken literally. The ideas in this paragraph are based largely on those in Gregory, *Geographical Imaginations*, pp. 171–3.
93. Thiong'o, *Petals of Blood*, p. 146.

5

Modernisation: Sport as a Global System

In the world of high modernity it has become virtually impossible to make sense of what happens in a place without looking beyond the local horizon.

DEREK GREGORY, *Geographical Imaginations*

In recent decades major changes have occurred which have increased the *global* character of the relationships impinging on various domains of human experience.[1] Among these domains are sports in general and track and field athletics in particular. The significance of track and field in this respect is that it is the sport which attracts representatives of more nations to its major spectacles than any other – even more than football. It is the most global of sports. At the time of writing, 206 countries were affiliated to the IAAF. Surely, in such a global culture as track and field athletics, we obtain, through the shared experience of outstanding and dramatic performances, the 'world memories' which, to an extent at least, 'unite humanity' – the opposite of the 'cleavages' formed by other world experiences such as world wars and colonialism. Such 'unifications' of humanity – or at least sectors of humanity – can be regarded as another kind of 'imagined community', a term we introduced towards the end of Chapter 3. In this case, however, they are communities which are *simulated* via mass media images and international sports spectators. Hence, the world track and field community can be regarded as an example of a 'simulated power bloc'.[2] This is not to deny the ideological purpose served by such 'unification'. Kenyan athletics is clearly implicated in the globalisation process and we will argue that an understanding of the country's emergence in track and field can only be achieved by taking the global dimension into account. It cannot be explained by looking at events and environments in Kenya alone.

As we noted in our opening chapter, Kenya's presence on the global athletics scene was first recognised in 1954, although international, if not global, influences were clearly being felt in east Africa well before that as indicated in Chapter 4. We showed how British *imperialism* had contributed greatly to the development of athletics during this period. Since the mid 1950s, however, the predominantly British connections with Kenya, while continuing, have been supplemented by impacts from America, Asia and other nations of Europe. Although the Olympics act as a kind of *neo-colonialism*, we can see in the post-1950s the relevance of *modernisation* and the policies favoured by international organisations for Kenya's athletic 'development'. The nature of the inter-continental connections changed. This theme – the changing nature of Kenya's global athletic connections – which, we feel, has led to a state of *'dependency'* in Kenyan athletics, forms the subject of the second half of this chapter. These themes, imperialism, dependency and modernisation, need not be viewed separately but can be seen as overlapping sets of structures which have contributed to the nature of Kenya's track and field 'industry' in the 1990s.[3] First, however, we will explore some arguments for using the systemic character of the world of sport as a basis for this chapter.

The global athletic system

In a seminal paper written a quarter of a century ago the Finnish sports sociologist Kalevi Heinilä noted how national sports systems had become 'totalised' as nations sought glory in events like the Olympic Games. He proposed that the success and effectiveness of the individual athlete depended more and more on the resources and effectiveness of the total system of national sport and less on individual effort independent of the system as a whole. He pointed to national systems of effective sports production, citing the former Soviet Union as a case in point. He argued that the 'total efficiency and the total resources of the national sports system' had replaced the efforts of the individual athlete; the athlete was now part of a system.[4]

We would argue that the world of sport had already moved on at the time Heinilä was writing. By the late 1960s athletes were increasingly crossing national boundaries, not simply to compete but to train. The upsurge in the number of foreigners obtaining athletic scholarships in American universities during the post-1960s period is a case in point.[5] In addition, coaches and trainers were attending courses in countries other than their own. Increasingly, the major organisations involved in the international dimensions of athletics were not state agencies. The governance of the IAAF and the IOC was increasingly apparent.

So was the presence of more explicitly commercial global organisations. The international trade in athletic footwear and equipment had been well under way since the 1950s. By the 1980s, shoe (and later, athletic clothing) firms such as Adidas, Puma, Reebok and Nike – which were to become multi-national corporations with an international division of labour[6] – were enrolling athletes of any nation as part of their media and publicity campaigns. The following text is an advertisement for running shoes, superimposed on the heads of a group of Kenyan runners:

> To believe you can win is like any other kind of faith. You can think about it, talk about it, write about it. But it doesn't matter, belief is a simple thing. The Kenyans believe they will win as simply as the sun shines. And even if you match their training, to beat them, you would have to match their faith.
> 'In my mind I am a Kenyan.'
> Nike Air – Just do it.

National pride and identity, quasi-religious language and a multinational corporation come together in the selling of athletic footwear through the image of the essentialised Kenyan athlete. Today's image of Kenyan athletes pounding through the savanna wearing a pair of Nike or Reebok shoes as part of a global advertising medium has become part and parcel of the modern world of sport (Figure 5.1).

As an aside, we note that advertisements such as that shown in Figure 5.1 also serve to illustrate the incongruous juxtaposing of sport images in late-modernity (or post-modernity). The high technology equipment of the world class athlete whose performances are minutely recorded and quantified are shown on the 'natural' or 'wilderness' landscape in which he is running – the celebration of progress, on the one hand, and of an 'eternal' Africa on the other.

According to the world systems view, a particular change within one of the nations in the system can only be understood within the context of the system as a whole. Hence, for example, the decline of British long distance running in the 1980s is not (in Taylor's words from a quite different context) 'merely a "British phenomenon", [but] it is part of a wider world-system process'.[7] It was related, for example, to the legitimating of professionalism in athletics, to the commercialisation of road racing in the USA, to the increasing media coverage of 'speed-oriented' events as speed and time became prominent cultural fetishes,[8] and to the emergence of long distance runners from nations like Kenya which had not previously posed a threat to European hegemony in these events. There are, at the same time, a number of developments which are not directly concerned with athletics and which have also influenced the globalisation of the sport. We will explore this world-systems idea further before fleshing out the detail of the Kenyan case.

Figure 5.1. Moses Kiptanui, multiple world record holder, on 'Planet Reebok'. The globalised shoe company reaches out into all continents.

Sport has undoubtedly become a form of global culture. This does not mean that it is homogeneous and that local differences in 'sport culture' have been totally eliminated. One has only to observe an inter-collegiate track and field meeting in the USA and compare it, and its respective 'meaning', with one in Britain to appreciate national differences. And it is possible, of course, to 'read' the Olympics and international sport differently in different countries. It cannot be denied, however, that a number of global processes have impinged on track and field in recent decades. Among these are the intensification of pre-existing pressures for the adoption of a common ideology of achievement sport and the necessary standardisation of the micro-spaces of sports arenas. Today the IAAF insists that all running tracks must be exactly the same size and of a standard composition for major competitions to take place and for records to be validated.[9] Unlike other cultural practices, there are few, if any, counter currents in track and field; the sport is moving in the direction of uniformity, universality and standardisation with little sign of the hybridisation which Pieterse sees in other cultural forms.[10] Other processes of a global nature include the new forms of communications which make intercontinental travel much easier than had been the case in the 1950s. In addition, developments in telecommunications have meant that global events, notably the Olympics, can be beamed to all parts of the world, hence encouraging a shared experience. This has been achieved by what is known as 'time-space compression'.[11] Kenya is today 'closer' to the USA and Europe in 'time-space' than it was thirty years ago. Such compression, or convergence of space, has enabled Kenyan athletes to participate in global sport – both as athletes and as part of a *global* television audience. The cumbersome and awkward sea crossings to major international sports events, characteristic of the 1930s, have been replaced by flexible, cheap and convenient inter-continental flights. The Olympics, along with *Dallas*, are part of the 'global cultural currency of the late twentieth century'.[12]

Furthermore, athletes' agents or managers are themselves international agencies who are able to create global festivals of a scale previously unknown outside the Olympics. These are exemplified by Grand Prix events such as the Bislett Games in Oslo or the Zürich *Weltklasse*. Globally contested prizes become the norm, rather than opportunities that occur only once every four years.

Two other global processes have assisted in propelling track and field into the global arena. A small number of languages of communication, notably English, have emerged and serve to ease international dialogue. In addition, the development of more widely shared notions of national citizenship has taken place as, for example, in South Africa and eastern Europe.[13] Among the first things that 'new' nations do on obtaining independence is to add their names to the list of countries affiliated to the IAAF.

In order to understand what is happening in the world of athletics, an awareness of the global system is therefore necessary. In order to understand the processes that are taking place in individual nation states it is also important to be aware of events occurring beyond local and national levels. A track and field meet is a *local experience* but it is part of the *global reality* of achievement sport; the local track meeting subscribes to global rules and regulations. If it organises things its own way it is removing itself from the international standards by which performances will be judged. Global reality and local experience are, however, mediated via a *national ideology* (Figure 5.2).

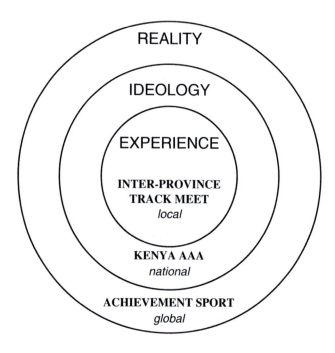

Figure 5.2. Kenyan running as part of a three-tiered system (after Taylor, 1989, p. 37).

Let us illustrate this idea with an example. Consider the case of young Kenyan athletes who accept scholarships to American universities. They are lost to Kenya and are unable to represent their district in local competitions. They are no longer so readily able to act as local role models for younger athletes. The power which the colleges are able to exert over the athletes may also prevent them from representing their region or nation. This is the *local experience*. In Kenya, track and field is seen nationally as a 'good thing' and in order to maximise 'athletic output' it has been quite acceptable for Kenyan athletes to leave their own country and obtain 'athletic scholarships' in America. This form of athletic migration is part of the *national ideology*. Such athletes could not make such a transition, however, unless the rules and underlying philosophy of athletics were the same in Kentucky as they are in Kenya – unless, that is, global sport was organised under a centralised bureaucracy which subscribes to the global reality of the *citius-altius-fortius* model of sports and aggressively seeks to convert the nations of the world to its ethos. This example shows that the experience at the local level can only be fully understood through an awareness of the *global reality*. This is not to say, however, that individuals are incapable of working to alter such global structures.

An alternative view of the concentric circles shown in Figure 5.2 is to see them as a central core, a semi-periphery, and a periphery. The core and the periphery can be interpreted as the exploiter and the exploited respectively, with the semi-periphery forming an ambiguous zone between the two.[14] The idea of the core nations of the world exploiting those of the periphery is an attractive idea in a sports context. Would Grand Prix track events be as profitable if Kenyan 'labourers' were absent? A steeplechase race without Kenyans is no longer regarded as attractive as it would have been in the 1950s when the Europeans dominated the event. We are now, however, beginning to more than hint at exploitation and we will return to this question, and that of athletic underdevelopment, in our final chapter. We may also be giving the impression that athletes are passive pawns in the hands of globally organised manipulators. This too would be an oversimplification as the contents of Chapter 7 will also show.

Having cleared the conceptual ground we are now ready to explore in more detail the nature of the global impacts on Kenyan track and field which have occurred since the mid 1950s. In the remainder of this chapter we look at two sides of the global system within which Kenya finds itself. First, we explore elements of sports culture which have 'moved in' to Kenya from outside; secondly, we look at the opposite tendencies, the outflows of athletic-related personnel from Kenya. The sections which follow depart from an emphasis on what could be termed global 'structures' (which have been considered in the earlier part of this chapter) and instead look at agencies involved in changing the face of Kenyan athletics.

Foreign sports aid

Kenya achieved independence in 1964 but remained within the Commonwealth. The imperial links were formally severed but the severance was superficial. In terms of cultural practice the new Kenyan political élite continued to promote imperial traditions, including achievement-oriented sports. Kenyan leaders, as with many others from the 'newly independent' nations, 'soon enough found that they needed the West and that the idea of total independence was a nationalist fiction'.[15] Far from reinstating Kenyan folk movement cultures, which could have been one form of revolutionary cultural strategy, the Western traditions which had been imposed from the 1920s were continued. Jomo Kenyatta, Kenya's first president, was interested in athletics himself and his daughter, Jane, was a talented school athlete. He did not fail to miss the political capital to be gained from success in international sport.[16] The same can be said of President Moi, an athletics enthusiast who as vice-president of the Arab and African Sports Association in the 1950s was among the first African sports officials in Kenya. Such continued Europeanisation suggests that sport, being the export of culture, serves to counter the 'mental decolonisation' which radicals in newly independent countries sometimes urge on their populations. Kenya, like most other African and Asian countries, has been an enthusiastic participant in colonially imposed sports and, apart from the boycott of the Edinburgh games in 1986, a continuing participant in the Commonwealth Games. This could be interpreted as an example of the victims of imperialism being turned into its supporters.

Sports aid is part of the overall package of foreign aid which, at root,

TABLE 5.1
Forms of technical cooperation in sports aid

1) Human resources	(a) Short-term visits by experts
	(b) Long-term visits by experts
	(c) Exchange visits
	(d) Education, scholarships, bursaries
	(e) Short-term workshops and clinics
2) Material resources	(a) Documentation centres and libraries
	(b) Clearing houses and publication inventories
	(c) Personal relationships between individuals
	(d) International congresses and conferences
3) Facilities and equipment	(a) Stadiums and complexes
	(b) Community-level sports grounds
	(c) 'Used but usable' equipment

(After Scott, 1991.)

results less from egalitarian principles than from the donor states' desires to improve their image with recipient countries or to gain some kind of economic advantage. Most sport aid assumes the form of technical cooperation between Kenya and various donor nations. The forms of aid are summarised in Table 5.1. In the case of Kenya, such aid has assumed a wide variety of forms and has come from various donor states. We cannot be exhaustive in charting all forms of overseas inputs to the Kenyan system but the flavour of such aid can be provided by the examples cited in what follows.

Britain

The first British athletics coaches were sent to Kenya as part of an assistance programme during the 1950s. They continued the work of the many British teachers and administrators we have described in the previous chapter. The Commonwealth aid programme did likewise in the 1960s. In 1952 one of Britain's national coaches, Denis Watts (funded by the British Council) conducted a number of seminars and coaching clinics in Kisumu, Mombasa and at the Jeanes School. He praised the facilities at the school and, although only having been in Kenya for six months, his visit was noted by the Community Development Office:

> ... there is no doubt that his visit came at a very opportune time and has resulted in a further rise in the standard of Kenyan athletics with more and more enthusiasm for the games leading up to possible participation in the fifth British Empire and Commonwealth Games.[17]

Some of Britain's most prominent athletes also visited Kenya at this time. For example, in 1955, British team captain and 120 yards hurdles champion, Jack Parker, conducted two training sessions in Kenya on his way from London to Malawi (then Nyasaland). Such occasional visits by British athletes may have had some impact on the enthusiasm of Kenyans for track and field. More significant in terms of motivating interest in athletics was almost certainly the longer-term work of Hywel Williams, the Welsh decathlon champion and a member of the Royal Air Force who was stationed in Kenya in the early 1950s. He left Kenya at the end of 1956, having trained a number of Kenyan army athletes and contributed greatly to the development of athletics in the colony. In 1954 he was able to practise what he preached by winning the Kenyan discus and pole vault championships.

In 1958 an English physical educationist and athletics coach, John Velzian, accepted the post of physical education instructor and coach at Kagumo Teacher Training College, Nyeri. His main early contribution to athletics was his work with the police from the Kenya Police Training School at Kiganjo. His job was also to tap and harness the athletic talent which was to be found in Kenya's schools. In 1962 at Nyeri, he allegedly 'discovered' Kipchoge Keino running the mile on a grass track in 4 minutes 21.8 seconds.[18] As well as helping nurture Keino's talent, he went on to assist in the coaching of Ben Kogo, Naftali Temu, Wilson Kiprugut and Daniel Rudisha. An excellent administrator, Velzian acted as head coach of the Kenyan team and also started a national secondary schools athletic championship. He was to fall out with the Kenyan authorities and was not reassigned any major duties until the 1990s. Nevertheless, Velzian is recognised by many as *the* major contributor to the emergence of Kenyan athletics since 1960.

Other coaches made important contributions. Edward Evans, a brother of the colony's first sports officer, coached and taught at Siriba College in western Kenya during the early 1960s. In 1965 he moved to Kenyatta College where he started organising cross country races, later to be become a major dimension of Kenya's athletic power. Ray Bachelor was a sports officer in the Coast and Rift Valley provinces who influenced and advanced the career of Seraphino Antao, Kenya's only 'world class' 100 and 200 metre sprinter, in the 1960s. Albert Simpson, a knowledgeable athletics enthusiast, was a renowned timekeeper who became president of the Nairobi track and field club.[19]

Other British coaches visited Kenya as part of overseas aid schemes but on an uncoordinated basis. According to the Kenyan observer Phillip Ndoo, it was these British coaches in the 1960s and 1970s who laid the foundations of modern Kenyan track and field, undertaking 'ambitious projects, some using tree branches for javelins, and of course, bamboo for vaulting poles. They had the athletes to work with, but almost no facilities'.[20] The significance of the imported printed word, as much as the foreign coach, should not be ignored. In 1960 a coaching manual titled *Athletics: A Coaching Handbook for Tropical Areas*, was published in London.[21] The authors were education officers in Kenya and argued that athletics should form part of the school curriculum from the primary phase onwards. With the paucity of technical equipment it was suggested that hurdles could be manufactured from improvised materials and bamboo poles could be used for pole vaulting. This was at the time when the synthetic track, the fibre glass vaulting pole and the aero-dynamic javelin were making their appearance in north America and Europe. Although the authors believed that Africans were 'natural athletes', an insistence on *technique* made sure that their natural body cultures would be moulded in forms cultured by the occident. Such books as this illustrate how physical education and sports science were, and continue to be (along with a variety of other 'academic disciplines'), involved in the (neo-)colonial project.

Germany

> With the aid of the Federal Republic of Germany, the Ministry of Culture and Social Services and the Kenya AAA have been able to work out a long term programme for up-coming athletes. Within the next 4–5 years the results of this scheme should show that with help and guidance of qualified coaches, the athletes will have gained broader knowledge and improved their standards.[22]

In these words the German coach, Walter Abmayr, summarised the contribution of Germany to Kenyan track and field, although it is not made clear whether 'improvement in standards' is meant in an absolute or relative sense. This distinction is made in the final chapter.

During the early 1980s the (then West) German government was significantly involved in the 'development' of Kenyan athletics, as explicated by the above quotation. Although it would be over-simplistic to aver that German aid alone *caused* the 'development' of Kenyan athletics, it certainly seems to have been *associated* with an improvement in athletics performances during the decade of the 1980s.

Although a number of German agencies were assisting in sport development during the 1960s, they tended to work independently of each other. From the mid-1970s a special branch of the *Deutsche Gesellschaft für Technische Zusammenarbeit* (GTZ) has dealt with sports aid. The GTZ has mainly involved the provision of top coaches and advisers on both a long- and short-term basis. The most influential of such coaches has undoubtedly been Abmayr who made a short-term visit in 1972 but returned as national athletics coach from 1980–85. Under his leadership, he recruited and trained other coaches. If Carey Francis had been the driving force behind Kenyan athletics in the 1940s, Abmayr could be argued to have been his equivalent in the 1980s. He set up the Kenya Athletic Coaches Association, and between 1981 and 1985 was responsible for the training of 260 athletic coaches.[23] He was also able to organise short-term visits of other German experts to give lectures and demonstrations. In addition Abmayr instituted a particularly Western form of recording of information about Kenyan athletics. We have referred already to the ranking lists published annually for world class and continental class athletes. Abmayr sought to monitor the performances of athletes at the national scale, establishing an annual publication of the 50 best Kenyan performers in each athletic event. While common in Europe, such national statistical publications are rare in Africa. Ranking lists such as these concretise the notion of the record and an athletic hierarchy and further marginalise non-serious forms of movement culture.

USA

Sports aid to Kenya from the US has been undertaken mainly by the Peace Corps. This sought to enhance the American image in Africa at the time of the 'cold war' and involved the dispatch of prominent athletes and coaches for short visits overseas.

Early visits were made under the auspices of the US Information Service. In the mid 1950s, visits to Kenya were arranged for Bob Mathias, the dual Olympic decathlon champion. Part of his programme included demonstrations at the East African Railways and Harbours championships in Nairobi.[24] In 1957, Jack Davis, the then world record holder for the high hurdles, and Mal Whitfield, dual Olympic 800 metres champion, undertook short visits. The former was based at Jeanes school and the Kenyan hurdler, Bartonjo Rotich, acknowledged Davis's help. Like John Velzian, Whitfield was instrumental in assisting Kipchoge Keino. Visits were also arranged for eminent coaches such as Chuck Coker and Donald Canham, track and field coach at Michigan University, who undertook coaching clinics throughout the country.

The Peace Corps was founded in 1961. A philanthropic organisation shaped by a cold war mentality, Kenya was seen as one of a number of countries to be protected from the perceived evils of communism. Sports featured so prominently in the work of the Peace Corps that it was dubbed the 'sports corps'. On the other hand, sports were incidental to the work of the Corps and those who initiated athletic programmes were often well-meaning amateurs. However, the director of the Peace Corps was well aware that

> athletic programs possess a unique ability to transcend political differences and thus gain access in countries with which official relations are strained or even non-existent. Peace Corps experiences with athletic programs have repeatedly proved this case.[25]

Peace Corps workers were mainly placed in rural communities where they coached track and field along with basketball and volleyball.

One member of the Peace Corps who was particularly influential in spreading athletics at the grass roots level was John Manners who taught in a number of secondary schools in the Rift Valley province from 1968 to 1971. Also worth noting was the work of Joanna Vincenti who was stationed at Kapkenda Girls' School near Eldoret. The interest in athletics which she established has resulted in an ongoing enthusiasm for the sport at the school. Vincenti helped nurture the career of Susan Sirma, Esther Kiplagat, and Helen Kimaiyo, some of Kenya's best runners in the early 1990s. A further important role in the work of the Peace Corps has been the forging of links between the universities and colleges attended by its members and Kenyan athletes who, through such links, have been able to obtain athletic scholarships.

The pro-American stance of the Kenyan government ensured the presence of Peace Corps workers during the 'take off' period of Kenyan track and field. This contrasted with the attitude of its neighbour, Tanzania, which wanted to reduce American influence in its schools and Africanise the curriculum. As a result, the Corps was subsequently withdrawn from Tanzania.

One element of foreign sports aid to Kenya involves the role of private firms for whom profit orientation is invariably paramount. One example is John Hancock Financial Services, based in Boston, Massachusetts, which has sponsored the Boston and New York marathons, among others. Indeed, the association between the Kenya AAA and the firm came as a result of top Kenyan runners taking part in the Boston marathon. In 1990 John Hancock Financial Services provided the KAAA with 1.2 million Kenyan shillings to develop athletics in the country. Whether this money has filtered down to the grass roots of the sport or whether it has been used to line the pockets of Kenyan officials is not clear. It seems likely, however, that an objective of the Hancock organisation is to put pressure on the Kenya AAA to encourage their athletes to compete in events sponsored by the organisation.

China

Sports Aid from China served as a means of establishing friendly relations with African countries. Since 1980 China has played a significant role in the development of Kenya's sport infrastructure in the form of stadium construction. The Moi International Sports Centre at Kasarani in Nairobi is the largest Chinese project undertaken in Kenya.

The Chinese contributed 52 per cent of the cost of the first phase of the development, a 60,000 seat stadium and a 200 bed hostel, in the form of an interest-free loan. Over 200 Chinese workers were involved in aiding Kenyan workers in the stadium's construction.

The building of such mega stadiums is seen by Kenyan observers as a contribution to the 'development' of athletics in their country. 'For Kenya's sportsmen and women', wrote a columnist in the *Weekly Review*, 'the completion of the stadium is another step forward in their efforts to maintain Kenya's good reputation in sports. Kenyans can now look forward to more world records with athletes now unhampered by a lack of proper and modern facilities'.[26]

The stadium has not been without its problems, however. Its construction was well behind schedule, its suburban location distances it from its potential city-based users, and it is mainly used for prestige competitions. In addition, the facilities are highly reliant on Chinese spare parts and Kenyan technicians have to be trained in China in order to satisfactorily undertake maintenance and repair work. There is a temptation to label it as an example of urban monumentalism in a country where the money could have been better spent – even in a sports context.

The forms of overseas aid provided by the countries cited above are essentially concerned with top-level sports. This is consistent with the expectations of modern African states. By and large they display a preference for the development of competitive sports rather than traditional games, recreational sport or sports for all.[27]

Missionary school athletics

Following the move towards independence the need for more secondary schools was recognised and a number of overseas missionary organisations showed interest in further spreading the Christian doctrine to Kenya through the setting up of schools. Among these was the Cardinal Otunga High School in Kisii, established by the Brothers of Tilburg in the Netherlands, and St Patrick's High School, Iten, established by the St. Patrick's Brothers from Ireland. These two schools exemplify the efforts of overseas organisations and individuals to mould the form of post-independence Kenyan athletics.

Cardinal Otunga High School grew from the request of Bishop Maurice Otunga for missionaries to work in his diocese. The Dutch brothers had been in Kisii since 1958, working on the development of an intermediate school, but it was not until 1961 that the secondary school was started under the headmastership of Brother Innocent de Kok. Although athletics had been part of the school programme, it was not until 1966 that it could be said to have entered the Kenyan athletics scene. An Irishman, Chris Phelan, was particularly associated with its athletic emergence. He had arrived at the school in 1965 and had a rich and lengthy history in athletics, having been a teacher of sports in Sarawak and Hong Kong.[28] Phelan started the Kisii District Secondary Schools Association, a body responsible for organising school sports at the district level. It was a major influence in encouraging further the spread of athletics in the district. According to another sports master at the school, Brother Anthony Koning, Phelan was so keen to carry out his athletics programmes that he 'could be seen rushing through the dormitories ... to get the "chosen ones" out of bed to train on the then rough track'.[29]

Assisted by other teachers such as Peter Haen and later Bob Hancock, some good athletes soon emerged from such a regime. In 1971 Hancock initiated a cross-country meeting at the school which came to be known as the Mosocho race, an important event in the calendar of Kenyan cross-country racing. The inaugural winner was John Ng'eno, a student from Kabianga High School, who was to become a world class 10,000 metre runner and a student athlete at Washington State University in the USA. The traditions established in the late 1960s and 1970s have contributed to the development of a number of world class athletes from the school. Among them have been Oanda Kironchi, Thomas Osano, Micah Boinett, Osoro Ondoro, Yobes Ondieki and Robert Ouko. The tradition of 'producing' athletes from Cardinal Otunga has been rivalled only by St Patrick's High School, an institution which is often termed the cradle of modern Kenyan athletics.

St Patrick's High School at Iten was started in 1960. The first head teacher, Brother Simon, had a keen interest in sports and coached the school athletics team himself. Under Brother Simon, all first year boys at the school were supposed to take part in athletics. This ensured that those of superior quality could be readily identified, these being put through a rigorous programme of training which culminated in competitions from July to August. Among those influenced by Brother Simon in the early days of St Patrick's were Mike Boit and Mike Murei. In the 1970s St Patrick's attracted other foreign teachers to build on the traditions of the 1960s. Among these teachers was Peter Foster, brother of the famous British long distance runner, Brendan Foster. More recently, coaching was undertaken by a new head teacher from County Cork in Ireland, Brother Colm O'Connell, prior to his departure to a local teachers' college where he could find more time for his coaching mission.[30] During this period athletes such as Olympic champion Peter Rono, Kip Cheruiyot, Ibrahim Hussein, Matthew Birir and Charles Cheruiyot have been added to the existing list of athletic giants whose introduction to the sport was at St Patrick's. Interestingly, the school has never possessed a running track and most training is done on cross-country routes, up and down the Elgeyo valley. Yet it has been suggested that the school provides an 'ideal situation for a favourable attitude towards sports' with its English traditions, its Christian asceticism, its boarding school ethos and its moderate climate at a high altitude.[31] European national athletics squads have often used the school as base for training.

In recent years, O'Connell has assisted in the development of women's running by coaching Lydia Cheromei (1991 World Junior Cross Country champion), Helen Chepng'eno (1994 World Women's champion) and the up-and-coming Rose Cheruiyot from nearby Kipsoen High School. It has been alleged, however, that the school has willingly accepted students of low academic calibre if they were good athletes. This form of athletic bias is far from unknown in the US colleges to which many Kenyan athletes have migrated over the last three decades (see below).

The role of the IAAF

The world governing body of the sport can be viewed as being analogous to a multinational corporation with its headquarters in the 'developed' world. As an 'imperialising power' its intention is to colonise the world with more and more adherents to participation in serious sports. The erosion of regional cultures is explicit in its ambitions, its aim being to 'help remove cultural and traditional barriers to participation in athletics';[32] African culture is seen as something to 'remove' in order that Western forms of movement culture may take its place. In recent years, through the increased television coverage of meetings and the increased professionalism of all athletics organisations, the IAAF has generated a vast source of revenue which it seeks to invest in various nations of the 'Third World'. The increased commercialisation and neo-colonialism of the sport is attributed principally to the energies of Primo Nebiolo, the president of the IAAF.

An aim of the IAAF Operational Plan for the World-Wide Development of Track and Field Athletics typifies the organisation's global ambitions. In order to implement its plans, a number of IAAF Regional Development centres have been established, the two in Africa being in Cairo and at the Moi International Sports Complex in suburban Nairobi. Courses for coaches are mounted at these centres. Between 1986 and 1989, seven such courses were held at the Nairobi centre.[33] These were intended for coaches in Kenya and other English-speaking nations in Africa. The IAAF has also assisted Kenya in financing athletes' journeys to take part in competitions outside Kenya.

Within Kenya itself, the German coach, Walter Abmayr, established a development plan with IAAF resources involving a hierarchy of coaches from national to local levels. This ranges from the national head coach and four national coaches for each of the main event-groups to coaches who assist in promoting athletics at the local level.

Kenyans abroad

As part of the 'new global cultural economy' a large number of 'moving groups and persons' are an essential feature. To 'the landscape of persons who constitute the shifting world in which we live', Arjun Appadurai has applied the term 'ethnoscapes'.[34] Such international movement was, as we have shown, exemplified during the early and later twentieth century with the migration to Kenya of missionaries, teachers, administrators and coaches from Europe. But these have been outnumbered by the substantial overseas migration of Kenyan athletic personnel. Kenyan athletes form part of a sporting 'ethnoscape' made up of athletes criss-crossing global space as they ply their athletic trades.

Such migration has assumed two main forms. The first is travel in order to take part in competitions such as international meetings, the Olympics, or Commonwealth Games, following which the athlete returns to Kenya. This was the traditional model in which there was no ambiguity about the athlete's domicile or allegiance. The second involves overseas travel in order to take up sojourn (temporary or permanent) in another country. Sojourn implies a longer period of residence than simply travelling and residing abroad for the duration of the athletic event. This dualism is not quite as simple as it appears, however. Because most Grand Prix meetings are in Europe it is more convenient for the 'journey to compete' to be but part of a temporary sojourn in a European country. In some cases, such residence abroad may last several months or longer. For convenience, however, we shall explore each of these two general categories in turn.

Kenyan athletes, global travellers

The athletes who ply their trade on a global level are one group within what Doreen Massey has called the power-geometry of globalisation.[35] By this she means the extent to which different groups in society (or in our case, in sport) are 'in charge' of the kind of migrations which we will describe below. The globalisation of athletics is reflected differently by the various groups in Kenyan (athletic) society. At one end of the spectrum there are the 'jet setters', the globally known athletes who can command where and when they travel and, through their agents or managers, the amount of money they receive wherever they appear. Such athletes often live overseas and return to Kenya infrequently. This 'jet-set' group also includes the people who are, basically, in charge of time-space compression in the sport, those who schedule meetings and use this to their advantage, those organising the payouts and payoffs. These include meeting organisers and athletes' agents.

A second group is also involved in a good deal of physical movement but is not quite so 'in charge' of the process as the jet-setters. These are the 'journeymen' athletes – those who have to travel in order to achieve the performance which will shift them into the jet-set class. Because there are no Grand Prix track events in Africa, all Kenyan athletes who aspire to the élite level must migrate in order to achieve these kinds of performances – to obtain the chance of what they perceive as a new life. This may mean migrating to an unknown part of the USA to attend a college which is only really interested in using human beings as points machines (see below) or it may mean living in an alien environment in northern England.

A third group is described by Massey as being on the receiving end of time-space compression. In an athletic context this group might include the Kenyan female athlete in Kisumu who owns a pair of Nike running shoes and watches the Olympics from Korea on a Japanese television but, because she is still unknown, cannot find a place in an American university. Or, to illustrate a different kind of complexity, there may be people on farms in the Rift Valley, the region which has contributed most to Kenya's running tradition, who have produced some of the greatest runners in world history and know about the record breaking exploits of Kiptanui, Ondieki and Sigei, but may have never visited Nairobi. As Massey puts it, 'at one level they have been tremendous contributors to what we call time-space compression; and at another they are imprisoned by it'.[36] The ways in which people are inserted into the sports world of time-space compression are many and varied.

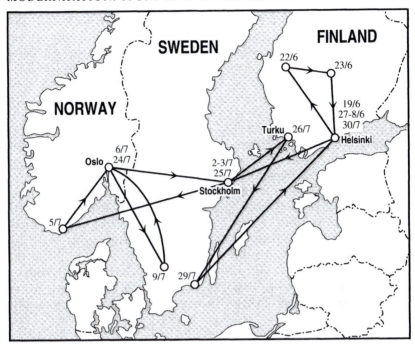

Figure 5.3. The travels of Ben Jipcho, 19 June–30 July 1973. Jipcho's races at each location are shown by the dates (source of data: *Athletics Weekly*, 28 (5), 1974, p. 19).

Widening geographic margins

We traced the germs of the internationalisation of Kenyan athletics in the previous chapter but by the mid-1960s Kenyan athletic performances had become increasingly visible on a global scale. Kenyan athletes were welcomed at events such as the Olympics, the Commonwealth Games, and the African Championships, festivals which involved a stay in a foreign country for a few weeks while representing their countries. Likewise they participated at invitational events in north America or Europe. In 1962, for example, as the wave of Kenyan athletics success was just beginning to surge, the best performances by world-class Kenyan athletes were registered not only in Nairobi (3) and Nakuru (2) but also in Dar-es-Salaam and Kampala, in Belfast and Berlin (2), and in Perth (2) and Prague (2). By the mid-1970s the Kenyan élite was undertaking tours of Europe involving a large number of races at a wide variety of places in a relatively short time span. Intensive Scandinavian tours became popular, partly because of the legendary running environment but also because of the availability of illicit payments for performing at a time when track and field was not yet openly professional. Figure 5.3 shows the itinerary of the great Kenyan steeplechaser Ben Jipcho, which involved jetting between Helsinki, Stockholm, Oslo and several smaller places during a six-week period in the summer of 1973. Since then the significance for the Kenyan élite of participation mainly within Africa and the Commonwealth has declined further. Figure 5.4 shows the global locations where African-class Kenyan runners achieved their best performances during 1993. Although Nairobi remained an important focus, venues for Kenyan athletic performances spanned four continents. A comparable map for *all* of the throwing events, however, would show that all the best performances were made in Kenya. The spatial margins of the journey to compete among African-class Kenyans vary considerably between event-groups.

During the 1960s and early 1970s, the most successful Kenyan athletes were almost all based in Kenya. Keino was in the police force, Jipcho was a prison officer, and Temu was in the armed forces. 'These services had a positive policy of recruiting possible internationals'[37] and provided them with better-than-average training facilities. From the early 1970s, however, the geography of 'producing' – or at least 'processing' – (as well as 'marketing') of Kenyan athletes changed as the geographic margins of the Kenyan presence expanded dramatically.

The scramble for Africa: American connections

Sporadic visits of Kenyan athletes to overseas countries, other than those where they competed in events like the Commonwealth and Olympic Games, were not totally unknown in the 1950s and early 1960s. Some Kenyans were students in British and American universities and happened to compete in athletics while at college. None of these left a very significant imprint. Of particular note, however, was the role of the British military and police colleges which some Kenyans visited on training courses but, at the same time, were able to practise competitive athletics. For example, several Kenyan athletes attended the Sandhurst Military Academy, including Munene and Sumbeiywo who, in 1987, still held the college records for the long jump and 400 metre hurdles respectively. Several Kenyan athletes represented the college in the West European Military Cadet Academy athletics meeting.[38] In the later 1960s a noteworthy visitor to Britain was Kipchoge Keino who paid brief visits to England to attend police training courses at Aldershot. While in residence he competed in some road races for Walton Athletic Club. Such visitors were, during their foreign visits, students first and athletes second and in this respect differed from the much larger flows of Kenyan athletes who were to traverse the globe in subsequent decades.

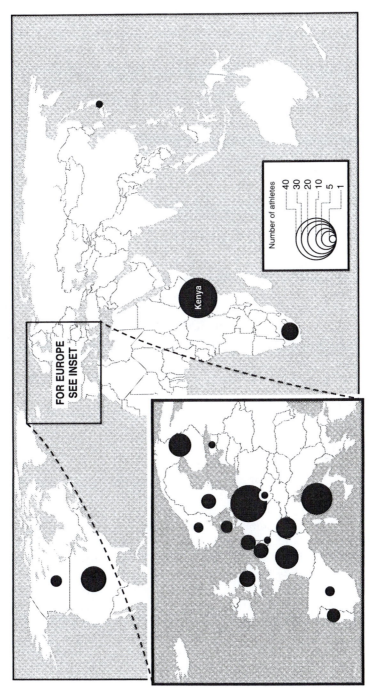

Figure 5.4. National locations of competitions where African-class Kenyan 800–10,000 metre runners achieved their best performances in 1993.

A major part of the increasing globalisation of Kenyan athletics involved the many Kenyan athletes who were attracted to the United States, not to represent their country but to improve the prestige of the athletics departments of the nation's universities. These journeys involved more than a flying visit to take part in a single athletic event. They involved temporary residence in a foreign country, often extending over four years or more.

The flow of Kenyans to US colleges and universities from the late 1960s and early 1970s was a new dimension in the globalisation of Kenyan track athletics and it can only be fully understood by appreciating the nature and significance of sports in the American higher education system. College and university sport in the United States is of considerable importance in raising and maintaining the visibility of institutions of higher education in the many small towns where they are located. Athletics scholarships are awarded by quasi-autonomous athletic departments to high-achieving athletes. In the main, these scholarships are awarded to 18-year-old American high school graduates.[39] From the late 1950s, however, many foreign recruits were lured to the US by the promise of support in college while following an athletic 'career'. Traditionally, the largest number of such foreign track and field recruits had come from Canada and north-west Europe. They often differed from US high school recruits by being seasoned athletes, sometimes of international calibre, in the twilight of their careers.[40] A trickle of Kenyans was attracted during the late 1960s. Among the first to come were distance runner, Steve Machuka, who attended Cornell University (though not on an athletic scholarship), and Patrick Onyango, a triple jumper who attended the University of Wisconsin.

Although a few Kenyans arrived in the US in the early 1970s, including Julius Sang and Robert Ouko (400 metres and 800 metres respectively) who attended North Carolina Central University, the explosion in East African recruiting came in the mid 1970s. Kenyans were often cheaper to recruit than Americans. Instead of scouring the nation for the blue chip recruit, a telephone call, or later a fax, from the track coach to an alumnus in Kenya could get a recruit for almost nothing. This is not to say that US coaches did not go to Kenya. Those who sought Kenyan talent to bring to the USA in districts like Nandi or Kisii are regarded by John Hoberman as the modern counterparts of the nineteenth century 'inquiring travellers' who recorded, and brought back in the form of lantern slides and travellers' tales, the legendary performances of the pre-modern athletes of 'Mother Africa'.[41] Whatever way they were recruited, the number of Kenyan collegians grew dramatically. From 1976 onwards there were more Kenyans appearing in the National Collegiate Athletic Association championships than from any other foreign country. From 1971 through 1978, 17.2 per cent of all men's championship appearances by non-Americans were by Kenyans, compared with a figure of 12.5 per cent from Canada. Of the 166 Kenyans, 132 or 85 per cent were distance runners.[42] This trend continued. As Table 5.2 shows, between 1973 and 1985, Kenya supplied 12.6 per cent of all superior foreign track and field athletes in US colleges, Canada accounting for 12.2 per cent.[43]

TABLE 5.2
Major national donors of superior foreign track and field student athletes, 1975–85
(n=609). (Source, Bale, (1991) p. 77.)

Country	Number	Per cent
Kenya	77	12.6
Canada	74	12.2
UK	54	8.9
Sweden	51	8.4
Jamaica	43	7.1
Nigeria	34	5.6
Eire	32	5.3
Norway	25	4.1
Ghana	18	3.0

Let us recall, however, that the repertoire of athletic performances is made up of various events. The kinds of Kenyans the colleges wanted were those with proven skills in events where there was a relative paucity of US high school talent. Hence, as noted earlier, the middle- and long-distance runners were those favoured. American colleges did not recruit Kenyan shot putters or pole vaulters. In 1982, at the peak of the migration of Kenyan athletic talent to the US, 24 of the 50 best Kenyan 5,000 metres runners were domiciled in the USA; the respective figure for national-class athletes in *all* field events was two.[44] Of the Kenyan contingent during the period shown in Table 5.2, 86 per cent were distance runners. What we see here is an international division of labour – a common feature of globalisation. The Caribbean and West Africa provides the sprinters, the Scandinavian countries the throwers, and Kenya the distance runners. The composition of the Canadian and British recruits has been much more diversified.

This flow of African recruits included some of the best athletes in the world, including subsequent holders of world records such as Henry Rono and Samson Kimombwa, and Olympic champions such as Paul Ereng and Peter Rono. Many more Kenyans, sometimes élite runners, but often more modest athletes, were attracted to American campuses, the number remaining relatively high until the mid 1980s. These were often *de jure* students but *de facto* full-time athletes.

College destinations of Kenyan athletes were often avoided by native-born American athletes who perceived them as out-of-the way places. The prime example was the University of Texas, El Paso (UTEP), which recruited many foreign athletes to enhance its track and field squad. 'Small and remote, without any great claim to academic distinction, except in geology, the school ... found a source of pride and joy in the track team since it rose to prominence in the 1970s',[45] helped greatly by the presence of a large number of foreign 'imports'. El Paso, situated in what approximated to a hot desert environment, was the main destination of Kenyan élite athletes during the 1970s and early 1980s.[46] Other major destinations for superior Kenyan athletes were Washington State and Iowa State universities (Figure 5.5).

From about 1985 onwards, the subsidy of the athletic scholarship became much less significant as the open payment of prize money to athletes became acceptable, something forbidden under the system of inter-collegiate sports in the USA. Track athletes no longer needed to attend an American university to realise their athletic ambitions. Consequently, the number of Kenyans based in the United States began to decline, although a few years in an American college or university are still likely to be attractive to those Kenyan athletes below the élite level or to those who feel like sampling an alternative lifestyle or obtaining an American degree at the same time.

It is difficult to say if the Kenyan athletic experience in the United States has had a major impact on development of Kenyan track and field. Kenyan migrants to the US would have had to be good athletes to be recruited. The basis of their athletic talent and initial 'development' lies in Kenya. The American experience for some athletes meant glory followed by disaster. Henry Rono was a world record holder while a student at Washington State University but finished his 'career' in the USA as a victim of alcohol abuse. Yobes Ondieki became a world class athletes *after* he spent four years at Iowa State. Certainly, the flow of Kenyan athletes to the US has had no impact on the 'development' of Kenyan field events.

A Kenyan diaspora

The open professionalism of athletics did not put a halt to the trans-continental migration of Kenyan athletes; it simply redirected it, increasingly to Europe. Of 30 élite Kenyan athletes whose biographies were sketched in the 1994 ATFS annual, 14 were domiciled in Kenya, while six were living in Europe and six in the USA.

Figure 5.5. Kenyans at Iowa State University, 1980s. From top left, clockwise: Yobes Ondieki, Moses Kiyai, Barnaba Korir and Richard Kaitany (source: Iowa State University).

For those below the highest élite, such migration to Europe is often seasonal in nature, a kind of 'athletic transhumance' made to coincide with the Grand Prix seasons in track and cross-country running. Others live in Europe and north America to benefit from the lucrative road racing circuits. A survey which we undertook in 1992 revealed that 76 per cent of a sample of Kenyan runners stated that they were motivated to travel abroad by the proximity of the region to international competition. In the world of athletics, Europe has a major advantage over north America in this respect.

In Europe, several groups of Kenyans spend much of their time living in close proximity to each other, close to nodes of regular athletic competition. In Britain, groups of Kenyan 'migrant workers' are based in the north-west, and in south and west London. Unlike scholarship holders in the United States, where, of necessity, they have to represent their colleges and universities, there is little indication that such athletes integrate themselves into any local athletics culture. For example, in Britain few join local clubs because they are not permanent residents. Their racing programmes are organised by their agents who, in some cases, also assist with their training regimes. Their lives revolve around their running. In recent years controversy has surrounded the participation of such athletes in British road race events. There is a feeling that the presence of Kenyans creates a disincentive for the British runners to compete. Other European groups are located in Belgium, Sweden, Switzerland, Denmark, Italy, Spain and Germany. In such cases club membership is common. For example, in Italy, Kenyans have joined the Brescia-based Fila team and in Switzerland the LC Zürich club; indeed, clubs may well be the principal recruiters in such countries.

Such seasonal migrants are complemented by a smaller group of longer-term migrants who are, in this respect, more analogous to the American scholarship holders. Kenyan athletic migration to Japan exemplifies this group and the paradigm example is probably Douglas Wakihuri, a winner of world and Commonwealth marathon championships. Wakihuri had considered attending college in the US but having met Shunichi Kobayashi, a Japanese living in Kenya, he was persuaded that he should write to the Japanese coach, Kiyoshi Nakamura. As an 18 year old, Wakihuri went to Tokyo where he joined the 'S and B Track Club' which is sponsored by a spice-manufacturing firm. Other Kenyan athletes spending time in Japan have included one of the nation's best women runners, Susan Sirma, and the 1995 world championship marathon runner Eric Wainaina. More recent migrants to Japan have joined the Oki Electronics club.

Kenyan athletes in Germany were attracted to the Heidelberg area by the contacts built up in Kenya by the German coach, Walter Abmayr. The 1988 Olympic 10,000 metre bronze medalist, Kipkemboi Kimeli, was one of the first of such migrants. He was joined by Julius Korir and Benson Kamau, among several others. In Denmark, two Kenyan athletes have opted to represent their adopted country in order to stand a better chance of getting international competition. By doing so, such athletes are able to be sure of international selection without having to face the high pressure Kenyan trials. The most well known is Wilson Kipketer who was recruited by a Scandinavian coach while at St Patrick's High School and taken to Denmark at the age of 17. By 1995 he had lived there for five years and obtained a Danish qualification shortly before winning the world 800 metres championship in that year (see below). Such strategies, initiated by athletes' agents, to induce migration to relatively weak athletic nations may become a feature of an increasingly minimalist approach towards national identity favoured by an increasing number of athletes.

The diaspora of Kenyan athletes illustrates the twin sociological concepts of globalisation – diminishing contrasts and increasing varieties. The global scale tendency for sports – track and field in particular – to create a common macro-culture among some members of each of the world's nations has been noted earlier. At the same time, but on a local scale, we can see in Kenyan talent migration the process of increasing cultural variety. In Ames, Iowa, we find Kenyan student-athletes mingling with those from the American mid-west; in Italy and Japan new Kenyan arrivals join clubs with athletes from the host countries. As Kenya becomes Americanised with the import of Nike shoes (and many other forms of American cultural baggage), so Iowa becomes Africanised with the import of Kenyan athletes. Indeed, Maguire has suggested that migrant athletes are the most visible expressions not only of the globalisation of sports but also of the increasing diversity of sports culture. But such migration may affect national cultures and national identities.[47] We return to these questions in our final chapter.

We should point out that relatively few women athletes have been part of the patterns of migration we have been describing in this chapter. This is the result, of course, of their under-representation in Kenyan athletics. Whereas in school the ratio of female to male participation in track and field is 45:55, from the ages of 17 to 21, when migration would be most likely to occur, the respective ratio is about 15:85.[48]

Compared with athletic migration, the number of Kenyan sports administrators who have obtained aid to follow a sports programme in the USA has been small. Those who have were in the 1960s, under the jurisdiction of the United States Information Service.

Culture shock?

The implications of the kind of migration described above are ambiguous. Any generalisations which can be made about how Kenyan athletes adjust to life overseas will certainly obscure a wide range of individual experiences. For example, when Kiptalam Keter visited Europe for the first time in the 1950s his reception by whites in England was warmer than the contact he was used to with Europeans in his own country.[49] Such hospitality may not always be the case, however.

We have attempted to establish the feelings of Kenyan and European student-athletes to the sojourn experience in the United States.[50] We asked the two samples to score their general feelings on a 'feelings thermometer' on which values range from 0 (very cold feeling) to 100 (very warm feeling) with 50 as a neutral response. For 21 Kenyan respondents the modal score was 70 and the mean 77.6. These reflect fairly warm or favourable feelings overall. The European scores were noticeably different, not in direction but in strength. The mode was 100 and the mean 87 for a larger sample of 93 European athletes. How might the less warm – but certainly not cool – feeling felt by Kenyan athletes towards sojourn in the US be explained? It could result from more severe feelings of homesickness, declining athletic performance, exploitation or discrimination. Is there any evidence to support any of these speculations?

Racial discrimination against African athletes while in American universities has been reported from several sources. It has been noted that African athletes 'have been threatened on many occasions with deportation if they do not do as they are told, if they don't race in every meet that comes along'.[51] Our evidence suggests that one-third of Kenyan athletic migrants experience what they perceive as discrimination while in America. Two-thirds do not appear to have any expectations about the extent of discrimination against them before they arrive in the US, but once there one-quarter of our sample respondents found more than they expected while none found less than they expected. Apart from the structural racism of American society, US track fans have often felt aggrieved by a limited number of athletic scholarships being given to a large number of foreigners – though this feeling is not peculiar to Kenyans. Although discrimination is not enough to make the overall sojourn unpleasant, it is clearly there.

The question of whether Kenyan athletes are exploited while in the US is difficult to establish. On the one hand it is not easy to operationalise the notion of 'exploitation' and, even if it were, people may be exploited without being aware of it (as a result, for example, of what is termed 'false consciousness'). Yet traces of exploitation are felt by some students. What is unclear is whether exploitation is greater or less in the case of Kenyan student-athletes than it is for any other foreign (black) recruits into the US collegiate set-up.

A different kind of attitudinal response to Kenyan residence abroad can be illustrated by the case of Wilson Kipketer, as noted earlier, the winner of the 1995 world 800 metres championship in the colours of Denmark. In order to take part in the 1996 Olympics, he required seven years' residence – the time required to obtain Danish nationality. A survey undertaken by a Danish newspaper soon after Kipketer's 1995 world championship victory revealed that only 31 per cent of respondents favoured the acceleration of the normal process of naturalisation. On the other hand, 51 per cent favoured the standard procedures taking their course, even if it meant that Kipketer would then be unable to represent them in the Olympics.[52] It seemed that Kipketer had been running *for* Denmark but not with Denmark. Perhaps this story reveals how the people of various nations may fail to accurately reflect the more strongly nationalistic ambitions of their sports organisations, or (in this case, more likely) the failure to identify with their black 'representative'.

Agents and the Grand Prix circuit

We have already alluded to the dramatic changes in the structure of track and field athletics which have taken place in the last decade. Track and field has become a glamour sport, possessing strong appeal for television cameras – with resultant increases in its commercialisation. The professionalisation of world athletics and the concentration of major events in Europe has led to the emergence of agents or managers who act on behalf of athletes to plan their programme of competitions and secure for them a good financial deal with meeting promoters. In return for their work for the athlete, the agent takes a cut of the fee. These agents are very largely based outside Kenya itself.

Given the money that can be made by agents it is tempting to assume that they exploit Kenyan runners in the free market place of the European track circuit. The Kenya AAA has, at times, expressed concern about the exploitation of 'its' athletes by foreign agents. It has appealed to the IAAF, without success, to force Kenyan athletes to sign contracts with the Kenyan association, urging that bogus agents were exploiting them by having them race too frequently and take an unknown percentage of athletes' earnings. The Kenyan association is also anxious that some of the money won by such athletes should be ploughed back into the grassroots of Kenyan sport. The Kenyan commissioner for sport was moved to comment that

> some agents tend to cheat athletes. They make them race too much because the bottom line of their objective is how much money they will earn. Some of the agents are good and take into consideration important competitions such as the Commonwealth Games, the World Championships etc. by ensuring that athletes do not run themselves into the ground and as a result fail to perform well in international competition.[53]

Some agents do appear to exploit some athletes. Of the athletes we asked, however, over 70 per cent said that they did not encounter such agent-related problems as over-training or being under pressure to compete while still recovering from injury.

At the same time, we cannot ignore allegations of past corruption among Kenyan athletics officials, which suggests that they also have pocketed money from track meets which was rightly the property of the athletes.

Kenyan contributions

We feel that the last two chapters have clearly shown that many foreign impacts have contributed to Kenya's present-day position as a powerful athletic force. They have mainly been concerned with the various overseas 'agencies' which have impinged on Kenya during the last century. The global 'structures' within which these operated have also been outlined in Chapter 2 and the early pages of the present chapter. It would be absurd, however, to argue that the broad domestic context has been of no importance. Athletes from other African countries have been on the receiving end of the same global impacts as Kenya, and been part of the same global system, but have failed to reach the relatively high levels of athletic success achieved by Kenya. We therefore feel that it is necessary to comment on the Kenyan contribution to the nation's athletic success, a subject we return to in a rather different way in the following chapter.

The Kenyan government does support athletics but its financial support to track and field is only about one-sixth that given to soccer. In

1980, for example, the Kenya Sports Council funded soccer to the extent of 2,452,562 Kenyan shillings. The equivalent figure for track and field was 372,541 shillings.[54] Nevertheless, within Kenya a well-developed scheme of hierarchical coaching and 'development' has been established, run by coaches and trainers at a variety of levels. Serious sports are also given considerable emphasis in schools. Indeed, the high esteem afforded to sports in the school system is often more significant in contributing to Kenyan success in world running than the compulsory status afforded physical education. Emphasis is placed on high-level performance and competition; until 1985 the guidelines issued to schools by the Ministry of Education was 'to become a champion'. The majority of the school population was barely catered for and, even with improved guidelines, 'the syllabi are more competition oriented than pedagogical'.[55] Such an ideology is clearly a good foundation for achievement sport.

The Kenyan national context cannot be said to be totally inhospitable to 'athletic development'. Kenya is certainly not among the richest African countries when measured in terms of gross national product per capita. But neither is it among the poorest. On several social indicators, notably in terms of health provision, it lies near the top of the list of African states. Although there is widespread political corruption (which has spilled over into the higher echelons of Kenyan athletics, as noted above), Kenya is also a country which is relatively stable in a political sense; there have been no serious internal wars (though, as noted earlier, tribal conflict is always a possibility), nor droughts or other disasters which have plagued some of Kenya's neighbours. Countries involved in lengthy and serious wars or famines are hardly likely to emerge as major athletic forces. While tribal conflict is always possible, the ideological environment within Kenya has not restricted the growth of modern athletics. In this respect, Kenya is somewhat different from two of its immediate neighbours, Ethiopia and Tanzania.

Each of these countries, while superficially similar to Kenya in terms of physical geography, has experienced quite different political and social histories. Neither experienced early British settlement with its associated, and influential, cultural baggage (including athletics) in the way Kenya did. Tanzania (formerly Tanganyika) was, until 1918, part of German East Africa. Ethiopia, despite Italian incursions, remained relatively untouched by European influence until much later. Kenya also differed from its neighbours in being subjected to a much larger number of European settlers – and hence a relatively greater degree of European influence – than the two other countries. Ethiopia and Tanzania have also, to a greater or lesser extent, experimented with Marxist forms of government which may have placed less emphasis on achievement sport than has been the case in Kenya. Each country has, of course, produced some élite athletes (for example, Abebe Bikila, Miruts Yifter and Haile Gebresilasie from Ethiopia and Filbert Bayi from Tanzania). In per capita terms, however, they have not begun to approach the levels achieved by Kenya (see Chapters 2 and 6). The internal political, economic and historical conditions in each of these countries have not been so conducive to the growth of modern athletics as they have been in Kenya.

Conclusion

A global systems approach is a convincing starting point in conceptualising any theory of world athletic development. We have demonstrated, in this and the previous chapter, that a variety of global impacts and controls have impinged on Kenyan track and field during the past century. It would be wrong, therefore, to suggest that the globally systemic character of Kenyan athletics is particularly new. What is novel is the redirection of the cultural flows which are involved. The increased mobility of athletes throughout the world has resulted in Kenya finding itself in a sort of 'new world sports order'.[56] This not only involves redrawing the world athletic map; as identities are reconstructed and contested it also raises questions of national identity itself and the inability of national allegiance to describe the geography of the sport.

In his 'mapping' of the global condition, Roland Robertson[57] suggests a five-stage path towards the present. We feel that this can be adapted to form an outline of what we have so far described for Kenya:
Phase 1 – *the germinal phase* lasting from the early twentieth century until the formation of the AASA in the early 1920s. During this period the seeds of modern track and field were planted by European imperialists although Kenyan athletics remained rooted in Kenya;
Phase II – *the incipient phase*, lasting from the 1920s until the 1930s. The gradual bureaucratisation of track and field, involving its standardisation and recording meant that the sport was becoming a source of social control, regional bonding, and one of inter-regional – and potentially international – competition;
Phase III – *the struggle for hegemony phase*, from the mid 1930s to the 1950s. For much of this period folk traditions co-existed with modern sports. By the mid-1950s, however, the hegemony of modern sport was completed with the formation of the Kenya AAA;
Phase IV – *the take-off phase*, from the 1950s to the 1970s. This period

saw Kenya entering major international competitions, initially in Africa and subsequently in the Empire and Olympic Games. It became known as a significant athletic power and the international migration of athletes began to take place;

Phase V – *the uncertainty phase*, beginning in the 1970s. Kenya's participation in international competitions became less certain with political boycotts (for example Olympics in 1976 and 1980; Commonwealth Games in 1986). Kenyan athletes increasingly migrated overseas to 'represent' other units such as colleges and universities in the USA or clubs (or even countries) in Europe. Today, other athletes face conflicts with the KAAA as they seek to represent themselves. The number of global organisations which seek to claim Kenyan athletes continues to increase. The nation state (Kenya) may remain the country which Kenyan athletes generally 'represent' (or are seen by the media to represent) yet these athletes, once they reach a certain level, become less and less a part of any Kenyan system (if, given the tribal traditions of Kenya, they ever were). They 'work' increasingly within multi-national or global systems (shoe companies, the IAAF, the IOC) which, we suggest in Chapter 7, serve to reduce the ability of the nation state to exert control over them.

This is, of course, a skeletal outline serving to summarise much of what has been discussed above. It remains to be seen to what extent such a scheme applies to other nations and other forms of global culture.

Notes and references

1. Lash and Urry, *Economies of Signs and Space*, p. 279.
2. Smith, 'Towards a global culture?'; Cook, Pakulski and Waters, *Postmodernization*, p. 101.
3. Theories of the global system in a sports context are briefly examined in Maguire and Bale, 'Introduction: sports labour migration in the global arena'.
4. Heinila, 'Notes on inter-group conflict in international sport'.
5. Bale, *The Brawn Drain*.
6. Barff and Austen, 'It's gotta be da shoes'. For a case study of the Nike company see Donaghu and Barff, 'Nike just did it'.
7. Taylor, *Political Geography*, p. 4.
8. Virilio, *Lost Dimensions*; for an application to sports see Penz, 'Sport and speed'.
9. Bale, *Landscapes of Modern Sport*, pp. 100–19.
10. Pieterse, 'Globalization as hybridization'.
11. On time-space compression see Janelle, 'Central place development' and Harvey, *The Condition of Postmodernity*.
12. Lash and Urry, *Economies of Signs*, p. 306.
13. Ibid. On sport and global processes see Harvey and Houle, 'Sport, world economy and new social movements'.

14. Taylor, *Political Geography*, pp. 36–8. We have used Taylor's idea of a 'three-tiered structure of separation and control' as the basic theoretical framework for this book. It is, of course, inextricably related to ideas of globalisation and modernisation. There are, however, a number of other potential frameworks for such an analysis as ours. Consider, for example, Gregory's notion of three levels of spatial structure – (i) events, (ii) systems of social practice, and (iii) structures of social relations. It would not be difficult to see (i) 'events' as, for example, the plotting of the growth of sports associations, (ii) 'systems of social practice' as, say, the transformation of folk-games to modern sports or the resistance to such transformations, and (iii) 'structures of social relations' as the global means of athletic production. For an elaboration on this approach see Gregory, 'People, places and practices'.

15. Said, *Culture and Imperialism*, p. 20. The Kenyan case is dealt with in Thiong'o, *Moving the Centre*.

16. Monnington, 'Black African sport'.

17. CDO, 1953, p. 7.

18. Baker, 'Political games', p. 276. The assertion that Kenya's track successes owed much to Velzian caused some resentment in Kenya: see Noronha, *Kipchoge of Kenya*, p. 110.

19. Amin and Moll, *Kenya's World Beating Athletes*, p. 18.

20. Ndoo, 'The Kenyan Success', p. 56.

21. Millar and Crawley, *Athletics*.

22. Abmayr, *Track and Field Performances*, p. 4.

23. Ibid.

24. COR, 1956, p. 123.

25. Kang, 'Sports, media and cultural dependency', p. 413.

26. *Weekly Review* (1987), p. 43.

27. Puronaho and Vuolle, *A Survey of the Needs of Sports Development Cooperation in Africa*.

28. 'Twenty years of Cardinal Otunga', *School Magazine* (1983), p. 11.

29. Ibid, p. 12.

30. Butcher, 'Low profile priest'.

31. Mählmann, 'Perception of sport in Kenya', p. 141.

32. Abmayr, 'Analysis and perspectives of the project in Kenya'.

33. Wangemann and Glad, *IAAF Development Cooperation*.

34. Appadurai, 'Disjuncture and difference in the global cultural economy'.

35. Massey, 'Power geometry and a progressive sense of place'.

36. Ibid, p. 62.

37. Monnington, 'Black African sport', p. 163.

38. Clayton, 'Sport and African soldiers', p. 127.

39. The geographical dimensions of the scramble to recruit these athletes is well described in Rooney, *The Recruiting Game*.

40. Bale, *Brawn Drain*, p. 77.

41. Hoberman, *Mortal Engines*, p. 35.

42. Hollander, *A Geographical Analysis of Foreign Intercollegiate Track and Field Athletes in the United States*, p. 22.

43. In this context 'superior' means that the athletes achieved a performance of a sufficient quality to rank them in the 'top 50' in the United States annual performers' lists. These are published annually in *Track and Field News*. See Bale, *The Brawn Drain*, p. 77.

44. Abmayr, *Track and Field Best Performances*.

45. Bale, *The Brawn Drain*, p. 84.
46. Ibid, p. 88.
47. Maguire, 'Preliminary observations on globalisation and the migration of sports labour' and 'Sport, national identities and globalization'.
48. Abmayr, 'Analysis and perspectives'.
49. Interview (JS) with Kiptalam Keter (April 26), 1992.
50. The European sample included a small proportion of swimmers, in addition to track and field athletes.
51. Ballinger, *In Your Face!*, p. 60. See also Bale, *The Brawn Drain*, pp. 137–8.
52. The survey was undertaken by *Jyllands Posten*; see *L'Équipe* (24 August 1995), p. 24.
53. Interview (JS) with Mike Boit (4 May 1992).
54. Godia, 'Sport in Kenya', p. 271.
55. Mählmann, Asembo and arap Korir, 'An analysis of sports in Kenyan educational institutions'.
56. Mackay, 'A new world order'.
57. Robertson, 'Mapping the global condition'.

6

Altitude or Attitude: Regions and Myths

The legendary feats of African-savannah-dwellers
...suggested the existence of exotic, unfathomed human
physiologies, comparable to exotic customs or ceremonies
beyond the understanding of European ethnologists.

JOHN HOBERMAN, *Mortal Engines*

In the last two chapters we have arrayed considerable evidence of the
large number of international factors which have contributed to present-
day Kenyan movement culture. We therefore feel that we have shown
that it is impossible to make sense of Kenyan track and field without
looking at global processes. We cannot, however, avoid the feeling that
many people still view Kenya's contribution to the world of athletics as
the result of factors endogenous to Kenya and its physical environment.
For this reason we think it is worth returning to the confines of Kenya
itself to look at athletics – notably running – on a national scale,
focusing particularly on the geographical differences in athletic output
within the country. In order to do this we will need to consider two
traditional 'geographical' themes – regional variation and environmental
determinism – in the context of the Kenyan running phenomenon. In
doing so we will expose certain myths which have grown up around
Kenyan athletics.

Myth is common in sports and often involves a spurious association
between sport and place. For example, it was a myth that the old
'communist' countries of Eastern Europe (the 'red machine')
outproduced the nations of the West in terms of superior track and field
athletes. Using the per capita approach described in chapter 2 it has been
shown that no statistical association existed between a nation's position
in relation to the former 'iron curtain' and its propensity to achieve a
high or low per capita output of superior athletes.[1] In England it was a
myth that blacks could not play football; they were said to lack courage
and guts. Today we see several black players in most English
professional football clubs.[2] As we have already shown, it was a myth
that black athletes lacked stamina and could not excel in endurance
events such as middle- and long-distance running. The Kenyans, and

athletes from some other countries, have demolished that myth. Yet many dubious stories and hypotheses about the 'success' of Kenyan athletics remain. Part of this chapter seeks to establish the extent of their mythical status.

Running and regions

One of the problems of the kind of quantitative data we employed in Chapter 2 is that the nation state, which is used as the areal unit for their collection and presentation, acts as a sort of 'container' of the data. In doing so, differences *between* nations are accentuated; variations which may exist *within* them are obscured. The container-based data also fail to pick out trans-national regions which straddle national boundaries. Nevertheless, we can often disaggregate national level data and hence examine the variations in athletic production within countries. Kenyan athletic 'output' is no exception.

The geographical origins of Kenyan athletes are not evenly distributed across the country, nor are they randomly distributed. There are, in fact, areas which overproduce superior athletes and others which underproduce, compared to the national average. In the case of track and field athletics we have evidence to show that it is not Kenya which should be regarded as the principal geographic unit of 'production' of superior athletes in east Africa but a particular region of Kenya, namely the Rift Valley Province. In effect, Kenya's positive athletic image is obtained by the exploits of athletes from one province. But we should not be too dogmatic about this. We are not saying that *all* of Kenya's superior athletes come from the Rift Valley; but a very large proportion certainly do.

In order to demonstrate the myth of *Kenyan* running and the dominance of *Rift Valley* running we temporarily revert to some further simple statistical analyses. We have been able to obtain the places of birth of 197 Kenyan runners who were ranked in the top 100 in Africa in their respective events in 1988 (comparative data for field event athletes were regrettably unavailable).[3] A per capita analysis was undertaken similar to that discussed in Chapter 2, except that for our present purpose we used the 197 runners to compare provincial *per capita* production with that of the Kenyan national average. The national level is presented as an index of 1.0 for purposes of easy comparison. The results of our analysis are shown in Table 6.1 and Figure 6.1. They show that the Rift Valley was the major source of Kenyan élite runners in 1988. This region produced more superior athletes than any other province, in both absolute and relative terms. Its per capita index was nearly four times the national average. Another way of stressing the dominance of the Rift Valley in terms of 'runner production' is to emphasise that the province produced 71.5 per cent of Kenya's superior runners but only contained 19.3 per cent of the national population.

TABLE 6.1.
Per capita variations in provincial production of superior Kenyan runners,
1988 (n = 197)

Province	Number of runners	Per capita index
Rift Valley	141	3.7
Nyanza	23	0.6
Central	13	0.4
Eastern	12	0.4
Western	8	0.1
North Eastern	0	0
Nairobi	0	0
Coast	0	0
Kenya	197	1.0

An examination of Figure 6.1 might suggest that the Rift Valley is the cultural core of Kenyan running. It is an area well above average runner 'productivity' and is flanked by Western and Nyanza provinces in the west, and Eastern and Central provinces in the east which (for our sample) are areas of below average or zero production. The map suggests a gradation in the culture of modern running away from the Rift Valley core. As we will show, this is a somewhat misleading interpretation but the absence of superior runners from the national periphery is obvious. The absence of runner production from Nairobi is not surprising. Various other studies in other parts of the world have shown the relative paucity of sports talent produced in large cities.[4] This is mainly the result of the large number of alternative opportunities for, or choices of, sports in such cities.

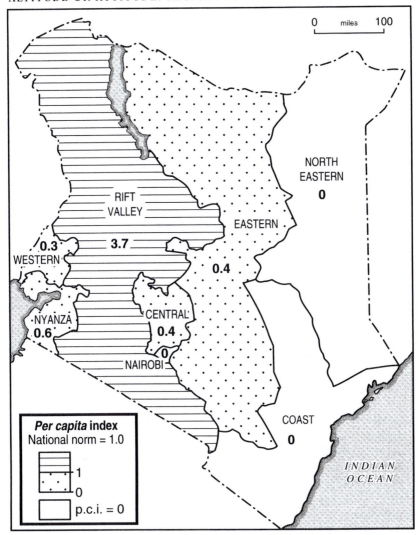

Figure 6.1. Per capita 'production' of superior Kenyan runners at the provincial level, Kenya, 1991.

High altitude: back to environmental determinism

The Rift Valley is a region of relatively high altitude. Kirinyaga (Mount Kenya) in Central Province rises to 5,200 metres (17,040 feet) and much of Rift Valley Province lies above 2,000 metres. A recurring theme – at least, since 1968 – has been that the altitude at which Kenyans live 'explains' their running successes and their world-class performances. The fact that an above average number of runners come from the Rift Valley further encourages an assumption that there is a link between altitude and athletic excellence.

The association between Kenya's high altitude and its apparent ability to produce an above-average number of superior runners has led some observers to believe that this is a causal relationship – that one variable (altitude) causes the other (superior runners). Kenyans from the Rift Valley are hence believed to possess a genetic advantage denied to foreigners.[5] In the first book to alert the world of athletics to various interpretations of *The African Running Revolution* it was noted that 'it has been *obvious* that athletes who spend most of their lives at 6,000 feet or more have a distinct advantage over athletes living closer to sea level when it comes to long distance running'. In such a comment looms the spectre of environmental determinism. As a result the editor of the book was moved to add a parenthetical note stating that 'many people believe this and it may be true but there is no scientific proof that it is'.[6]

Environmental determinism is a doctrine which was particularly popular during the late nineteenth and early twentieth centuries. It attributes human activities and behaviour to the physical environment in which people live. Environmentalism sees the environment as the 'dominant actor', forgetting history, ignoring key social, economic and political factors, and remaining unmediated by culture.[7] Human beings are viewed as clay in nature's hands. This doctrine emerged at a time when the 'laws of theology' were being replaced in scientific and popular consciousness by the 'laws of nature'. Environmental determinism, though often laced with racist attitudes has, nevertheless, a long history in scientific, geographical and sporting lore. Consider the following examples which might seem appropriate to the Kenyan situation. We can adopt (and adapt) the tenet of the early twentieth-century geographer, Ellsworth Huntington, to illustrate our point: in the development of great athletes 'a certain peculiar type of climate ... seems to be a necessary condition of great progress'.[8] He introduced the idea of 'climatic energy', arguing that high outputs of human energy were impossible in tropical latitudes. This meant that on his world map of variations in 'climatic energy', Kenya was defined as a 'low' or 'medium' energy country. Hence Kenya, experiencing as it did 'the enervating monotonous climates of much of the tropical zone ...[would produce] a lazy and indolent people'[9] – hardly the sort to break world long distance running records.

It is ironic, however, that other environmental determinists would have read the Kenyan environment differently. For example, Ellen

Churchill Semple deduced that the mountain dweller (for example, Kenyan?) brings 'certain qualities which make him [sic] a formidable competitor in the struggle for existence – the strong muscles, unjacked nerves, iron purpose and indifference to luxury bred in him by the hard conditions of his native employment'.[10]

Let us now consider some examples of environmental determinism applied explicitly to athletics. Much of what follows provides a dramatic contrast to the eulogising of the distance running capabilities of the Maasai and other Kenyan groups alluded to in Chapter 3. Instead, it reflects the ambiguous view of the European toward the African athlete. The black athlete *per se* was widely perceived as a born sprinter. An extreme view, which is admittedly a product of its time, would be that the black athlete

> wherever he lives today ... appears to have retained much of his primitive reaction to danger ... his response to sound appears to be keener than that of the white man and these reactions are of vital importance in short distance races. ... His speed 'off the mark' and the maintenance of rapid action for short distances are, *without doubt* due to the primitive reaction to jungle instinct.[11]

Likewise, black athletes would not be suited to long distance running because they are 'more profusely supplied with sweat glands and the pores are wider, hence enabling the tropical native to disperse more heat than the northerner, especially in a tropical environment'. The profusion of sweat glands may cause the black athlete to get rid of too much heat and therefore too much energy in cooler climates. 'This may be one of the reasons why he [sic] is better adapted to short distance races where maximum effort is required for a shorter period of time'.[12]

Some of the geographical perspectives of the early 1950s were residuals of more general thinking from a century earlier. Some advocates of environmentalism went so far as to doubt the possibility of any kind of 'development' of athletics in Africa. It was only grudgingly admitted that Africans might one day be able to 'put up performances in their native lands *almost comparable* with those of the European and American, *at least in short distances* and field events.'[13] Such an observation was an athletic shadow of the mid-nineteenth century view that Africans could not improve their existing mental and physical states (without, of course, the problematic presence of biological adulteration – or racial amalgamation).[14]

Such views about blacks being physiologically favoured in sprint events continued into the early 1970s and undoubtedly still exist today. In 1971 Martin Kane had an article on black athletic success published in *Sports Illustrated*. In it he argued that all black athletic success was explained by the discredited notion of 'race'. He averred that black athletes, be they from Britain or Brazil, Kentucky or Kenya, shared certain physical and psychological characteristics. The physical make-up of black athletes, he argued, predisposed them towards sprint events. Faced with the problem of explaining the success of Kenyan (and Ethiopian) athletes in the long distances, he claimed that the Kenyans, while having black skin, also conveniently possessed a number of white characteristics![15] Kane, and other such thinkers, ignored (or have been unaware of) the work of the physical anthropologist, W. Montague Cobb who argued, as long ago as 1936, that success in track and field was not based on physical characteristics but on such factors as proper training and motivation to succeed. Referring to American athletes, he noted that 'there is not a single physical characteristic which all the Negro stars in question have in common which would definitely identify them as Negroes'.[16] Put another way, the biological characteristics of 'black' and 'white' athletes are not mutually exclusive.

Environmentalist thinking in studies of athletic performance was not necessarily restricted to black athletes. For example (and implicitly drawing on the ideas of Semple) it was noted that the large number of Scandinavian (particularly Swedish and Finnish) athletes who featured among the world's greatest middle- and long-distance runners during the 1930s and 1940s, was explained, basically, by the fact that cooler regions were innately superior to the tropics. Athletes from Scandinavia were 'favoured by cold winters, warm summers and precipitation of the temperate continental variety'. In addition, 'where there exists a mountain barrier and a consequent rain-shadow region, within but a few miles a temperate climate passes into extremes'.[17] As a result, at the continental level, performances in distance running could be correlated positively with longitude. The Welsh, English and Swedish records for three distance running events were provided as the most flimsy of evidence.[18] More romantically, a German writer from the 1930s observed that in Finland

> all kinds of being in these stretches of land were capable by nature of special feats of endeavour ... Running is certainly in the blood of every Finn. When you see the clear, deep green forests, the wide open luxuriant plains with their typical red peasant homes, the heights covered by massive clusters of trees and the never-ending light blue to the horizon with the lakes merging with the sky, one is overcome with an involuntary feeling of elation and because you don't have wings, you want to run. Yes, hurry light-footed through

this northern scenery, for kilometres, for hours on end. Nurmi and his friends are like animals in the forest. They began to run because there was a deep need, because a peculiar dreamlike scenery constantly enticed them and pulled them into the spell of its mysteries ... It is not merely the pursuit of the naked record, for fame and honour, which spurs every son of the north to near superhuman feats. Their splendid times are also a way of thanking mother earth and the beauty of her many endless trails.[19]

Be it climate, longitude or coniferous forests, these were erroneous attempts to 'explain' the success of Nordic distance runners by applying the same kind of environmentalist attitudes and language used to explain the success of black runners in the sprints in the 1950s – and, paradoxically, to explain the success of Kenyan runners today. The tendency to identify causation with association is a common statistical confusion but in these cases it is understandable as a result of the longstanding popular belief in the kind of environmentalism to which we have alluded.

Compare the emphasis on the physical environment in the above 'explanation' of the success of the Finnish runners with the way in which the African environment is used by the American journalist, Kenny Moore, to 'explain' the success of the Kenyans – though in a rather different and more Darwinian way:

Africa can seem to be a sieve of afflictions through which only the hardy may pass. The largest, fastest, wildest, strangest beasts are here. Every poisonous bug, screaming bird and thorned shrub has arrived at this moment through the most severe environments ...Sport is a pale shadow of the competitive life that has gone on for ever across this high, fierce, first continent. Is it any wonder that frail European visitors feel threatened?[20]

We do not feel that it is necessary to more than summarise the oft-quoted arguments about the effects of altitude on athletic performance. It is widely believed that athletes *from anywhere in the world* who live at altitude will benefit in races from 1,500 metres upwards. A currently conventional version of such implicitly determinist thinking is that living at high altitude provides the ability to perform well in aerobic athletic events over distances from 1,500 metres to the marathon. The coach, John Velzian, talking about the success of Kenyan athletes, put it this way: they were born and have lived at an altitude well above 5,000 feet. This operates to their advantage in several ways. Since their whole physiology of respiration has become adapted to living in an atmosphere with a decreased supply of oxygen, it is of considerable benefit to them when competing at lower levels.[21]

In such a view, the emphasis is placed on the altitude and not on the athletes. It fails to take into account their motivation, their coaching, their training, their underlying achievement orientation, and a number of other factors.

While rejecting environmental determinism we should point out that if we ignored the physical environment entirely we would be guilty of 'environmental blindness'. We would be viewing the environment as a 'bit player' and interpreting such factors as altitude as passive or neutral. Yet the conclusion reached two decades ago by Jack Daniels, a physiologist and track coach from the University of Texas, was that

> the biggest issue that research has not yet resolved is whether the African runner, or any altitude resident, has a distinct physiological advantage over a well-trained sea level native in a race at sea level. Of course, neither has sufficient proof been provided to show that a sea-level native who trains at altitude can improve sea-level performance beyond that which could be brought about by sufficiently intense sea-level training.[22]

That issue does not seem to have been resolved. The more recent view of Swedish medical scientist Bengt Saltin and his associates is that while some physiological differences do exist between Kenyan and Swedish runners, and that any importance ascribed to being at altitude cannot be excluded, it 'is considered unlikely to be of any major significance'.[23]

If athletic productivity was related causally to altitude alone, all high altitude countries should be producing long distance runners at high per capita levels. Consider, however, three of Kenya's neighbours, Ethiopia, Tanzania and Zimbabwe, each of which possess similar altitudinal characteristics to Kenya. These countries have much lower levels of per capita output of African-class distance running talent than Kenya. Zimbabwe (men's index of 1.66 and women's of 1.36) produced at just above the continental norm of 1.00 with Ethiopia (0.73 and 1.09) and Tanzania (1.04 and 0.41) also at relatively modest levels, around or below the continental average. For Kenya the respective indices for distance runners were 10.65 and 7.52. There are a number of high altitude countries in other parts of the world where the production of superior distance runners remains extremely low; consider, for example, the cases of Nepal, Peru, Mexico, Bolivia and Colombia. Indeed, most high altitude countries produce relatively few world class athletes of any kind.

It is clear, therefore, that altitude cannot *cause* the high levels of athletic output and success that has characterised Kenyan running, any more than nature can cause the cultivation of rice. Indeed, as we have noted earlier, in the 1950s Kenya was equally strong in the sprints, javelin and high jump, events for which altitude has never been used as an explanatory variable. In recent decades Kenya has produced many excellent 400 metre sprinters (25 per cent of African-class 400 metre runners in 1993 were Kenyans), another event for which a background of living at altitude has never been claimed as an advantage. The same observation might also be made about Kenya's runners at 800 metres, an event at which aerobic and anaerobic qualities are delicately balanced. Placing undue emphasis on altitudinal and other physical environmental factors is often used to devalue and denigrate Kenyan success by implying a 'gift of nature' or an unfair advantage.

Huntington's ideas were discredited in Jokl's analysis of the results of the 1952 Olympics.[24] Objections to environmentalist ideas have subsequently been stated more forcefully by the geographer Richard Peet who describes them as a 'disguised kind of natural racism'.[25] Environmental determinism of the type described above reflects the values of a Western society which has consistently seen success in sport as being related to 'racial' characteristics – a physical analogue of what David Livingstone has called 'moral climatology'.[26] When black athletes fail to behave according to the stereotype their superiority is presented as a 'gift of nature' just as it was for the Scandinavian distance runners of the 1930s and 1940s. The patent inadequacy of physical environmental and 'racial' factors, therefore, forces us to look for other possible reasons for the outstanding success of the Rift Valley runners – or, more accurately, certain groups within the Rift Valley.

Rift Valley running

As was noted earlier Rift Valley Province is a large area of high altitude bordering Sudan and Ethiopia in the north and Tanzania in the south. Within it there are a large number of districts occupied by various ethnic groups (see Figure 2.10). Just as there are considerable variations in 'athletic productivity' within Kenya there has also traditionally been considerable variation within the province.

As we have shown, in 1991 the Rift Valley Province as a whole had a per capita index for Kenyan runner production of 3.7. The respective index for the Rift Valley district of Turkana, however, was only 0.5 – half the Kenyan average and further evidence of the inappropriateness of the altitude factor in explaining athletic output. Here we have a high altitude area which produces few Kenyan runners. At the other end of the scale, however, was Nandi district which had an index of 22.9. Put in more dramatic terms, Nandi district has only 1.8 per cent of Kenya's population but in 1988 'produced' 42.1 per cent of the nation's superior runners. Other major producing districts within the Rift Valley included the contiguous areas of Baringo (index of 4.6), Elegyo Marakwet (4.3), Uasin Gishu (2.4) and Kericho (2.1). A neighbouring district in Nyanza Province, Kisii, had an index of 1.7. This contiguous group of districts is another clear example of a 'running region', at a different level of scale from that shown in Figure 6.1, and is shown in Figure 6.2.[27]

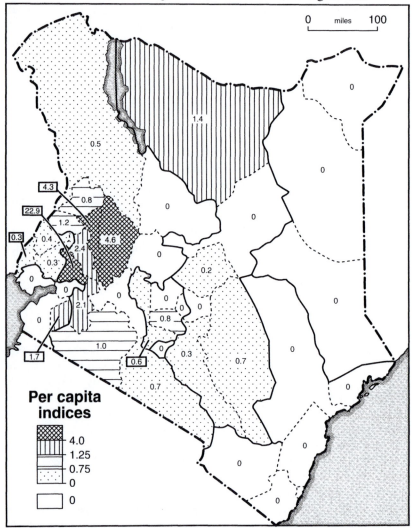

Figure 6.2. Per capita 'production' of superior Kenyan runners at the district level, Kenya, 1991.

In Chapter 3 we referred to the nineteenth- and early twentieth-century academic and popular view that the Maasai were great runners. However, Reclus could never have predicted that the Maasai would eventually compete in major athletics championships. Nevertheless, his observations about their running abilities were certainly not wrong. Among the most famous Maasai runners have been Daniel Rudisha, Billy Konchellah, and Stephen Ole Marai. These were not distance runners but they exhibited their talents over 400 and 800 metres. By 1993, Maasai runners had won nine medals in major athletic championships. Members of a neighbouring ethnic group, however, the Gusii (Kisii), had won 78 medals; another Rift Valley group, the Kalenjin, had won 317. These latter figures amounted respectively to 15.4 per cent and 62.6 per cent of the 506 medals won by Kenyan athletes in major competitions up to 1993. The respective figures for Kenyan-held world records were 11.8 per cent (Gusii) and 76.4 per cent (Kalenjin). Moving to another level we find that many of these medals and records were achieved by one group within the Kalenjin, the Nandi, who have given their name to one of the districts within Rift Valley Province. It is to this particular group that we now turn.

The achievements by the Kalenjin in general, and the Nandi in particular, in a relatively small part of the Rift Valley, demands further exploration. We will attempt to apply some sociological ideas to the phenomenon of Kalenjin and Nandi running dominance (having already acknowledged that they live at high altitude – as do other ethnic groups with *low per capita* levels of output) which will move us away from crude environmental determinism with its focus solely on altitude.

Achievement orientation and the Kalenjin

We have argued earlier that the transition from traditional to modern forms of Kenyan running represents a process of change rather than one of continuity. This does not ignore the possibility that a degree of continuity may be present at a deeper attitudinal and ideological level. It is, therefore, the cultural (rather than biological) bases of particular Kenyan ethnic groups that we now explore.

The Kalenjin are generally regarded as quiet, ascetic, serious people who display little migration from their home areas. They are also known 'to be hard working and enduring, a fact which is perhaps best demonstrated by Kenya's famous long distance runners almost all of whom are Kalenjin'[28] (as noted above). Could their traditional asceticism, seriousness and diligence be part of a broader profile which is conducive to their success as modern athletes? Using data compiled by Berg-Schlosser in the mid-1970s it is possible to detect characteristics of the Kalenjin which are at least consistent with a good background for distance running excellence, *in contrast to other Kenyan ethnic groups*. As part of his research into tradition and change in Kenya Berg-Schlosser undertook an analysis of inter-ethnic differences in 'achievement orientation'. Of the tribes studied, the Kalenjin had the smallest score for 'low' achievement orientation – 78 per cent of those interviewed displaying 'medium' or 'high' achievement orientation.[29] This was the highest figure for 'medium' and 'high' achievement orientation among the ethnic groups which were surveyed. Likewise, in a study of different attitudes to sports among three ethnic groups, Peter Mählmann has shown that Kalenjin school students perceived the ascetic experience of sport as being more significant than did Luo and Arab students.[30]

It goes without saying that achievement sport requires a high level of achievement orientation. Groups displaying asceticism (associated as it is with the postponement of gratification) and achievement orientation would seem more likely to be attracted to individual sports than team sports (and to long distance than to short distance running events). Some evidence for this is found in Kenya with the Kalenjin being attracted to running but the less ascetic Luo excelling in football.[31] The Kalenjin also have a high degree of ethnocentricism – an expression of, and a preference for, social relations among their own ethnic group.[32] Group loyalty plus the fact that the Kalenjin also display a high adherence to ascriptive criteria in determining social positions implies a very positive self image. So while the Kalenjin represent a highly traditional society in some respects, this is coupled with attitudes quite consistent with achievement sport. We stress here that the Kalenjin situation is clearly different from other Kenyan tribes in these respects, notably in its achievement orientation.

The traditional side of the coin is shown in the Kalenjin attitude to women. Of those interviewed 75 per cent of both men and women thought that women should have less freedom than they possess at present. Only among the Maasai (as we have already noted, the most traditional tribe in Kenya) was the score higher (82 per cent).[33] The Kalenjin see womens' roles in a highly restrictive way and this clearly shows how difficult it is for women to break into the world of Kenyan running. Yet, as we will show in the next chapter, they have succeeded in doing so, albeit to a limited extent so far.

A note on the Nandi

Within the Kalenjin, the Nandi are arguably the group in present-day Kenya which has the greatest tradition of individualism and competitiveness. The Nandi attitude is that of the Kalenjin writ large: "'...we are the Nandi: all other people are nothing". Their ethnic feeling is, indeed, aggressive, and even superficial observers of the Nandi have been struck by their haughtiness and arrogance. The Nandi consider[ed] himself the equal of any man, and superior to all who are not Nandi'.[34] The Nandi displayed considerable resistance to mission education, seeing it as a threat to their authority. More significantly, the Nandi was the only tribe to engage in prolonged 'guerrilla' resistance against the British. In 1895, as the British tried to assert their control over Nandi-land, they met with considerable resistance from Nandi warriors under the leadership of Koitalel Samoei. The Nandi experienced five 'punitive' expeditions in a period of ten years, the fifth being the largest ever mounted in Kenya.[35] It was not until 1905 that the Nandi resistance to British rule was ended following the assassination of Samoei by a British officer at a meeting that had been called to discuss peace.[36]

The Nandi were also among the most aggressive groups involved in cattle raiding (the 'sport' of the Nandi). They were, therefore, one of the groups to be most vigorously channelled into sportised running through the kinds of social control activities of the British administration discussed in Chapter 4. Nandi excellence in sportised running had been noted well before the adoption of the Kenya AAA in 1951. As early as 1937 the teams taking part in the Rift Valley sports meeting were dominated by athletes from Nandi, Elegyo and Baringo. In the 1947 national championship the entire Rift Valley team was represented by Nandi. In 1949 the District Commissioner of Nandi, J.K.R. Thorp, recognised something special about Nandi athletes, although the merit in cultivating this talent was again seen as a valuable source of social control. He commented that 'the Nandi *tradition* of athletic prowess is one which should be preserved ... the hard work put in annually by a great many people is well worth while and its ultimate value cannot be judged by a fine display of cups alone.'[37] In 1948, the Commissioner for Central Province commented that the encouragement of sport and football had proceeded with varying success, although none of the tribes in the Central Province equalled those in other provinces (implying the Rift Valley). This comment followed the 1949 national championships in which Nandi athletes won 11 events. In 1950 the principal of the Government African School at Kapsabet noted that 'the Nandi are too much of individualists to learn to play football or hockey as a team.

They usually prevent themselves being beaten too badly by a good team by sheer guts'.[38]

We accept that labelling an entire ethnic group with certain characteristics is to reduce a large number of individual human beings to identical clones. Nevertheless, students of cross-cultural psychology do recognise that 'average' cultural traits do vary between groups. They do, of course, conceal (as do all averages) considerable variations within populations but, nevertheless, may reveal very broad differences between them.

The success of the Nandi in an individual sport, such as running may, therefore, be a reflection of their earlier, pre-sportised aggressiveness in the areas of cattle raiding and resistance to imperial rule and their achievement orientation. This is not to say that modern Nandi *racing* represents a form of continuity with their (quite differently configured) pre-sportised *running*, but with their deeper ideological orientation. However, our 'explanation' of a particular form of sporting participation would not be inconsistent with Eichberg's idea that the indigenous movement culture of a particular group is sustained by their *selective* adoption of *particular* modern Western sports.[39] In this view a traditional form of behaviour possesses a degree of stability which permits the adoption of particular sports and a redefinition of earlier cultural forms, supplementing our earlier observations about the achievement orientation of the Kalenjin. In the Nandi case, resistance was consistent with the individualism of running; raiding became racing. Aggression and victory as particularly prized cultural traits of the Nandi have been retained in the tradition of track running. It is also clear that the Nandi had built up a considerable reputation as athletes before the 1940s, their relatively early participation in sportised running giving them a substantial advantage on the road to modern track and field athletics.

The success of the Nandi and their neighbours could, in no small part, also be the result of more widely observed social psychological factors. One is the imitative effect of role models on young boys (and later girls). Let us recall the early modern Kenyan athletes. Keter and Keino were Nandi; they were followed by Mike Boit, Amos Biwott, Benjamin Kogo and many others. Maiyoro was a neighbouring Gusii, as were Naftali Temu, Arere Anentia and Richard Juma among the early Kenyan running élite.

The first Nandi athlete of continental significance was Kiptalam Keter who dominated Kenyan half-mile running from 1949 to 1962. He had been inspired by, among others, the Kenyan 440 yards record holder, Kipwambok Bor, and was impressed by his aggressive style.[40] Keino acknowledged Keter as one of his role models, along with other 1950s

Kenyan athletes such as Kanuti Sum, Bartonjo Rotich and Lazaro Chepkwony.[41] Mike Boit, another great Nandi runner, also acknowledged Keter as an inspiration.[42] Keino himself certainly appears to have been a role model for many other Nandi athletes. Indeed, the historical explanation of the early success in athletics in the Nandi region is supported by medical and social scientists. For example, Saltin and his associates argue that

> the reason for the superiority of the Nandi tribe in running compared with the other Kalenjin groups is probably not different genetic endowments. The reason is more likely that the first famous Kenyan runner, Kipchoge Keino, as a Nandi gave rise to a tradition in his tribe that was followed by recruitment of talents to the high school where good organised training and competitions were early established.[43]

Nandi athletics had the advantage of an unplanned early start – earlier than the Keino era, as we have shown. Later, running became an invented Nandi tradition, a subject to which we return in our final chapter.

There is at least a suggestion that the Nandi are influencing, through imitation, the attitudes of neighbouring ethnic groups. The Kenyan world championship cross country team of 1992, for example, possessed only three Nandi runners in a squad of 20. Athletes like Moses Kiptanui, Richard Chelimo, Ismael Kirui, William Mutwol, Nixon Kiprotich, Susan Sirma and Esther Kiplagat are either Tugen, Keiyo or Marakwet – other Kalenjin tribes.[44]

Stacking, running to school and hard training

The above description of Nandi and Kalenjin dominance in Kenyan athletics is not presented as a definitive theory. Indeed, we do not subscribe to the view that any one factor can explain why Kenya is such a dominant running power, although there is a widespread desire and temptation to seek mono-causation among those looking for a neat and tidy view of the world. In this section we hint at certain possible additional explanations and conclude by dismissing others as myths.

Stacking

Some early classic sociological studies of sport in the United States observed how black athletes were over-represented in certain playing positions in football and in baseball. Central positions required judgment, leadership and considerable interaction with other players. The non-central roles assigned to black players implied that they were thought by coaches and trainers to lack qualities of judgment and leadership. This was viewed as a form of racial segregation and was termed 'stacking'. This term was used to describe the way in which black athletes were stacked in certain non-central positions. Racial bias in the spatial positioning of players has been found to occur in other sports, from US basketball to British soccer and Australian rugby.[45] Here we may be getting closer to the Kenyan situation.

In Kenya the early success of Kalenjin athletes has encouraged school teachers and coaches to channel Kalenjin school students into middle distance running on the basis of the many role models of the past. If they are Kalenjin they are expected to succeed at the middle distances. One of the authors (JS) experienced such 'pushing' into running (despite the absence of any obvious ability) while a student at primary and secondary school because he was a Nandi.[46]

The above 'explanations' are commonly used all over the world – role modelling and stacking create self-fulfilling prophecies in all cultures. A positive attitude towards achievement sport is not unique to Kenya; it is a common attitude found wherever Western sport has taken root. Yet other alleged explanations of Kenyan success in running refuse to lie down and die. Many of these (such as diet and ability to withstand pain) are not unique to the Kalenjin or to Kenya and are characteristics found in peoples in many other African countries. For illustrative purposes we will simply note two. It is here that we enter the realm of myth.

A lifetime's training

A common 'explanation' of Kenyan success in distance running is that

> the Kenyan has ... been training solidly every day of his [sic] life since he was parked in a corner of his mud and wattle hut as a baby and encouraged to survive. His lifetime's training will have built up an incredible physical toughness, a resilience under stress and an astonishingly high tolerance of pain.[47]

This well-intentioned but ultimately patronising and racist piece of writing is close to a picture of the 'noble savage'. It stereotypes Kenyans as living in mud huts and is basically similar to the 1950s allusions (see Chapter 1) to 'raw talent'. The high pain threshold is frequently attributed to the pain caused during circumcision. As this, and the other conditions described above, is widely experienced throughout Africa, there is no reason why Kenyans should be singled out.

Another common 'explanation' is that Kenyan athletes are dominant because they ran long distances to school as young boys. The seriousness with which this is taken is reflected in its inclusion as a possible contributory factor to Kenyan running success by the medical scientist, Saltin.[48] The evidence that Kenyan middle and long distance runners did run long distances as young children is mixed. Saltin's data suggest that the average distances of habitual running/walking performed during childhood, *including* the distance covered to and from school by 29 runners of varying standards, was about 10 kilometres. But it is not clear whether this was, for example, two runs of five kilometres each, or four runs of 2.5 kilometres each day, or lesser distances with additional running at other times unrelated to going to school. Nor is it clear if the 29 athletes who claimed they ran to school were part of a larger sample, of whom some may have never run to school at all.

It is possible, of course that 'schoolboys' of 18 or 19 years of age may run to school as part of their formal athletic training but with educational development at the primary level there is little need for anyone in most of Kenya to run to school given the generous provision of educational establishments. It again invokes an image of a 'simple' lifestyle, lacking in 'technique'. It remains an image of the 'native' and the 'primitive', of the 'natural' rather than the 'cultural', with whom the European cannot possibly compete.[49] During fieldwork in rural areas of Nandi district in 1992, however, one of the authors (JS) never saw any children running to school. When asked whether they ran to school as children, 14 (70 per cent) of twenty Kenyan international athletes questioned said that they did not. In any case, the need to walk and run reasonable distances at an early age is probably greater in many of the other high altitude countries which produce no distance runners of note.

Such explanations are not unique to Africa. In 1929 it was observed that regular running as youngsters could also 'explain' the *English* production of distance running talent. Webster noted that *'from time immemorial* English schoolboys have been taught to run distances from a very tender age upwards. ... With this custom as a foundation it was easy and *natural* for England to produce a *race* of good distance runners'.[50]

Despite this parallel view, the problem of occidental views of African runners centres on them being judged as an athletic 'other' – a figure of 'non-reason'.[51] The African is regarded as being not just black – which often encourages the view of the 'native' and the 'primitive' – but also *essentially* different, being imbued with physical qualities denied the European. As we noted in Chapter 3, this tradition went back to the early twentieth century and before. David Spurr has suggested a European *need* to essentialise the African. Adopting his ideas, we can suggest that the idealisation of the Kenyan athlete is a form of compensation (on the symbolic level) for the Western processes of rationalisation which destroyed the traditional forms of Kenyan movement culture and made Kenya but one component of the global sports system. The kind of writing noted above (and in much of Chapter 3) reinforces the exotic qualities of the 'other' 'as if the Western imagination harboured a secret resistance against its own movement towards a completely rational and instrumental view of the world.' The idealised Kenyan runner is therefore seen as 'a substitute gratification for what would otherwise be an overwhelming sense of loss'.[52]

Nurture, not nature

During the 1930s, hard work and sacrifice were rarely used to explain the success of black American stars such as Jesse Owens. The same applies today in relation to Kenyan athletes. In athletics it is culture not biology, attitude not altitude, nurture not nature, which are the crucial variables which 'explain' individual athletic success in the rationalised and regulated world of achievement sport. The running of the athletes, who seemed to Western observers to have suddenly appeared in London and in Vancouver in 1954, was not 'natural'. It had been strongly 'cultured' by the activities of the Colony Sports Officers and the Kenya AAA. As part of this enculturation, for example, the half-miler Kiptalam Keter was relieved of his normal work duties and given a post in the police force when it was found that his work clashed with his running.[53] As Kipchoge Keino increasingly showed the potential to be a world-class athlete he was ordered by the police force to remain at the Police Training School at Kiganjo which provided good facilities for training rather than follow his own wish to become an ordinary policeman and return nearer to his home at Kapsabet. Having resigned himself to staying at Kiganjo he was given preferential treatment and was made a physical education instructor at the school.[54] The prison service and the army have also assisted in providing athletes with sinecures in order to allow serious athletic training to take place. Indeed, in the 1940s and early 1950s the army and police actively recruited from the district championships, approaching the winners as races finished and offering them places in the respective force. The fact that the majority of Kenya's runners in the 1960s had been indirectly subsidised by state agencies might be regarded as one of the key factors explaining their success.

Like Chepkwony, Maiyoro and Keter, Kipchoge Keino did not

simply appear from nowhere when he made his initial major international appearance in 1962 at the age of 22. He had marked out his own rough running track as a boy and maintained quantitative records of his progress from the age of 15 when his best time for the mile was 5 minutes 49 seconds.[55] His training regimen was methodical, not random. He constantly sought superior methods to improve his performance. His aim, to maximise his athletic output by increasingly rational means, bore a close resemblance to that of the former great Finnish record breaker, Paavo Nurmi.

An integral part of achievement orientation is a willingness to work hard and to submit oneself to a rational training programme. Active runners at St Patrick's High School train twice a day on at least five days of the week. One of the sessions includes running up to twelve kilometres, the second up to eight kilometres. Table 6.2 shows a programme of training prescribed for more mature Kenyan runners. It involves three training sessions per day. Distances may not exceed 100 kilometres per week but the major part of training at both school and senior level is at high intensity.[56] By any standards it is rigorous and is regarded by the editor and publisher of *Running Research News* as the prime factor in explaining Kenyan running success.[57]

TABLE 6.2

General preparation programme of pre-season training in Kenya. Training undertaken for period 24 February–9 March (after Kosgei and Abmayr (1988), p. 55).

	A.M.	P.M.
MON.	17–18 km. in approx 80 minutes.	9 km. high speed. 15 × 200m. hillwork.
TUE.	10 km. fartlek,* high speed.	Approx. 15 km. in 60 minutes.
WED.	20 km. easy regeneration. 20 minutes flexibility.	8 km. easy running.
THUR.	15 km. in 60 minutes. 20 × 100m. at 70% effort.	15 km. easy fartlek.*
FRI.	15 km. in 65 minutes. 20 minutes gym.	8 km. easy jogging.
SAT.	Competition or 13 km. at competitive speed.	Rest.
SUN.	10–12 km. in 50–55 mins. 20 minutes flexibility exercises.	Active rest.

* Fartlek is a term used to refer to fast and slow running in a natural setting. It is a Swedish term meaning 'speed play'.

Conclusion

The key theme of this book is that Kenyan athletics cannot be 'explained' with reference to Kenya alone. But what happens in Kenya and, crucially, the differences that exist within Kenya, do matter and have had an effect on Kenyan athletics. We are not suggesting that the physical environment is of no significance. To put undue emphasis on a physical factor such as altitude is, however, to ignore the complex webs of African history and the different degrees of adoption of Western cultures by the many ethnic groups in present day Kenya. It is to over-emphasise the biological. For this reason we have suggested that cultural and social *differences* should not be ignored in assessing the factors contributing to athletic success among various Kenyan groups.

David Wiggins has summarised the critique of the genetic thesis in the following words:

> We know as little about the contribution of genes to athletic ability as we do about the genetics of intelligence. Athletic ability is clearly a function of many genes in interaction with a number of other variables such as economic background, motivation, facilities, and coaching. How many genes may be involved in athletic ability is difficult, if not impossible, to determine since there is no way to separate out the contribution made by the aforementioned variables to sport performance.[58]

To say that Kenyans run so well because of their physiological or genetic characteristics is a racist statement. It is the 'penchant to *generalize* based upon essences perceived as *biological* [so common among observers of Kenyan running] which defines "racism"'.[59] Our position, with regard to 'race' is that it is a social or cultural, not a biological, construction.[60] Nor should we forget the ambivalent attitude of the European to the Kenyan runner. The travellers' tales ascribing black athletic superiority contrasted with the views of some environmental determinists and athletic coaches who saw black athletes as being incompatible with long-distance running. However, environmental determinism was itself ambivalent in this respect, operating as it did at global (Africa compared with Europe) and local (Wales compared with England) scales.[61]

We may briefly return to the contradiction between the type of travel writing which generally took a positive (albeit essentialised) view of the African's athletic ability (as exemplified in Chapter 3), and the environmentalists' negative views noted in this chapter. It may be useful to speculate on an alternative route to explore this contradiction. African athletic ability as expressed in its indigenous forms, and as perceived by the travel writers, was treated in a benign way. In its pre-sportised form it could not pose a threat to European running as racing. As modern sportised African running emerged in the 1950s and 1960s, however, it threatened to eliminate one of the fundamental differences between Kenyans and Europeans: that is, European supremacy and African absence in the heroic, long distance events. Africans were therefore labelled as 'natural athletes' but in possession of 'unfair advantages'. Such an image allowed the European to feel secure once again because it restored the 'athletic balance' in favour of the occident.[62]

A central aspect of this chapter has been the acknowledgement made to intra-national space. Kenya has not been homogenised and a 'geographical' approach has been stressed. If we are to favour any one broad approach to the study of Kenyan athletics, therefore, it is similar to what Chris Philo terms 'geographical history'. By this we seek to 'enrich and to shed light upon ... historical happenings by injecting them with a measure of geographical sensitivity'.[63] This is, of course, implicit in our world systems approach, as outlined in Chapter 2. In our case we have suggested that by the 1930s, particular ethnic groups (notably the Nandi and the Gusii) in a particular part of Kenya had already found that athletics was not inconsistent with their traditional ideology and that from the early adoption of track and field, the effects of role models and self-fulfilling prophecies, plus support from various Kenyan agencies, have cumulatively contributed to the emergence of an 'athletics region' whose 'sports space' is mainly occupied by athletics. This is typified by Nandi and, to a lesser extent, the surrounding districts of other Kalenjin groups. In other parts of Kenya, other sports, notably football, dominate the available sports space.

Notes and references

1. Bale, 'Towards a geography of international Sport'.
2. Maguire, 'Sport, racism and British society'.
3. Data collected from the Kenya AAA. The marathon was excluded from the events in which athletes were ranked. We note that Douglas Wakihuri, one of Kenya's most successful marathon runners, was born at coastal Mombasa.
4. Rooney, *Geography of American Sport*; Bale, 'The changing origins of an occupation'; and Curtis and Birch, 'Size of community of origin and recruitment to professional and Olympic ice hockey'.
5. Note the comment: 'Keino can be said to have a genetic advantage denied to lowlanders': Norris and Ross McWhirter, *The Guinness Book of Records*, (London, Guiness Superlatives: 1969), quoted in Daniels, 'Science on the altitude factor', p. 28.

6. Fenwick, 'The talent distribution'.
7. Blaut, *The Colonizer's Model of the World*, p. 69; Doherty, 'African environment and African development'. In an early article (in 1919) on the geography of games and sports it was noted that 'climate determines the kind of games we play': Hilderbrand, 'The geography of games', p. 91.
8. Huntington, *Civilization and Climate*, p. 9. For an excellent review of Huntington's work see Livingstone, *The Geographical Tradition*, pp. 225–31; see also his 'Environmental determinism', and Tatham, 'Environmentalism and possibilism'.
9. Austin Miller, *Climatology* (London, Methuen: 1947) p. 2, quoted in Livingstone, *The Geographical Tradition*, pp. 225–6.
10. Ellen Semple, *Influences of Geographic Environment* (London, Constable: 1911), quoted in Cloke, Philo and Sadler, *Approaching Human Geography*, p. 5.
11. Richards, *Athletic Records*, pp. 10, 12 (emphasis added). This dissertation was never published but is almost certainly the first attempt by a British geographer to seriously address the geographical dimensions of achievement sport. Although the quotations from his writing included here are used to illustrate the nature of deterministic thinking, Richards did not totally deny social influences on athletic performance. His dissertation, examined by E.G. Bowen and influenced strongly by another member of the 'Welsh school of geography', H.J. Fleure, does not, however, reflect the latter's humanism and anti-racism. On this see Livingstone, *The Geographical Tradition*, p. 286. A number of crude biological theories of the black athlete's success at sprinting are outlined in Webster, *Why? The Science of Athletics*, pp. 385–8.
12. Richards, *Athletic Records*, p. 57. Other, physiological, characteristics of 'negroes' – including the presence of a 'more forward pitch of the pelvic bones and consequently a more forward hang of the thigh' which were alleged to encourage ability at sprinting but to retard their ability at long-distance running – are outlined in Webster, *Why? The Science of Athletics*, pp. 386-8.
13. Richards, *Athletic Records*, p. 60.
14. See, for example, Brantlinger, 'Victorians and Africans'; Cairns, *Prelude to Imperialism*, p. 207; and Young, *Colonial Desire*.
15. Kane, 'An assessment of black is best'. A detailed critique of Kane's paper is found in Cashmore, *Black Sportsmen*, pp. 47–55; see also Wiggins, 'Great speed but little stamina'. Although social scientists may often feel that 'racial science' has long been dead, Marek Kohn has brilliantly signalled that it is alive and kicking in his pessimistic *The Race Gallery*. His chapter on sports covers the debate about Kenyan running (pp. 77–83) and basically reaches the same conclusion as that in the present chapter.
16. Cobb, 'Race and runners'. We are grateful to John Hoberman (University of Texas) for this reference. See also Wiggins, 'Great speed but little stamina'.
17. Richards, *Athletic Records*, p. 63.
18. Ibid, p. 65.
19. Schumacher, *Die Finnen, das grosse Sportvolk*, pp. 83–4. We are grateful to Tuija Kilpeläinen (University of Jyväskylä) for this reference and to Ruth Bale for translating part of the text. In fact Nurmi is more remembered for his scientific training regime than for 'running in nature'. He ran with stopwatch in hand and constantly tried to push his sportised body beyond existing barriers. From another 1930s perspective (though not stated in quite such lyrical terms as Schumacher's) it was also noted that 'there is undoubtedly something about the national temperament of the Finns and the atmosphere and conditions of life in their

northern land which enables them to lay claim to be considered the greatest distance runners the world has yet seen at distances over one mile': Webster, *Why? The Science of Athletics*, p. 378 (italics added).

20. Moore, 'Sons of the wind', p. 79.
21. Daniels, 'Science on the altitude factor'.
22. ibid. p. 41.
23. Saltin, et al, 'Aerobic exercise capacity', pp. 219–20.
24. Jokl, *Medical Sociology*, p. 108.
25. Peet, *Global Capitalism*, p. 18. See also Blaut, *The Colonizer's Model of the World*, p. 71.
26. Livingstone, 'Climate's moral economy', in Godlewska and Smith, *Geography and Empire*. On Darwinism and sports see Hoberman, *Mortal Engines*, pp. 33–61.
27. The outlying district of Marsabit (index of 1.4) in the northern part of Eastern Province is shown as also producing runners at above the national per capita average. This higher-than-average index was the result of only one runner coming from the district. The fact that one runner can lead to a high per capita index exposes a flaw of this and other such approaches which are very sensitive to the population size of the area being studied.
28. Berg-Schlosser, *Tradition and Change in Kenya*, p. 148–9.
29. Ibid, p. 222.
30. Mählmann, 'Perception of sport in Kenya', p. 134.
31. Ibid, p. 135.
32. Berg-Schlosser, *Tradition and Change in Kenya*, p. 204.
33. Ibid, p. 233.
34. Huntingford, *The Nandi of Kenya*, pp. 21–2.
35. Rosberg and Nottingham, *The Myth of 'Mau Mau'*.
36. Meinertzhagen, *Kenya Diary*.
37. KNA, PC/NKU2/32/2, GAS, emphasis added.
38. KNA, PC/RVPv2/3/6, p. 24.
39. Quoted in Heinemann, 'Sport in developing countries'. In a Nandi context note the comment that 'running was to be a surrogate for raiding': Manners, 'Raiders from the Rift Valley'. For an extended review of Nandi excellence in running, see Manners, 'In search of an explanation'. For a cautionary note on sport being an adaptation of pre-modern values, see, Guttmann, *Games and Empires*, p. 79.
40. Interview (JS) with Kiptalam Keter, 26 April 1992. Keter competed in the Commonwealth and Olympic Games and recorded a best time for the half mile of 1 minute 49.7 seconds at Kapsabet in 1961.
41. Interview (JS) with Kipchoge Keino, 24 April 1992. See also Noronha, *Kipchoge of Kenya*, p. 22. Note that the athletes named here were not all distance runners.
42. Aitken, *More than Winning*, p. 196.
43. Interview (JS) with Kipchoge Keino, 24 April 1992.
44. Saltin *et al.*, 'Aerobic exercise capacity', p. 221.
45. Examples of such studies include Loy and McElvogue, 'Racial segregation in American sport', pp. 5–23, and Maguire, 'Sport, racism'. In Britain it is obvious that a disproportionate number of black athletes are recruited (or attracted) to football, boxing and track and field.
46. This kind of bias on the part of teachers has been alluded to in the USA and in Britain in the context of black students being channelled into sports rather than into academic studies. See Cashmore, *Black Sportsmen*.
47. Lewis, 'An elan, a zest and a grace', pp. 9–11.
48. Saltin *et al.*, 'Aerobic exercise capacity'.

49. Hoberman, *Mortal Engines*, p. 56. See also Moore, 'Sons of the wind', p. 79.
50. Webster, *Athletics of Today*, p. 91, emphasis added.
51. Gregory, *Geographical Imaginations*, p. 29.
52. Spurr, *The Rhetoric of Empire*, pp. 131–2.
53. Interview (JS) with Kiptalam Keter.
54. Noronha, *Kipchoge of Kenya*, pp. 33–4.
55. Ibid, p. 158.
56. Saltin *et al.*, 'Aerobic exercise capacity', pp. 216–17.
57. Quoted in Kohn, *The Race Gallery*, p. 81.
58. Wiggins, 'Great speed but little stamina', p. 184.
59. Gates, 'Talkin' that talk', p. 403.
60. For a fascinating review of the 'emergence' of racism see Young, *Colonial Desire*, pp. 62–8.
61. Livingstone, *The Geographical Tradition*, p. 223.
62. Jan Mohamed, 'The economy of the manichean allegory', p. 87. We do not feel qualified to more than suggest that ideas from post-colonial literary studies (as used here) might be further applied to post-colonial sports studies.
63. Philo, 'History, geography and the "still greater mystery" of historical geography', p. 261.

7

Development, Underdevelopment, Resistance

That is the partial tragedy of resistance, that it must to a
certain degree work to recover forms already established or at
least influenced or infiltrated by the culture of empire.

EDWARD SAID, *Culture and Imperialism*

We want to conclude by evaluating the outcome of a century which has
seen Kenyan running change from folk culture to modern sport. How
can the Kenyan experience of this oft-called modernisation and its
concurrent globalisation be interpreted? Was Kenyan athletics
witnessing a process of 'development' between 1902, when
Meinertzhagen timed his anonymous soldier at 14 minutes for the 2.25
mile (3,600 metre) race, and 1995 when Moses Kiptanui, running in
Rome, broke the world 5,000 metre record with a time of 12 minutes
55.30 seconds? And does the difference between the 1936 time for the
mile of 4 minutes 38.5 seconds by Kamunya, then the fastest time a
Kenyan had recorded for the distance,[1] and the 3 minutes 46.38 by
Daniel Koeman in Berlin in 1997 (the Kenyan record at the time of
writing) denote progress? In a way it does. It illustrates the career of
Kenyan running – moving from African-class to world-class
performances, or the periphery catching up with the centre. But is there
also a case for suggesting that Kenyan athletics has been
underdeveloped in some way during the Europeanisation of its
movement cultures? Could things be getting worse rather than better? It
is also worth asking whether any forms of Kenyan resistance to the
invasion of Western forms of running culture have occurred during the
same period. These questions are addressed in this chapter.

In the context of Kenyan athletics, it is possible to see 'development'
and 'underdevelopment' occurring at the same time. The development
of Kenyan athletics will appear obvious but the active
underdevelopment of the nation's body cultures by foreign interests may
be less so.[2] The widespread use of statistical measures in economics and
in sports can often provide a kind of evidence for development. The
underdevelopment of a nation's culture, on the other hand, frequently

requires qualitative assessments and an ability to probe below the ideology of modern sport. It is, nevertheless, possible to detect underdevelopment and regression in Kenyan athletics within the statistics which are so often used to denote its growth.

We can apply notions of both 'development' and 'underdevelopment' at three different levels. These are at the levels of (i) the national culture, (ii) the national athletic system, and (iii) the individual athlete.[3] We will include each of these levels in our discussion.

Racing to development

The concept of *athletic development* is not a subject which has been widely discussed or debated. If development is viewed as a change in a positive direction, the improvement of the Kenyan mile record cited above implies a form of athletic development: the record (output) has been getting better over time. In athletic terms we can say that Kenyan 'mile space' has been conquered by time. In broader terms, the number of Olympic medals won by Kenyans has also been steadily increasing, as was shown in Figure 1.6. In addition to the improvement of records and the winning of an increasing number of medals, athletic development often seems to mean things like the successful recruitment of more and more people into achievement sport and the construction of more and more synthetic running tracks. If we were to mirror conventional economic approaches to 'development' we would also apply quantitative indicators such as the per capita and specialisation indices which we discussed in Chapter 2. A country experiencing relative athletic development should, according to this approach, be increasing its per capita index and reducing its specialisation index. However, it is widely argued these days that development cannot be defined in universal terms.[4] Certainly, reducing human performances (and, indeed, human beings) to results (statistics) fails to make clear the social relationships between those involved in producing them.

Development of athletic culture

In several chapters in this book we have used different kinds of statistical descriptions to locate Kenya's place in the world of sport. Based on an initial exploration of these statistics there would appear to be little doubt that during the last half century Kenya has improved its situation in 'track and field space'. From a situation of invisibility in the early 1950s to one of a significant presence in many events at the present day, it would certainly appear that Kenyan track and field has developed considerably. Using the per capita approach noted earlier, the Kenyan (men's) index was already well above the global norm by the mid 1960s and the overall index has shown a steady rise since the early 1980s. In 1980 the per capita index for world-class Kenyan athletic output (men and women) was 3.09; in 1984 it was 2.65 (Kenyan athletic development may have gone backwards as a result of the two Olympic boycotts in 1975 and 1980); by 1988 the respective figure was 3.27 and by 1992 it had increased dramatically to 6.03. In 1992 the men's index was 9.90 whereas in 1980 it had been 4.91. It appears self-evident that Kenyan women's athletics has also 'developed', despite some of the more gloomy comments which we made previously. In the early days of modern Kenyan athletics, women's events lagged way behind the men's. As late as 1980 the per capita index for the production of world class Kenyan women's athletic output was still only 0.61 (about the value of the male index in 1956). Although still lagging some distance behind the men, by 1992 it had risen to 1.52. Today women's track and field is beginning to 'take off' in Kenya, also suggesting the existence of development (Figure 7.1).

Figure 7.1. The athletes starting this cross-country run reflect various aspects of 'development' in Kenyan running (source: Boit, 1988, p. 24).

The indices of Kenya's relative development can be complemented by statistics which make Kenya's changing *share* of the world's athletic output more explicit. Here we can distinguish between national shares of the world total number of *superior* athletes (i.e. those ranked in the top 100 in the world in any Olympic track and field event) and national shares of the global number of *élite* athletes (that is, those in the top 20 in the world in any of the same events). Between 1980 and 1992 Kenya gradually increased its share of both superior and élite athletes as Figure 7.2a clearly shows. Indeed, the élite share has been growing faster than the superior share, a subject we return to later. The patterns for selected other countries are shown in order to illustrate the variety of trends which have emerged since 1980. Note the rapid increase in China's output of superior athletes and the very small share of global output supplied by Kenya's neighbour, Ethiopia.

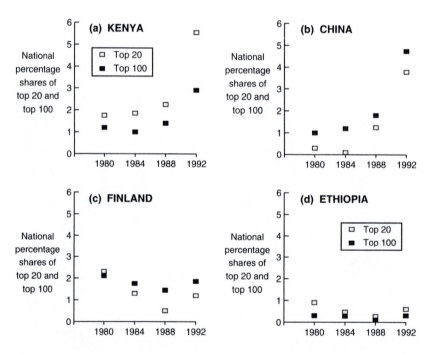

Figure 7.2. Kenyan (a), Chinese (b), Finnish (c) and Ethiopian (d) percentage shares of world output of élite (top 20) and superior (top 100) athletes in the world, 1980–92 (courtesy of Heikki Herva).

Development of the national system

We have shown in previous chapters that the national athletic system in Kenya has also apparently been 'developing'. It has been progressively bureaucratised and internationalised. Its officials are now Kenyan rather than British. Instead of grass and dirt running tracks there now exist synthetic tracks – although there are only two in the entire country. We also showed in Chapter 5 that Kenya now has the Moi International Sports Complex in Nairobi where the IAAF holds its coaching clinics. There exists a hierarchical system of coaching. Foreign coaches attend to Kenyan athletes and international corporations provide Kenyan runners with equipment and clothing. Today athletes run in Nike shoes, for example, rather than in bare feet; this must be progress. On the face of it the infrastructure for sport seems to have been developing alongside the improvement in overall athletic output.

The fortunes of individual athletes

The wealth and lifestyles of many athletes also seem to have improved at the same time as 'development' at the national and system levels. For many Kenyan runners, the fact that they come from a relatively poor country means that their prime motive for running is economic. The impact of neo-colonial relations has provided many opportunities for athletes to earn big money on the international circuits. In the summer of 1994 eight victories on the American road race circuit contributed $82,500 to Benson Masya's annual income.[5] When William Sigei broke the world 10,000 metres record in Oslo in 1994 and Cosmos Ndeti became the first man to win the famous Boston Marathon three times in succession in 1995, they each received about $75,000 in appearance money and bonuses. Moses Kiptanui won $100,000 when he became the first man to break eight minutes for the 3,000 metres steeplechase in Zurich in 1995.[6] Of course, such stellar performances would have increased these earning potentials in subsequent races. Athletes like Yobes Ondieki, the former world record holder for 10,000 metres, have been able to live a life of luxury in the United States, benefiting from the financial rewards of his work as a professional athlete. Money earned in Europe or America by Kenyan runners is often used to purchase farms, property and land in Kenya.

In other cases, the experience of education in the United States has contributed to former scholarship-holders gaining university degrees and secure jobs back home in Kenya. Mike Boit, for example, owes his doctorate and his job as national commissioner for sport to his career in track. Thanks to the emergence of global professional athletics, even athletes achieving more modest athletic performances are almost certainly better off financially than if they had resided permanently in Kenya.

Measurements involving statistics such as athletic performances and financial earnings are the conventional indicators of 'development' or 'progress'. A low per capita index of athletic output, however, does not mean that a country is poor in terms of its movement culture. Indeed, the presence of rich forms of indigenous movement culture are not incompatible with 'development' in other spheres as the rise of Islam has indicated in recent years.[7] We do not wish to develop that theme here but instead will proceed towards a view which suggests that certain forms of 'underdevelopment' of Kenyan movement culture have occurred at the same time as its apparent 'development'.

Underdeveloping Kenyan athletics

As we noted in Chapter 4, indigenous folk games did, for a rather short time co-exist with European athletics. They are now virtually non-existent. Although the term 'cultural imperialism' may be contested when applied to a number of cultural phenomena,[8] there seems little doubt that the case of track and field in Kenya clearly exemplifies such a process. The depth of penetration of athletics and the apparently passive reaction of the recipient culture to its introduction (though not to colonialism *per se*) does suggest the presence of cultural imperialism. Such a position may be contrasted with that found in some Islamic fundamentalist states where the 'reach' of sport may be total but the response has been conflictual.[9] And as we have seen from Chapter 4, the early twentieth century proselytisers quite straightforwardly *imposed* athletics, along with other sports, on the school curriculum and elsewhere (though many of the athletes emerging from this system would not necessarily deny that they enjoyed their athletics). Likewise, from Chapter 6 we noted that today the IAAF's *intention* is to spread the value of modern achievement sport at the expense of indigenous cultures. At the same time, we do recognise that the IAAF's cultural colonisation of Kenya has been less *coercive* than was that of the missionaries. It may, therefore, be worth briefly examining the distinction between cultural imperialism and globalisation, as outlined by Tomlinson:

> Globalisation may be distinguished from imperialism in that it is a far less coherent or culturally directed process. ... [T]he idea of

imperialism contains, at least, the notion of a purposeful project: the *intended* spread of a social system from one centre of power across the globe. The idea of 'globalisation' suggests interconnections and interdependency of all global areas which happens in a far less purposeful way. It occurs as the result of economic and cultural practices which do not, of themselves, aim at global integration, but which nevertheless produce it. More importantly, the effects of globalisation are to weaken the cultural coherence of all individual nation-states, including the economically powerful ones – the 'imperialist powers' of a previous era.[10]

This succinct view would therefore see the early part of Kenya's athletic history being strongly reminiscent of cultural imperialism with the latter eras being more related to processes of globalisation. This is an important distinction because those who adopt the globalisation view see cultural change of the kind we have been describing as being an inevitable outcome of *modernisation*. Whatever perspective is adopted, however, cultural erosion is typical of economic development, modernisation and cultural imperialism.

By the mid-twentieth century, Western sportised running had triumphed in Kenya. Unlike athletic performances and the quantification of national variations in 'athletic output', cultural erosion is difficult to put into numbers. How can we quantify the museumisation of Kenyan native body cultures as forms of entertainment for visiting tourists (see Chapter 3)? In this sense, traditional Kenyan movement culture has not only been underdeveloped – it has been exterminated; it has been a victim of cultural genocide. What has replaced it is athletics as entertainment, providing 'super-hero images before a people desperate for someone, something, to admire'.[11] This view would see modern athletics as part and parcel of capitalist relations: the major track and field spectacles require a class-divided society for such a diet of bread and circuses to exist and flourish.[12] Kenyan spectator sport becomes no different in this respect from the situation in Europe or north America except that Kenyan spectators rarely see white runners. There is, however, another way of looking at such cultural homogenisation. If Europeans can make money from Grand Prix events, why shouldn't Africans benefit too? Who are we to say what the true 'interests' of Kenyan athletes are?[13]

One interpretation is that Kenyan runners are the objects of a European gaze. This is what John MacAloon termed 'cross cultural voyeurism' or 'popular ethnography'.[14] In other words, Kenyan athletes are live subjects on display, in some ways analogous to the contents of the lantern slides shown at the Royal Geographical Society and other such august bodies in the 1890s, or the pictures of half dressed 'natives' found in the pages of the ever-popular *National Geographic*. Today, however, Kenyans are captured by the gaze of the television camera or the European athletics fan. Through this gaze the Europeans are symbolically able to possess the Kenyans; after all, Europeans rarely, if ever, visit Kenya to watch athletics. In addition, athletics as entertainment can be viewed as the opium of the people: 'culture becomes the aesthetics of anesthesia'.[15] Can racing around a standardised 400 metre synthetic track 25 times, routinely metronomised in a concrete stadium, be regarded as progress? As Juha Heikkala has put it, 'what sense is there in straining oneself to run in circles faster than any other?'[16] This is not to adopt a naïve view of a lost romantic past but to emphasise that racing need not be the only (nor even the only *modern*) running genre. Élite athletes of all nations no longer run for the sake of running; they do not love it in the sense of the true amateur. They exchange their achievements on the world market for the best price they can get. Performance becomes a commodity whose value is determined by the market. In a single global market for sport, the production of results is for exchange rather than use.[17]

When athletes from countries like Kenya reject their indigenous body cultures in favour of those of Europe or America they have, in a sense, been collaborating with imperialism – Said's 'culture *as* imperialism'.[18] They may perceive themselves to be advantaged by such engagement – and indeed, this may well be the case – yet they are automatically placed at a disadvantage in international competition since virtually all the sports on the Olympic agenda are Euro-American in origin. This exemplifies a hidden dimension of the world sports system. Countries like Kenya, though part of a global system, can be seen as being marginalised. They cannot be said to have joined the global sports system as equal partners with existing members; they take part on unfavourable terms.[19] Indeed, we will suggest that the global core has actually exploited peripheral countries like Kenya, hence making the Kenyan athletics revolution, if it may be so termed, even more remarkable.

Because no Kenyan (or African) body cultures are included in international athletic competitions Kenya is obviously disadvantaged in the very events in which the so-called developed countries already possess the greatest advantages. In track and field athletics it is the field events that require the greatest technological and scientific support. The high jump and javelin need expensive equipment, which is simply not necessary for distance running. Indeed, these two field events in which Kenya showed distinct promise in the early 1950s have become increasingly technologised over the last forty years – the period during which Kenya's performance in them has declined relative to other countries. It is no accident that the events which require the least technology are those in which the Kenyans most excel.

As we noted in the first chapter, however, this was not the case in the less technologised age of the 1950s. What we find interesting in this respect, and what we feel we must stress, is that when we look back to the *Manchester Guardian* preview of the 1954 AAA championships it was the high jumper who was identified as Kenya's brightest prospect. In those championships the high jumpers performed relatively better than the distance runners; and the javelin throwers performed as well as the distance runners. From Kenyan performances in the 1954 Commonwealth Games we can see that the country's high jumpers and javelin throwers were performing relatively better than those of today. When Kenya entered the global sports arena it had a diversified group of athletes who could compete internationally at a relatively high level of performance. What is more, the group was, to a limited extent, multicultural. The sprinter Antao and the hurdler Monks displayed the Kenyan-Asian and Kenyan-European presence respectively. Today the Kenyan team is fully Africanised. It is also dominated by the middle- and long-distance runners, although a number of 400 metre runners are also of world class. But a distance running tradition was not 'invented' until after the 1968 Mexico Olympics (see below). The present day situation is that while Kenya may have more than 'caught up' with the rest of Africa (and the world) in some of the running events, it has been relatively underdeveloped in the field events. This partial or selective form of development is what athletic 'progress' means for much of Africa.

The idea of relative underdevelopment can be examined on both the African and global scales. Here we can again use numbers to describe what we mean. Consider first the composition of the list of African all-time top ten athletes in each Olympic track and field event as it was in 1966 in comparison with how it stood in 1993. Figure 7.2 shows the number of Kenyan athletes in each event in the lists at each of these two dates, hence indicating the extent of relative African-level 'development' at the top end of the sport. In 1966, for example, there were three Kenyans among the top ten all-time African steeplechasers; by 1993 there were nine. In this event, therefore, Kenya has clearly enhanced its position *vis-à-vis* other African countries. Consider next the women's 100 and 200 metres. There has been no change in Kenya's

contribution during the period 1966–93 (no athletes in either year); at
the élite African level, the sprint events in Kenya have been in a state of
stasis. Finally, consider the men's javelin throw and decathlon. In 1966
Kenya had one athlete in the all-time African top ten in each of these
events; by 1993 no Kenyans were found in the all-time lists. From
Figure 7.3 it can be seen that the events in which Kenya's share of the
top ten all-time African performers has most dramatically increased are
those from 400 through 10,000 metres. In other events they have
remained relatively static or have even declined, a situation most
obvious in the entire range of field events.

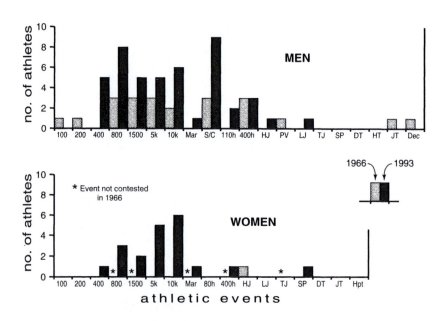

Figure 7.3. Changing Kenyan composition of the all-time African top ten athletes, as
in 1966 and in 1993 (source of data: Pinaud, 1966, and Abmayr and Pinaud, 1994).

Exactly the same kind of analysis can be undertaken on a world
scale. In 1966 there were only three events in which one Kenyan athlete
featured in the world top ten all-time list of performers (Figure 7.4). By
1994, far more athletes from Kenya were represented. In the
steeplechase alone there were six Kenyans. Kenya's share of the élite in
the 800, 5,000, 10,000 metres and steeplechase had increased

dramatically. On the other hand, no women from Kenya were in any of the top ten all-time world lists. And among the men's events, no relative improvement had taken place in the sprints and field events. In the latter group of events, Kenya lags way behind the world élite. What we see here, graphically displayed (literally) are the twin processes of development and underdevelopment going on side by side.

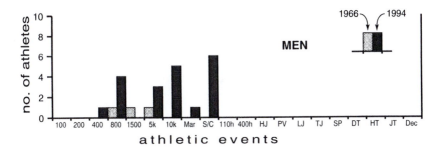

Figure 7.4. Changing Kenyan composition of the all-time world top ten athletes, as in 1966 and in 1994 (source of data: Quercetani, 1966, Matthews, 1994).

Kenya's athletic output, while diversified on an African scale, is specialised on a global scale. Indeed, in the last decade, while showing an obvious increase in per capita output, there is little evidence that Kenya's per capita production has become anything but more specialised. Figure 7.5 shows the position of Kenyan athletics in two-dimensional 'success space'. In the diagram, per capita and specialisation indices are plotted on respective axes at four year intervals between 1980 and 1992. If countries are experiencing athletic 'development' we would expect to see them moving upwards to the left in the graph. It is clear that this is certainly not the case for either Kenya's men or women athletes.

Let us also return briefly to Figure 7.2. In 1980, 1984 and 1988 the differences between Kenya's percentage shares of the world's superior and élite athletes was not very great. By 1992, however, its share of the world's élite was over 2.5 percentage points greater than its share of superior world output. The growing gap between the nation's share of world élite and superior athletes may indicate an inability of the Kenyan athletic 'system' to produce a balanced output *within events* (that is, it appears relatively 'top heavy') – something we have already stressed exists between events. In China's case (Figure 7.2b), however, a more balanced output seems to exist, the difference between its share of the world top 100 and the world top 20 being much less dramatic than that of Kenya. The other two countries, Finland (Figure 7.2c) and Ethiopia (Figure 7.2d) exemplify other patterns between 1980 and 1992.

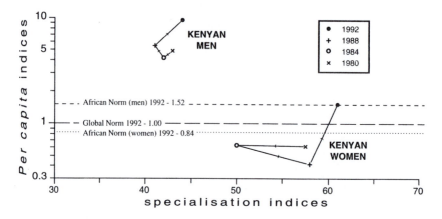

Figure 7.5. Kenyan athletes in 'success space', 1980–92. Per capita output has been increasing but so too has the specialisation of that output.

How has underdevelopment – or at least exploitation – manifested itself at the level of the individual Kenyan athlete? An associated outcome of the Kenyan dependence on Euro-America has been that, because of the geographical distribution of major athletic competitions, Kenyans must necessarily spend a considerable time away from home, thus reducing the number of domestic role models available for aspiring athletes. Those who continue to reach the top tend to see their future outside their own country. In extreme cases, as we have seen, Kenyan athletes seek foreign domicile, even a different nationality, principally in the interests of achievement sport. One view is that in doing so they implicitly denigrate their own nation, region and home, judging it by the standards of the economic 'core'. There is a tendency towards what Peet calls 'the production of one world mind, one world culture, and the consequent disappearance of regional consciousness flowing from local specificities of the human past'.[20] Likewise, athletics provides a conduit for the penetration of European and American ideas into Kenya.[21] We are not suggesting, however, that Kenya is in any way unique in this respect; the same observations could be made about the penetration of American forms of culture into Britain, for example.

Dependency or development?

In what way could Kenyan athletics be said to be in a dependent relationship with other nations and organisations? Dependency in sports, like in economics, can be seen as a symbiotic relationship with development. In Kenyan track and field, therefore, dependence would be seen as the result of the suppression of local games resulting from the imperialist underdevelopment of indigenous African culture. To take part in modern sports, Kenya is today dependent on the organisations of the global economic and cultural core – that is the IAAF, the IOC and the various international handouts such as sports aid and athletic scholarships. Kenyan athletes can only 'develop' by incorporation into the world system which is dominated by the global athletic core. At the same time, the dependence on the European scene for the financial rewards of track seems much like the dependence of the Kenyan economy on US and European corporations. Such political and economic domination of the sport can be regarded as having an ideological consequence: it passes on the belief that culture in general and movement cultures in particular are somehow 'better' in Europe and the US than in Kenya.[22] In this respect the governing bodies of track and field can be likened to multi-national corporations. In the world of sport, multi-national organisations have reduced the capacity of the nation state to exercise control or influence over the body-cultural activities of its population.

Dependency is also seen in the necessary adoption by Kenya and other nations of products produced by Western firms. In track and field this is classically exemplified by the producers of athletic equipment, ranging from the virtually ubiquitous athletic shoe to the more selectively adopted forms of equipment used in the field events. Of the major footwear companies, Adidas and Puma are European-owned; Nike and Brooks are USA firms; Asics is a Japanese company. By adopting Western sports Kenya becomes dependent on Western goods and therefore feeds Western profits.

The notion of dependence could be viewed as being more complex than this, however. For the global athletic system to function and profit it is itself dependent on the African athletes who grace the Grand Prix market places. It is almost impossible to conceive of a Grand Prix 5,000 metres or steeplechase race without the presence of Kenyan participants. Under such circumstances it is difficult to see who is dependent on whom.[23]

Racing as resistance?

We may have given the impression that we deplore the rise of achievement sport as a form of mass culture. To a large extent we do. However, we do not fail to recognise that sports can provide a forum for oppositional opportunities for those who may be exploited. In his excellent study of the relationships between American baseball and the Dominican Republic, Alan Klein observes that events and institutions that promote national pride foster cultural resistance by promoting the integrity and cohesiveness of native culture at the expense of foreigners. Since third world culture is often devalued by foreigners and locals (because of social self-loathing), an act or symbol that promotes local people is an act or symbol that resists.[24]

In our case, Kenyan running can be regarded as such a symbol. We therefore wish to explore whether, through their running, Kenyan athletes can be interpreted as resisting or opposing many of the tendencies we have been describing. These could theoretically include opposition to imperialism and colonialism (past or present), to exploitation, to governing bureaucracies such as the IAAF or the Kenya AAA, to nationalism, to various issues of global or national concern (such as racism or ethnic bias), or (theoretically, but least likely) to achievement sport itself.

Although there was no shortage of resistance to British imperial rule in Kenya, we have implied in Chapter 4 that, while apathy may have existed, there was no serious active resistance to the adoption of Western sport. We use the word 'implied' because the kinds of travel writing cited in Chapter 4 fail to communicate the voices and attitudes of indigenous people in relation to the newly imposed sports. Opposition to British colonialism did find outlets in more appropriate cultural forms such as dance, literature and in drama.[25] For example, from the end of the nineteenth century to the 1940s 'anti-imperialist Muthuu dances had spread in central Kenya like fire across a dry plain',[26] but this was body culture as resistance to colonialism, not an attempt to campaign directly for an alternative to Western sport within the colonial structures. As noted earlier, the Maasai were notable for their unwillingness to adopt European culture and, because of this, they absented themselves from Western body cultures. But as part of Kenyan political activism, achievement sport was not a serious target, even though the Mau Mau philosophy of the early 1950s advocated, perhaps rhetorically, a 'return to ancient customs'.[27]

As we suggested at the end of Chapter 3, the new Kenyan élites and the masses, each in their own ways, have been happy to have embraced (or to have been seduced by) athletics. The large crowds attending the mission school sports (Figure 4.3) and other events described in Chapter 4, seem to support this view. This is not to say, however, that the colonisation of the mind (and body), and the subsequent sporting success of the colonised over the coloniser are contradictory. As Pratt has noted, subjugated people may have been unable to control what emanated from the dominant culture but they can determine, to varying degrees, what they absorb into their own and what they use it for.[28]

As we have seen, athletics was gradually adopted via the missionaries, the schools, the army and the police service. Many Kenyans saw it as a form of cultural and political capital through which they could achieve international visibility, personal prestige and money. Following independence Kenyans embraced the sports which the Westerners had forced on them, unable to rid themselves of the culture of imperialism. Yet even in a situation of neo- or post-colonisation, it cannot be said unambiguously that the way Kenyans have utilised athletics may not be interpreted as a form of cultural resistance, both to those who implanted it and to those who control it today at the state and global scales. Hence, while modern athletics may be English in origin, the form of running and its idiosyncrasies may often reflect Kenyan attitudes and ambitions.[29] Indeed, it is possible that Kenyan athletes are pioneering a new form of running, one that rejects national labels and provides a kind of freedom from the bureaucratic restrictions about which athletes often complain.

Kenyan running as an invented tradition

Our initial interpretation of Kenyan running as resistance is based on the seminal work of the Trinidadian Marxist, C.L.R. James who, in *Beyond a Boundary*, identified cricket as a site for the 'playing out and imaginary resolution of social antagonisms in the colonial and post colonial West Indies'.[30] Although the details of the Kenyan athletic situation are obviously different from those of cricket in the various Anglicised islands of the West Indies (for example, athletics in British Kenya never seems to have been socially exclusive as cricket once was in the British Caribbean), we feel that the general thrust of James's notion of sport being one of the civilised ways in which the anti-imperialist struggle is played out,[31] is valid in the African as well as the Caribbean context. Let us recall that what was true of colonialism in Kenya was also true of one of its component parts, track and field athletics. While many indigenous cultural practices existed at the tribal level, it could be argued that independent Kenya, given the diversity of tribal customs, bestowed a privileged position on running and other sports because it had few *institutionalised* forms of cultural practice of its own.[32]

To overthrow the ideology of running as racing would be to reject the ideology of modern society in which it flourishes. As Colin Leys points out, it would therefore be inconceivable to make use of the dramatic and theatrical character of Olympic or world championship athletics as a way of subverting any system seen as oppressive. African-American athletes may have shown the clenched fist at the 1968 Olympics but they had first won their medals. They did not go so far as the fictional Colin Smith, who in *The Loneliness of the Long Distance Runner* deliberately chose not to finish a race which he would have easily won while well in the lead – and which the establishment would have wished him to win.[33] Resistance does not assume this form when the participants are insufficiently alienated from the society in which they live. Athletics, unlike theatre, dance or literature, cannot be counter cultural or hybrid. In athletics the ideological script never changes; the most African it can become is 'Afro-European'. Resistance therefore has to assume less dramatic forms.

In order to make running more their own, Kenyans had to loosen the 'English' elements within it because English culture was what they (consciously or subconsciously) struggled against. So the 'ideological protocols' of running 'were refashioned, not overthrown'.[34] Kenyan running has emerged entirely within the constraints of the rules of the sport introduced by the colonialist and under the present day authority of the IAAF. However, 'English running' – like English cricket – is essentially made up of orderliness, discipline, resolution and puritanism; Kenyan running reflected a 'different rationality'. The social significance of this rationality, as we saw from some of the journalists' comments about the 1954 races at London's White City, was misconstrued by the English commentators. Kenyan running was seen as a kind of 'indiscipline, excess and irresponsibility'.[35] In fact it was running with élan, something which had become suppressed in the rational world of restraint occupied by 'modern' runners. We are aware here of how close we come to essentialising the difference between English and Kenyan running; yet we feel that, in Kenya, modern body culture, while being Anglicised, has not quite become modern English body culture. The mirror image of the imperialist is not perfect.

A further way of interpreting the emergence of Kenyan running in general (and the steeplechase in particular) is to relate it to Eric Hobsbawm's notion of 'invented traditions'. It could be argued that, for some Kenyans, the adoption of track and field – or, more precisely, running as racing – has become an invented tradition,[36] something we alluded to briefly at the end of Chapter 3. Such traditions may have been formally invented (such as the African and Arab Sports Association in

1924 or the Kenyan AAA in 1951) but, more significantly in Kenya's case, we refer to a tradition which emerges informally in a less easily traceable manner within a brief and datable period.[37] We have described in Chapter 1 how distance running in Kenya became a tradition from 1968 following the successes of Kenyan athletes at the Mexico Olympics. There was no indication at all that long distance track racing was a particularly Kenyan athletic trait until the Mexico Games. In 1954 the success of the distance runner Maiyoro had been matched by that of the high jumper Lenemuria and the javelin thrower Kiguru. It was the hurdler Rotich, as well as the distance runner Anentia, who had won the first Commonwealth medals for Kenya; and it was the sprinter Antao who was the first Kenyan Commonwealth gold medalist. The sprint-hurdler Monks had been the first Kenyan woman to win an international title. We have indicated the diversity of the early Kenyan athletic presence by looking (also in Chapter 1) at the composition of Kenyan touring teams in the 1950s and early 1960s and the early successes of Kenyan athletes in the sprints, jumps and throws. To be sure, the comments of Reclus and the others indicated that there was *apparently* a 'custom' of distance running which existed among pre-modern Kenyan tribesmen but this is not the same thing as a modern running (as racing) tradition. For voyeurs of the Kenyan scene and for the sports journalists in the 1960s and 1970s, these customs, made visible by the pictures found in books such as Joy Adamson's and the kinds of comments made by travel writers about the capabilities of the traditional 'native', provided modern Kenyan running with (in Hobsbawm's words) the 'sanction of precedent, social continuity and natural law' as expressed in Kenya's history. The 1968 Olympics at which Kenyans won several medals and became highly visible internationally, presented 'a novel situation' which, as we saw in the previous chapter, took 'the form of reference to old situations'.[38] The custom of running among east African tribesmen became a modern Kenyan male running *tradition*. This was adopted, to a lesser extent, by Kenyan women later.

Sportised running enjoyed 'submerged' or, more accurately, 'nominal continuity' with Kenyan tribal running but it was, in fact, turned into something quite different. This is indicated by comparing the modern Olympians shown in Chapter 1 with the anonymous runners in Figures 3.1 and 4.5. The image of the Kenyan runner became a sort of reality – a self-fulfilling prophecy fuelled by role models and the sporting press.

Colonial institutions such as athletics do not have a direct and unambiguous effect. Indeed, 'they can be reappropriated by the colonized and used against the institutions from which they emanate'.[39]

The British had created a sport which for many years served to socialise Kenyans into accepting their athletic inferiority. But when Maiyoro so unexpectedly finished third in the spectacle of the 1954 AAA championship, his performance as a colonial 'exhibit' offered new visions (to the European as well as the Kenyan) which had not previously been in the athletics script. By the 1970s the British could no longer control athletics, nor any longer defeat the African. This was especially so in the case of the steeplechase, from Biwott onwards.

A sense of the steeplechase

Since 1968, Kenyan athletes have consistently beaten the white man at his own game and Allen Guttmann has suggested that it is through sports, more than in any other domain, that such tables can be turned.[40] What is more, the Kenyans' victories have often been most notably achieved in their way, in what has been claimed as *their* event. Indeed, the steeplechase has almost become a national sport, in much the same way that soccer has for Brazil, rugby has for Wales, or ski-jumping has for Finland. Kenyan running has often been seen as having a highly individualistic form – a 'Kenyan style' almost. The style has often taken the form of devastating front running – the very approach which so bemused and bewildered the White City crowd in 1954. It is often demonstrated in its most graphic form in the 3,000 metres steeplechase which Kenyans have virtually made their own event (Figures 7.3 and 7.4). When Kiptanui broke the world steeplechase record in 1995, he spurned the offer of a pacemaker, something almost unheard of in modern record attempts. In that race, typical of many middle distance races on the European Grand Prix circuit, eight of the first twelve finishers were Kenyans. To modify the comments of Alan Klein, the steeplechase has become metamorphosed from an index of European cultural superiority to a demonstration of Kenyan excellence. Kenyan pride in the steeplechase has become synonymous with resisting neo-colonial cultural colonisation.[41]

It could be argued that Kenya's contribution to the 1968 Olympic Games exemplified the Olympics as 'an intermittent sequence of different models'. Whereas the 1896 Athens Games had been a 'patriotic festival' and those at Berlin in 1936 a 'political-economic-military showpiece', those of 1968 could be said to have been a 'Third World Games'.[42] Central to this image was Amos Biwott's steeplechase victory, achieved with an unconventional water-jump technique with which he completely avoided getting his feet wet. We have described 1968 as the moment when the steeplechase, perhaps the most gruelling of all track and field events, became a 'Kenyan tradition'. Kenyans can look back on Biwott, Jipcho, Kogo, Rono, Kariuki, Keino, Koech and Kiptanui – all steeplechase 'legends'.

For each major steeplechase event in which Kenyans take part there is a sense of anticipation – a sense that something dramatic will happen. There is a tendency to see the ongoing present as history in the making, to designate races as 'historic' or 'classic'. Such legendary performances consolidate Kenyan ideas about their 'relationship' with the 'steeplechase' – the word even evokes a different kind of feeling from such words as the '100 metres'. It is possible that, in this way, the Kenyans create a picture of themselves as traditionally tough, having stamina and being able to succeed.[43]

The toughness of the steeplechase and its implicit linkages back to the traditional 'tough' lifestyle of many Kenyan ethnic groups (note again, the significance of the Nandi) take us back to Hobsbawm's invented traditions, providing, as they do, a sense of *invariance*. In this, as in so many other cases, however, its authenticity – the perceived or implied deep roots of the steeplechase in African culture – is highly questionable, if not illusory.

In the popular psyche there is a 'Kenyan style' of running. This is reflected in an interview by one of authors (JS) in 1992 with Kipchoge Keino. He noted that the Kenyan style of running was different from that of Westerners, observing that, when racing, he started slowly and then gradually increased the pace:

> Our style of running was not like theirs. When I ran, I liked to 'front-run'. European athletes, on the other hand, used to pace themselves with the aim of saving themselves for a final lap sprint finish. On the contrary, I started slowly and gradually wound up the pace. If you had the strength you would live with my pace ... as far as I was concerned, it was only athletes who could muster the stamina and strength to stay with my pace who could pose a challenge to my ability to win. They were amazed to see us run the way we did ...[44]

The Kenyan style of front running can also be seen as a rational way of unsettling European athletes who often find difficulty in responding to the adventurous pace at which some Kenyans start a race – just as Maiyoro had done at the White City in 1954. Sometimes, however, a fast early pace devastates the athlete him/herself, and it is easy to read this as being the Kenyan way. It is equally easy to suggest that for some young runners, raw to international competition, it is almost a rite of passage – part of the transition from novice to international – to run like

this. There is, however, a danger in presenting Kenyan running in such
a way. Like the English before him, Keino tends to see the African
runner and the European as antithetical, reifying their individual
differences *at their most different*.[45] By doing so he shows how the self-
conception of those outside the West can be shaped by Western power.[46]
The Kenyan speaks the language of the coloniser yet other Kenyan
athletes, for example Wilson Waigwa and Paul Ereng, have adopted
almost the opposite tactic in their running to that described by Keino;
that is, staying at the back of the field of runners and attempting to
dramatically outsprint the opposition in the final stretch. The truth is that
Kenyan runners, like those from all nations of the world, possess a
variety of styles and strategies. Such labelling as that exemplified above
tends, all too easily, to become the stereotype which has been outlined
in earlier chapters, that of the unsophisticated native. It also reflects the
European need to see the African in generalised terms.

Through running, Kenyans are able to ape the occidentals by
practising their sports but at the same time express national pride by
defeating them in those very same sports, thus reflecting the tension
between the hegemony of a Western-imposed body culture and the
resistance of a 'peripheral' state.[47] Having struggled in obscurity to
refine their running, Kenyans have made it their own. Each title won by
a Kenyan in the major championships is a triumph for his or her
compatriots at home.[48] In mimicking their former oppressors, however,
they now dominate them. One interpretation might be that the Kenyans
have successfully manipulated and controlled the means of socially
controlling them.

Rootedness and mobility

Resistance can assume many forms and can be found in several contexts.
In the late 1990s we sense that Kenyan runners are in the forefront of
resisting the power of the bureaucracies that have traditionally
controlled them and have dictated where athletes compete. What we are
about to describe can also be interpreted as a form of resistance against
nationalism in sport and, to some extent, an assertion of the freedom of
the individual. Indeed, Kenyan athletes may be in the vanguard of
radical change in the relationship between athlete and nation, illustrating
the rejection of nation and favouring an implicit 'post-nationality'
position in sport. How has this worked itself out?

There is always a tension between rootedness and mobility, between
home and abroad. Some Kenyan athletes live most of their lives in
Kenya; others roam the world as athletic migrants. Mobility can be

viewed as resistance.[49] In what ways can the 'mobile' athlete, on the move from country to country, be seen in such a way? First we must identify the ways in which athletes face domination in their day-to-day lives. In modern track and field dominance can come from at least two major sources of power. The first is the national governing sports bureaucracy, in this case the Kenya AAA, that seeks to control the practices of athletes. The second is the group made up of agents and promoters who provide the sources of income for such athletes.

By travelling the world to compete, the Kenyan athlete is more like a nomad than a tourist, reacting against his or her roots, rejecting nationalism and localism, doing his or her own thing (as far as is possible) in the presence of pressures from the national bureaucracy to do otherwise. Such athletes appear to lead a 'decentred' existence,[50] undermining the categories of order and authority which are taken to typify the modern global sports system. Representing Kenya may be rejected in favour of representing no place at all or of representing the self. This may emerge when the national bureaucracy attempts to dictate when and where an athlete should run. In recent years the Kenya AAA has become increasingly anxious about athletes choosing to run overseas rather than compete in (or for) their own country. In 1994 attempts were increasingly being made to get Kenyan athletes to obtain written permission from the national governing body before competing abroad; indeed, this is the IAAF rule. It has proved unworkable and, as a result, the Kenyan federation was reckoned to be losing control of 'its' athletes. What could happen in the future is that Kenyans running without the permission of the national federation will not be picked for the big international championships. In 1994, the Kenyan AAA ruled that athletes would not be considered for the Commonwealth Games if they did not first compete in the national trials. As a result, of the 12 leading steeplechasers in the Commonwealth, all of whom were Kenyans, only one was chosen to represent the nation in the 1994 Commonwealth Games. When money is more important than representing one's nation, however, championships (in which no money prizes are awarded) become irrelevant. Market forces may, therefore, assist in breaking the link between athlete and nation. Much the same has happened in tennis which, except in the small number of events such as the Davis Cup, can no longer be regarded as a 'representational' sport.

As we noted in Chapter 2, the athlete in representational sport acts as an intermediary between the people and the state. In athletic representation, the group partakes vicariously in the success of one of its parts, the athlete. This assumes that the part represents the whole and can do so because the athlete shares a fundamental likeness with the entire group.[51] But the foundations of this assumption are breaking down. What does 'Kenya' mean to a Kenyan runner when he works with his agent to compete for several thousand dollars rather than take part in a qualifying meet to represent his country? And what did representation mean for Wilson Kipketer, the Kenyan Dane? What did representation mean for the Danes whom he 'represented'? When he won his world 800 metres title in 1995, the Danish response was underwhelming; the nation cannot be said to have rejoiced. The population felt uneasy and ambivalent about his victory. Kipketer's own (cynical or naïve) attitude may have been reflected in the sub-heading of an article which appeared in a Danish magazine soon after the championships. It read: 'Kenyan or Danish? The king of runners is quite certain: "I am Wilson Kipketer"'.[52]

Clearly, such athletes (we are not applying these ideas only to Kenyans) are not reflecting the norms of conventional – or, at least, traditional – athletic behaviour. To represent one's country was conventionally regarded as one of the pinnacles of an athlete's career. Those who seek an alternative form of 'identity' are transgressing the bounds of conformist athletics and, literally, transgressing the bounds of the state which would otherwise bind them for purposes of being identified with it.

Identity can be argued to exist in two forms, identification and 'identisation'. The difference between the two can be seen in respective answers to the question 'who am I'? The response may be 'I am like ...' (identification) or 'I am different from ...' (identisation).[53] The latter implies a lack of conformity, independence and a less uniform and less conventional attitude to the world of athletics. At the same time, however, the apparently more 'open' behaviour of these less nationalised runners is not without ambiguity. They do, after all, continue to display images from a dominant culture. When they race they have simply changed the name on their chests from 'Kenya' to 'Reebok' and they are certainly abiding by the norms of conventional running.

Another example of mobility as resistance occurs when athletes recognise that it is easier to represent another nation than their own. Whereas the group described in the previous paragraph is 'national', athletes who adopt other nationalities are 'transnational'. To them nationality appears to be meaningless; racing is everything. We do not write this in a pejorative sense and are certainly not championing nationalism. We see what many would regard as a mercenary tendency, together with the rejection of representational sport – as a kind of 'post-nationalism' or 'a-nationalism' and a logical outcome of achievement orientation in a market-led capitalist world of transnational cultural forms. Traditionally, athletes have been territorialised by the 'container' of the state. What we are now beginning to see is a leaking container and a possible reduction in the sporting significance of the territorial state.[54]

'Home' for many athletes becomes a place to take an occasional holiday. It remains to be seen if such developments (if developments they be) will serve to undermine the representational and expressive functions upon which sport as a spectacle so often depends. We also ponder the question of whether 'styles' of running and racing will become increasingly homogenised as the internationalisation of track and field athletics proceeds along its current trajectory.[55] The global system which created Kenyan running is now aiding the 'de-Kenyanisation' of the self same form of movement culture.

Resistance in the press

Finally, we may identify a form of resistance that is to be found in the Kenyan press. Certain sections of the press find a more effective forum for criticism of Western attitudes towards Kenya in their sports coverage than on the front pages.[56] The cartoon is a particularly potent form of political and cultural comment and satire, and we include two examples to illustrate the form in which resistance to dominant Western attitudes may take.

While many examples have been assembled to depict the visual images of blacks by whites,[57] the black view of white stereotypes – the 'black on white' view ('occidentalism') – is less well known to (even liberal) white Europeans. The kind of occidentalism shown in the cartoons (Figures 7.6 and 7.7) published in leading Kenyan newspapers at the time of the World Athletics Championships in Tokyo in August 1991, illustrate what amounts to a Kenyan view of a Western perception of east African running.[58]

The first of these alternative perspectives depicts a situation in the 1990s but pokes fun at a long tradition. As Hoberman points out

> in the colonial context, assessments by European observers of their "primitive" subjects reflected the one sided nature of this comparative project: The men from Paris, London and Berlin were the scientists, while the indigenous populations of Africa ... provided an endless stream of interesting subjects.[59]

Have things changed very much? The cartoon in Figure 7.6 examines the Western notion that the Kenyan runner is in some way biologically or genetically 'different' from those in Europe and North America. Note that the two scientists – the 'experts' – are white, authoritative, rational and part of an international system of sports-medical research. The modern, clinical environment of the laboratory also serves to symbolically mock Western science – which cannot solve the perceived problem.

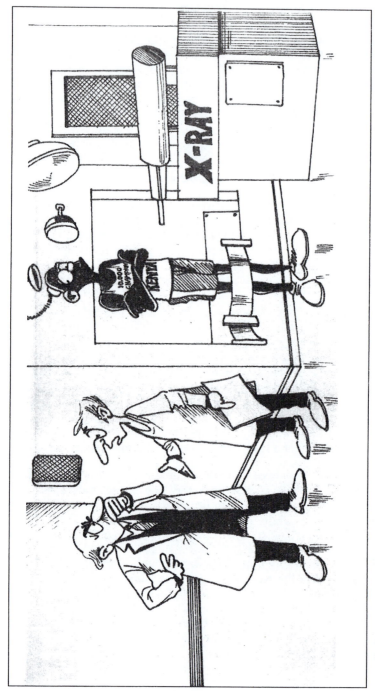

Figure 7.6. 'I've checked everything, Sir ... his bones, lungs, heart ... there's nothing extra to make him run faster' (courtesy of the *Sunday Nation*, Nairobi).

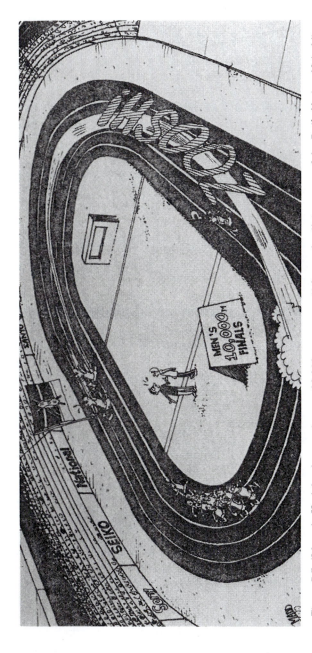

Figure 7.7. 'I hear in Kericho they used to run 20,000 metres to and from school' (courtesy of the *Daily Nation*, Nairobi).

The second cartoon (Figure 7.7) mocks the European 'impulse to romanticise the vitality' of the idealised Kenyan runners.[60] It shows two Kenyan athletes (carrying the national flag) close to lapping the rest of the field in the final of the world 10,000 metres championship (in Tokyo two Kenyan runners, Moses Tanui and Richard Chelimo, won the gold and silver medals respectively). The national icon, the Kenyan flag, carried by the leading runner, is placed next to the global iconography of the advertisements around the track. Indeed, 'Kenya' has already passed Sanyo and will soon overtake National and Seiko. Kenya, at the economic/athletic periphery, is seen defeating the representatives of the multi-national global sports economy. The two discussants in the infield are again clearly identified as white and, as in the previous example, they are trying to 'explain' the success of the Kenyans. This time they fall back on the romantic myth of a simple, eternal, essential Africa, of young children endlessly running across the plains to school – the myth of the native 'other' noted in earlier chapters.

The future?

Kenya's rise to what appears to many to be athletic fame is not unique. In several respects Finland was the Kenya of the 1920s and 1930s. Each of these relatively small countries has, at different times, found itself in a similar position. Each became identified with particular track and field events, notably middle and long distance running; their success came soon after they were granted their political independence; their running success has featured mainly men; they have each produced running heroes. In Finland, as in Kenya, we have noted how spurious explanations have been presented to account for the triumphs of earlier years: racial characteristics, the Finnish temperament, the forest landscape and the climate have all been used to 'explain' the procession of great runners coming out of this northern nation.[61] In the 1930s it was predicted that Finland's long distance running dominance would never end;[62] but it did. There were twelve Finns in the top twenty 5,000 metre runners in the world in 1930;[63] in 1994 the respective figure was zero. For Kenya the respective figures were none in 1930 and six in 1994.

A symbolic index of the changes that have occurred in these two nations during the last sixty years is the fact that, on opening a Finnish book on that nation's running heroes, one finds that the foreword was written by the Kenyan, Kipchoge Keino.[64] The northern Europeans who once dominated long-distance running now have a Kenyan as their hero. As a postscript to this story, the Finnish winner of the 1995 World Junior

Women's Cross Country Championship, Annemari Sandell, had not been training in the Finnish forests prior to her victory; instead she prepared for the race in Kenya. But will Kenya go the same way as Finland? Do nations rise and fall like an athletic tide?

In order to subscribe to the *citius-altius-fortius* ideology of the athletic arms race Kenya must maintain its share of the global athletic output. Its per capita index must not decrease; its specialisation index should, at the same time, be reduced. We have seen that Kenya's share of world athletic output is still growing. This is likely to continue for some years as Kenya's women runners improve their performances. But it cannot go on for ever. This is the paradox of athletic 'development'. As more and more nations embrace the achievement oriented goals of track and field, fewer and fewer of the total number of world athletes can win gold medals and the knock-on effects of fame and fortune. When we consider the vast nations of Asia, several of whom seem determined to 'progress' in track and field but who have yet to reach the global norm in terms of per capita output, prospects of everlasting growth for Kenya (and many other countries in the world) are slim. China's recent growth rates in athletic output have been dramatic. Though still displaying a very low level of per capita output, it is possible that if current trends continue it will, in absolute terms, make substantial inroads into the total global production of superior athletes. By the year 2000 it could well be accounting for around 10 per cent of all superior output – more than that contributed by Russia in 1992.

Pledging itself to achievement sport would mean that Kenya would have to invest heavily in capital-intensive forms of athletics field events which require considerable technical and scientific inputs. Some would go so far as to say that 'even if developing countries concentrated the means at their disposal for sports advancement on high-performance sport, their chances of success would be very limited'.[65] Kenya's success has been restricted to running at the cost of success in the field events. Improving Kenyan performances in the field events would incur very high opportunity costs; the money could arguably be better spent on other things.

As Henning Eichberg has repeatedly stressed, however, there are alternatives to the centimetre-gram-second model on the path to the 'development' of a nation's movement culture.[66] One is to place more emphasis on 'keep fit' or 'welfare sport'. In the West, the revolution in 'fun running' has been a characteristic of the last few decades. Unfortunately, such forms of movement culture easily become co-opted by achievement sports (such as the 'mass marathon' syndrome) and become commodified. They are also often beset by the fetish of narcissism – running to look good, which often involves considerable expenditure on the latest training shoes and clothing. Running becomes a Western fashion, fuelling further the dependence on overseas cultural models.

Another potential form of 'development' is a return to folk traditions. Is it possible that Kenya could (re)adopt other forms of movement culture and in doing so de-emphasise achievement sport? The opposition of Ngugi wa Thiong'o to the adoption of Western culture is almost entirely focused on 'high', cultural forms – theatre, song, dance, and literature. When he does criticise Kenya for adopting western sports he cites activities like polo and tennis - the sports of the cultural élite. He says nothing about the much more widespread presence of football and running. It may be that theatre and dance are cultural forms which are much more suited to the radical voice than sports. But if we were to follow Ngugi's line of argument it would be for Kenya to return to African forms of running, jumping and throwing, the likes of which were described in Chapter 3. These would not be museumised residuals or touristic reminders of a bygone age but part of a living popular culture.

There are few precedents for this kind of future. In recent decades the most dramatic about-turn in sport was in the period of the Cultural Revolution in Maoist China. During the late 1960s and early 1970s 'medals-and-trophyism' was denounced and competitive sports all but ceased.[67] A similar route has, in a less dramatic form, been followed in a small number of modern African and other peripheral nations.[68] It is unlikely (though not impossible) that this will happen in Kenya because it would require a conflictual response to what Edward Said has called 'the formidable structure of cultural domination'[69] – in this case, the widespread adoption of Western athletics. It would also require the re-adoption of traditional structures of consciousness – a decolonisation of the mind.[70] As a result, it has been suggested as a general principle that the most that could be hoped for might be the desportisation of play, rather than the liberation of sport.[71]

There is nothing natural about modern Kenyan running. Only in the unlikely event of Kenyan movement culture somehow returning to its indigenous traditions might it be comprehensible without having to look beyond the local horizon.

Notes and references

1. The 1936 time (when the 'African record' stood at 4 minutes 34.6 seconds, set in 1925 by R.P. Wilson of Rhodesia (now Zimbabwe) is taken from Abmayr and Pinaud, *L'Athlétisme Africain*, p. 141. We again note the unspectacular quality of Kenyan running at that time, hardly confirming any 'legendary feats of African savannah dwellers' (Hoberman, *Mortal Engines*, p. 56).
2. Gunder Frank, *Capitalism and Underdevelopment in Latin America*.
3. Klein, *Sugarball*.
4. Lee, 'Development'.
5. Mackay, 'King of the road Masya'; Mackay, 'Ndeti and Pippig are still the bosses in Boston'.
6. Quoted in Rodda, 'Goodwill game from Kenyans', and David Martin, 'Simply awesome'.
7. Eichberg and El Mansouri, 'Physical culture as an indicator of societal contradiction'.
8. Tomlinson, *Cultural Imperialism*.
9. Houlihan, 'Homogenization, Americanization and creolization', p. 371. A case in point would be the opposition of Islamic fundamentalists to the appearance of women athletes wearing Western running costumes which are regarded as immodest by Islamic standards. Conflict can also occur, of course, in the form of indigenous opposition to traditional forms of body culture: see Brownell, *Training the Body for China*.
10. Tomlinson, *Cultural Imperialism*, p. 175.
11. Peet, 'The destruction of regional cultures', p. 166.
12. Leys, 'Sport, the state and dependency theory', p. 310.
13. Tomlinson, *Cultural Imperialism*, p. 119.
14. MacAloon, *This Great Symbol*, p. 262.
15. Peet, 'The destruction of regional cultures', p. 166.
16. Heikkila, 'Discipline and excel'.
17. Taylor, *Political Geography*, p. 9.
18. Said, *Culture and Imperialism*, p. 319.
19. Taylor, *Political Geography*, p. 9.
20. Peet, 'The destruction of regional cultures', p. 169.
21. See also Klein, 'Baseball and underdevelopment'.
22. This point is made in relation to the USA and the Dominican Republic in the context of baseball: see Klein, *Sugarball*, p. 152.
23. Lee, 'Dependence', p. 126.
24. Klein, *Sugarball*, p. 112. By 'self-loathing' Klein refers to the way in which the dominated party is partly (at least) convinced of its own inferiority.
25. Thiong'o, *Detained*, pp. 64–5.
26. Ibid, p. 67. See also Thiong'o, *Moving the Centre*, pp. 88–92.
27. Leakey, *Defeating the Mau Mau*, p. 27.
28. Pratt, *Imperial Eyes*, p. 6 (italics added).
29. On the ambivalence of sport as cultural imperialism see Guttmann, 'Our former colonial masters'.
30. James, *Beyond a Boundary*; the quotation is from Lazarus, 'Cricket and national culture'.
31. Hall, 'C. L. R. James: a portrait'. For an excellent collection of essays addressing the anti-colonial dimensions of cricket in the West Indies see Beckles and Stoddart (eds), *Liberation Cricket*.

32. Lazarus, 'Cricket and national culture', p. 102.
33. Leys, 'Sport, the state', p. 313; Sillitoe, *The Loneliness of the Long Distance Runner*.
34. Lazarus, 'Cricket and national culture', p. 103.
35. This is the language used by Lazarus (ibid.) to describe West Indian cricket.
36. Hobsbawm and Ranger, *The Invention of Tradition*.
37. Hobsbawm, 'Introduction: inventing traditions'.
38. Ibid, p. 2.
39. Spurr, *The Rhetoric of Empire*, p. 186.
40. Guttmann, *Games and Empire*, p. 179.
41. Klein, 'Baseball and underdevelopment'.
42. Eichberg, 'Forward race', p. 117.
43. Much of this paragraph is based on Ehn, 'National feeling in sport', p. 63.
44. Interview (JS) with Kipchoge Keino, 1992.
45. Young, *Colonial Desire*, p. 5.
46. Carrier, *Occidentialism*, p.5.
47. Klein, *Sugarball*, p. 152.
48. Ibid, p. 156.
49. Cresswell, 'Mobility as resistance'.
50. Rojek, *Decentring Leisure*, p. 131.
51. Brownell, *Training the Body for China*, p. 95.
52. Ahrenst, 'Jeg er Wilson Kipketer'. We are grateful to Lone Friis Larsen (University of Copenhagen) for this reference.
53. The term 'identisation' is a neologism used by the French sociologist Pierre Tapp. See Gerard, 'Les deux faces de l'identité'.
54. The notion of the state as a 'container' is based on ideas in Taylor, 'The state as a container'.
55. Leys, 'Sport, the state', p. 312. Note also a particularly incisive essay by Surin, 'C.L.R. James' materialist aesthetic of cricket'.
56. As noted in the case of baseball and the Dominican Republic in Klein, *Sugarball*, p. 120.
57. Pieterse, *White on Black*. Note the section on sports, pp. 148–51.
58. Carrier, *Occidentalism*.
59. Hoberman, *Mortal Engines*, p. 36.
60. Ibid, p. 37.
61. Vettenniemi, 'The promised land of running', p. 101. We are grateful to Tuija Kilpeläinen (University of Jyväskylä) for this reference.
62. Schumacher, *Die Finnen*, p. 85.
63. Quercetani and Magnusson, *Track and Field Performances through the Ages*.
64. Hannus, *Flying Finns*.
65. Heinemann, 'Sport in developing countries', p. 149; Monnington, 'Crisis management', p. 115.
66. Eichberg, 'Olympic sport – neocolonialism and alternatives'.
67. Brownell, *Training the Body for China*, pp. 302–3.
68. Guttmann, *Games and Empires*, pp. 165–6.
69. Said, *Orientalism*, p. 25.
70. Mählmann, 'Role of sport', p. 129.
71. Leys, 'Sport, the state', p. 310.

Bibliography

Abmayr, Walter, *Track and Field Performances, Kenya, 1982* (Nairobi, Abmayr: 1983).

Abmayr, Walter, 'Analysis and perspectives of the project in Africa', *Women's Track and Field in Africa* (report of the first IAAF congress on women's athletics) (Deutscher Leichtathletik Verband, Darmstadt, 1983) pp. 532–8.

Abmayr, Walter, *Africa: Track and Field* (Ravensburg, Drexler: 1987).

Abmayr, Walter and Pinaud, Yves (eds), *L'Athlétisme Africain '94* (Paris, Editions Polymédias: 1994).

Adamson, Joy, *The Peoples of Kenya* (London, Collins and Harvill: 1967).

Ahrenst, Henrik, 'Jeg er Wilson Kipketer', *Sport på Stregen*, 7 (1995) pp. 8–12.

Aitken, Alastair, *More than Winning* (Lewes, Temple House Books: 1992).

Amin, Muhammad and Moll, Peter, *Kenya's World Beating Athletes* (Nairobi, East African Publishing House: 1972).

Anderson, Benedict, *Imagined Communities* (London, Verso: 1991).

Anderson, David, 'Stock theft and moral economy in colonial Kenya', *Africa*, 56 (4) (1986), pp. 399–416.

Andrews, David, 'Desperately seeking Michel: Foucault's genealogy, the body, and critical sports sociology', *Sociology of Sport Journal*, 10 (2) (1993) pp. 148–67.

Appadurai, Arjun, 'Disjuncture and difference in the global cultural economy' in Mike Featherstone (ed.), *Global Culture* (London, Sage: 1990) pp. 295–301.

Baker, William, 'Political games: the meaning of international sport for interdependent Africa', in William Baker and James Mangan (eds), *Sport in Africa: Essays in Social History* (New York, Africana Publishing: 1987) pp. 272–94.

Bale, John, 'Sports history as innovation diffusion', *Canadian Journal of History of Sport*, 15 (1982) pp. 38–63.

Bale, John, 'The changing origins of an occupation; the case of professional footballers in 1950 and 1980', *Geography*, 68 (1983) pp. 140–8.

Bale, John, 'Towards a Geography of International Sport', Occasional Paper 8 (Loughborough, Loughborough University, Department of Geography: 1985).

Bale, John, *The Brawn Drain: Foreign Student-Athletes in American Universities* (Urbana, University of Illinois Press: 1991).

Bale, John, *Landscapes of Modern Sport* (London, Leicester University Press: 1994).

Bale, John and Sang, Joe, 'Out of Africa: the "development" of Kenyan athletics, talent migration and the global sports system', in John Bale and Joseph Maguire (eds), *The Global Sports Arena: Athletic Talent Migration in an Interdependent World* (London, Cass: 1994) pp. 206–25.

Balfour, Patrick, *Lords of the Equator: an African Journey* (London, Hutchinson: 1937).

Ballinger, Lyn, *In Your Face! Sport for Love or Money* (Chicago, Vanguard: 1981).

Bank, Dick 'Dick Bank's Mexico reflections', *Athletics Weekly*, 23 (1) (1969) pp. 18–23.

Barff, R. and Austen, J., '"It's gotta be da shoes": domestic manufacturing, international subcontracting, and the production of athletic footwear', *Environment and Planning*, 25 (8) (1993) pp. 1103-14.

Barton, Juxon, 'Notes on the Turkana of British East Africa', *Journal of the African Society*, 19/20 (1920/21) pp. 107–15; 204–11.

Beckles, Hilary and Stoddart, Brian (eds), *Liberation Cricket: West Indies Cricket Culture* (Manchester, Manchester University Press: 1995).

Berenatzik, Hugo Adolf, *Afrika: Handbuch der Angwandten Völkerunde* (Innsbruck, Schüsselverlag, 1947).

Berg-Schlosser, Dirk, *Tradition and Change in Kenya: a Comparative Analysis of Seven Major Ethnic Groups* (Paderborn, Ferdinand Schöningh: 1984).

Berman, Bruce, *Control and Crisis in Colonial Kenya* (London, James Currey: 1990).

Bernett, Hajo, *Leichtathletik in Historischen Bilddokumenten* (Munich, Copress Verlag: 1986).

Binder, Renee and Burnett, G.W., 'Ngugi wa Thiong'o and the search for a populist landscape aesthetic', *Environmental Values*, 3 (1) (1994) pp. 47–59.

Birnbaum, Martin, 'Reception in Ruanda', *Natural History*, 44 (5) (1939) pp. 298–307.

Blacking, John, 'Games and sports in pre-colonial African societies', in William Baker and James Mangan (eds.), *Sport in Africa: Essays in Social History* (New York, Africana Publishing: 1987) pp. 3–22.

Blain, Neil, Boyle, Raymond and O'Donnell, Hugh, *Sport and National Identity in the European Media* (Leicester, Leicester University Press: 1993).

Blaut, J.M., *The Colonizer's Map of the World: Geographical Diffusionism and Eurocentric History* (New York, Guilford Press: 1993).

Boit, Mike, 'Where are the Kenyan women runners?' *New Studies in Athletics*, 4 (1988) pp. 22–7.

Boyes, John, *King of the Wa-Kikuyu* (London, Methuen: 1912).

Brantlinger, Patrick, 'Victorians and Africans: the genealogy of the myth of the Dark Continent', in Henry Louis Gates, *'Race', Writing and Difference* (Chicago, Chicago University Press: 1985) pp. 185–222.

Brohm, Jean-Marie, *Sport: a Prison of Measured Time* (Ian Fraser, trans.) (London, Ink-Links: 1978).

Browne, S. St J. Orde, *The Vanishing Tribes of Kenya* (London, Seeley, Service and Co.: 1925).

Brownell, Susan, *Training the Body for China: Sport in the Moral Order of the People's Republic* (Chicago, Chicago University Press: 1995).

Buchanan, Keith, *Reflections on Education in the Third World* (Nottingham, Spoksman Books: 1975).

Buchanan, William and Cantrill, Hadley, *Now Nations see Each Other: a Study of Public Opinion* (Urbana, University of Illinois Press: 1953).

Burton, Richard, 'Cricket, carnival and street culture in the Caribbean', *British Journal of Sport History*, 2 (2) (1985) pp. 179–97.

Butcher, Pat, 'Low profile priest runs highest school', *Guardian* (3 August 1995), p. 19.

Cagnolo, C., *The Akikuyu: their Customs, Traditions and Folklore* (Nyeri, Catholic Mission of the Consolata Fathers: 1933).

Cairns, Alan, *Prelude to Imperialism: British Reactions to Central African Society 1840-1890* (London, Routledge: 1965).

Carrier, James (ed.), *Occidentalism: Images of the West* (Oxford, Oxford University Press: 1995).

Carter, John Marshall and Krüger, Arnd (eds), *Ritual and Record: Sports Records and Quantification in Pre-Modern Societies* (New York, Greenwood Press: 1991).

Cashmore, Ernest, *Black Sportsmen* (London, Routledge: 1982).

Clayton, Henry, 'Sport and African soldiers: the military diffusion of sport through sub-Saharan Africa', in William Baker and James Mangan (eds), *Sport in Africa: Essays in Social History* (New York, Africana Publishing: 1987), pp. 114–37.

Cloke, Paul, Philo, Chris and Sadler, David, *Approaching Human Geography* (London, Paul Chapman: 1991).

Cobb, W. Montague, 'Race and runners', *Journal of Health and Physical Education*, 1 (1936), pp. 3–7, 53–5.

Colonial Office, *Report on the Colony and Protectorate of Kenya for the Year 1951* (London, HMSO: 1952).

Cook, Stephen, Pakulski, Jan and Waters, Malcolm, *Postmodernization: Changes in Advanced Societies* (London, Sage: 1992).

Cotlow, Lewis, *In Search of the Primitive* (Boston, Little, Brown and Co.: 1966)

Cranworth, Lord, *A Colony in the Making or Sport and Profit in East Africa* (London, Macmillan: 1912).

Cranworth, Lord, *Kenya Chronicles* (London, Macmillan: 1939).

Cresswell, Tim, 'Mobility as resistance: a geographical reading of Kerouac's "On the Road"', *Transactions of the Institute of British Geographers*, 18 (2) (1993) pp. 249–62.

Curtis, James and Birch, J., 'Size of community of origin and recruitment to professional and Olympic hockey in Canada', *Sociology of Sport Journal*, 4 (1987) pp. 229–44.

Daniels, Jack, (1975) 'Science on the altitude factor', in Dave Prokop (ed.), *The African Running Revolution* (Mountain View CA, World Publications: 1975) pp. 40–8.

Decker, Wolfgang, 'The record and the ritual: the athletic records of ancient

Egypt', in John Marshall Carter and Arnd Krüger (eds) *Ritual and Record: Sports Records and Quantification in Pre-Modern Societies* (New York, Greenwood Press: 1991) pp. 21–30.

'Dinesen, Isak' (Karen Blixen), *Out of Africa* (Harmondsworth, Penguin: 1954).

Doherty, Joe 'African environment and African development', in *African Futures*, proceedings of a Conference held at Centre for African Studies, University of Edinburgh (Edinburgh: 1986) pp. 403–28.

Donaghu, Michael and Barff, Richard, 'Nike just did it: international subcontracting and flexibility in athletic footwear production', *Regional Studies*, 24 (1990) pp. 537–52.

Drake, Dick and Henderson, Joe, 'Blacks of Africa, US prevail in Mexican extravaganza', *Track and Field News* (October/November 1968) p. 3.

Ehn, Billy 'National feeling in sport. The case of Sweden', *Ethnologia Europea*, 19 (1) (1989) pp. 57–66.

Eichberg, Henning, 'Body culture as paradigm: the Danish sociology of sport', *International Review for the Sociology of Sport*, 24 (2) (1989) pp. 42–63.

Eichberg, Henning, 'Forward race and the laughter of pygmies', in Mikluas Teich and Roy Porter (eds), *Fin de Siècle and its Legacies* (Cambridge, Cambridge University Press: 1990) pp. 115–31.

Eichberg, Henning, 'Olympic sport – neo-colonialism and alternatives', *International Review for the Sociology of Sport*, 19 (1) (1984) pp. 97–104.

Eichberg, Henning, 'Stronger, funnier, deadlier: track and field on the way from the ritual to the record', in John Marshall Carter and Arnd Krüger (eds), *Ritual and Record: Sports Records and Quantification in Pre-Modern Societies* (New York, Greenwood Press: 1990) pp. 123–34.

Eichberg, Henning 'The societal construction of space and time as sociology's way home to philosophy', in Otmar Weiss and Wolfgang Schultz (eds) *Sport in Space and Time* (Vienna, Vienna University Press: 1995) pp. 31–42.

Eichberg, Henning, 'Travelling, comparing, emigrating: configurations of sport mobility', in John Bale and Joseph Maguire (eds), *The Global Sports Arena: Athletic Talent Migration in an Interdependent World* (London, Cass: 1994) pp. 256–80.

Eichberg, Henning and El Masouri, Ali Yehia, 'Sport in Libya: physical education as an indicator of societal contradictions', in Horst Ueberhorst (ed.), *Geschichte der Leibesübungen* (Berlin, Bartles and Wernitz: 1989) pp. 261–73.

Faris, James, 'Photography, power and the southern Nuba', in Elizabeth Edwards (ed.), *Anthropology and Photography 1860–1920* (New Haven, Yale University Press: 1992) pp. 211–17.

Fenwick, Geoff, 'The talent distribution' in Dave Prokop (ed.), *The African Running Revolution* (Mountain View CA, World Publications: 1975) pp. 19–22.

Foran, W. Robert, *The Kenya Police, 1857-1960* (London, Robert Hale: 1962).

Foucault, Michel, *Discipline and Punish* (Harmondsworth, Penguin: 1977).

Fox, James, *White Mischief* (Harmondsworth, Penguin: 1984).

Furlong, J.D.G. and Szreter, R., 'The trend of the performance differential between leading men and women athletes', *The Statistician*, 24 (2) (1975), pp. 115–28.

Gale, F. Holderness (ed.), *East Africa (British)* (London, Foreign and Colonial Compiling and Publishing Co.: 1908/9).

Galtung, Johann, 'Sport as a carrier of deep culture and structure', in Maaret Ilmarinen (ed.), *Sport and International Understanding* (New York, Springer Verlag: 1984), pp. 12–19.

Galtung, Johann, 'The sport system as a metaphor for the world system', in Fernand Landry, Marc Landry and Magdelaine Yerls (eds), *Sport: the Third Millennium* (Sainte-Foy, Les Presses de l'Université, Laval: 1991) pp. 146-55.

Gates, Henry Louis, 'Talkin' that talk', in Henry Louis Gates (ed.), *'Race', Writing and Difference* (Chicago, Chicago University Press: 1986) pp. 402-9.

Gatti, Attilio, *South of the Sahara* (London, Hodder and Stoughton: 1946).

Geilinger, Walter, *Der Kilimondjaro: Sein Land und Seine Menschen* (Bern, Verlag Hans Huber: 1930).

Gérard, Jean-Louis, 'Les deux faces de l'identité: vers un méta-modèle pour l'identité', in Knut Dietrich and Henning Eichberg (eds), *Körper Sprache: Üder Identität und Konflict* (Frankfurt, Afra Verlag: 1993) pp. 45–62.

Gibson, John, *Performance Versus Results: a Critique of Values in Contemporary Sport* (Albany, State University of New York Press: 1993).

Gilman, Sander, 'Black bodies, white bodies: toward an iconography of female sexuality in late nineteenth century art, medicine and literature', in Henry Louis Gates, *'Race', Writing and Difference'* (Chicago, Chicago University Press: 1985), pp. 223–61.

Godia, George, 'Sport in Kenya', in Eric Wagner (ed.), *Sport in Asia and Africa* (New York, Greenwood Press: 1989) pp. 260–81.

Greaves, L. B., *Carey Francis of Kenya* (London, Rex Collings: 1969)

Gregory, Derek, *Geographical Imaginations* (Oxford, Blackwell: 1994).

Gregory, Derek, 'People, places and practices: the future of human geography', in Russell King (ed.), *The Future of Geography* (Sheffield, The Geographical Association: 1985) pp. 56–76.

Gunder Frank, André, *Capitalism and Underdevelopment in Latin America* (New York, Monthly Review Press: 1969).

Guttmann, Allen, *From Ritual to Record: the Nature of Modern Sports* (New York, Columbia University Press: 1978).

Guttmann, Allen, *Games and Empires: Modern Sports and Cultural Imperialism* (New York, Columbia University Press: 1994).

Guttmann, Allen, '"Our former colonial masters": the diffusion of sport and the question of cultural imperialism', *Stadion*, 14 (1) (1988), pp. 49–63.

Guttmann, Allen, *The Olympics* (Urbana, University of Illinois Press: 1992).

Hall, Stuart, 'C. L. R. James: a portrait', in Paget Henry and Paul Buhle (eds),

C. L. R. James's Caribbean (Durham, Duke University Press: 1992), pp. 1–16.

Hall, Sydney, *The Role of Physical Education and Sport in the Nation Building of Kenya*, Ph. D. thesis, Ohio University 1983, University Microfilms.

Hannerz, Ulf, 'The world in creoleisation', *Africa*, 57 (4) (1987), pp. 546–59.

Hannus, Matti, *Flying Finns* (Helsinki, Tietosanoma: 1990).

Harvey, David, *The Condition of Postmodernity* (Oxford, Blackwell: 1989).

Harvey, Jean and Houle, François, 'Sport, world economy and new social movements', *Sociology of Sport Journal*, 11 (4) (1994), pp. 337–55.

Harvey, Jean and Sparks, Robert, 'The politics of the body in the context of modernity', *Quest*, 43 (2) (1991), pp. 164–89.

Heikala, Juha, 'Discipline and excel: techniques of the self and body and the logic of competing', *Sociology of Sport Journal*, 10 (4) (1993), pp. 397–412.

Heinemann, Klaus, (1993) 'Sport in developing countries', in Eric Dunning, Joseph Maguire and Robert Pearton (eds), *The Sports Process, Human Kinetics* (Champaign, IL: 1993), pp. 139–50.

Heinilä, Kalevi, 'Notes on inter-group conflict in international sport', in Eric Dunning (ed.), *The Sociology of Sport* (London, Cass: 1971) pp. 343–51.

Hemingway, Ernest, *Green Hills of Africa* (London, Cape: 1954).

Hilderbrand, J. R., 'The geography of games', *National Geographic Magazine*, 36 (2) (1919), pp. 89–143.

Hinde, Sidney Langford and Hinde, Hildegarde, *The Last of the Masai* (London, Heinemann: 1901).

Hoberman, John, *Mortal Engines: the Science of Performance and the Dehumanization of Sport* (New York, The Free Press: 1992).

Hobsbawm, Eric, 'Introduction: inventing traditions', in Eric Hobsbawm and Terence Ranger (eds), *The Invention of Tradition* (Cambridge, Cambridge University Press: 1983), pp. 1–14.

Hobsbawm, Eric, 'Mass producing traditions: Europe, 1870-1914', in Eric Hobsbawm and Terence Ranger (eds), *The Invention of Tradition* (Cambridge, Cambridge University Press: 1983), pp. 263–307.

Hobsbawm, Eric and Ranger, Terence (eds), *The Invention of Tradition* (Cambridge, Cambridge University Press: 1983).

Hollis, Claud, 'The Maasai', *Journal of the African Society*, 42 (1943), p. 124.

Hollander, Tom, 'A Geographical Analysis of Foreign Intercollegiate Track and Field Athletes', unpublished master's dissertation (Eastern Michigan University: 1980).

Houlihan, Barrie, 'Homogenization, Americanization and creolization: varieties of globalization', *Sociology of Sport Journal*, 11 (4) (1994), pp. 357–75.

Hughes, Anthony, *East Africa: the Search for Unity* (Harmondsworth, Penguin: 1963).

Huntingford, G. W. B., *The Nandi of Kenya: Tribal Control in a Pastoral Society* (London, Routledge: 1953).

Huntington, Ellsworth, *Civilization and Climate* (New Haven, Yale University Press: 1915).

Huxley, Elspeth, *White Man's Country: Lord Delamere and the Making of Kenya* (Vol. 1) (London, Macmillan: 1935).

Hyam, Ronald, *Empire and Sexuality: the British Experience* (Manchester, Manchester University Press: 1990).

Jackson, Peter, 'Constructions of culture, representations of race: Edward Curtis's "way of seeing"', in Kay Anderson and Fay Gale (eds), *Inventing Places: Studies in Cultural Geography* (Melbourne, Longman Cheshire: 1992), pp. 89–106.

James, C. L. R., *Beyond a Boundary* (London, Stanley Paul: 1969).

Janelle, Donald, 'Central place development in a time space framework', *Professional Geographer*, 20 (1968), pp. 5–10.

JanMohamed, Abdul, 'The economy of manichean allegory: the function of racial difference in colonialist literature', in Henry Louis Gates (ed.), *'Race', Writing and Difference* (Chicago, Chicago University Press: 1985) pp. 78–106.

Jarvie, Grant and Maguire, Joseph, *Sport and Leisure in Social Thought* (London, Routledge: 1994).

Jokl, Ernst, 'High jumping technique of the central African Watussis', *Journal of Physical Education and School Hygiene*, 33 (1941) pp. 145–9.

Jokl, Ernst, *Medical Sociology and Cultural Anthropology of Sport and Physical Education* (Springfield, IL, C. Thomas: 1964)

Jokl, Ernst, *Physiology of Exercise* (Springfield IL, C. Thomas: 1964).

Jones, Thomas, *Education in East Africa* (London, International Education Board: 1925).

Kane, Martin, 'An assessment of black is best', *Sports Illustrated*, 34 (3) (1971), pp. 78–83.

Kennedy, Dane, *Islands of White* (Durham, Duke University Press: 1987).

Kenyatta, Jomo, *Facing Mount Kenya* (London, Heinemann: 1979).

Kirk-Greene, Anthony, 'Imperial administration and the athletic imperative: the case of the District Officer in Africa', in William Baker and James Mangan (eds), *Sport in Africa: Essays in Social History* (New York, Africana Publishing: 1987), pp. 81–113.

Klein, Alan, 'Baseball and underdevelopment: the political economy of sport and the Dominican Republic', *Sociology of Sport Journal*, 6 (2) (1989), pp. 95–112.

Klein, Alan, *Sugarball: the American Game, the Dominican Dream* (New Haven, Yale University Press: 1994).

Knowles, Joan and Collet, D. P., 'Nature as myth: notes towards a historical understanding of development and conservation in Maasailand', *Africa*, 59 (4) (1989), pp. 433–60.

Kohn, Marek, *The Race Gallery: the Return of Racial Science* (London, Cape: 1995).

Koskei, Mike and Abmayr, Walter, 'Cross country training in Kenya', *New Studies in Athletics*, 4 (1988).

Krapf, Lewis, *Travels, Researches and Missionary Labours During an Eighteen Year's Residence in Eastern Africa* (London, Cass: 1968).

Lambert, H. E., *Kikuyu Social and Political Institutions* (Oxford, Oxford University Press: 1956).

Langley, Myrtle, *The Nandi of Kenya: Life Crisis in a Period of Change* (London, Hurst: 1979).

Larsen, Niels and Gormsen, Lisbet, *Bodyculture: a Monography of the Bodyculture among the Sukuma in Tanzania* (Slagelse, Bavenebanke: 1985).

Lash, Scott and Urry, John, *Economies of Signs and Space* (London, Sage 1993).

Lazarus, Neil, 'Cricket and national culture', in Paget Henry and Paul Buhle (eds), *C. L. R. James's Caribbean* (Durham, Duke University Press: 1992) pp. 92–110.

Leakey, L. B. S., *Defeating the Mau Mau* (London, Methuen: 1954).

Leakey, L. B. S., *The Southern Kikuyu Before 1903* (Vol. 2) (London, Academic Press: 1987).

Lee, Roger 'Development', in R. J. Johnston, Derek Gregory and David Smith (eds), *The Dictionary of Human Geography* (Oxford, Blackwell: 1994) pp. 128–30.

Lewis, David, 'An elan, a zest and a grace', in Dave Prokop (ed.), *The African Running Revolution* (Mountain View, CA, World Publications: 1975) pp. 9–11.

Lewis, Roy and Foy, Yvonne, *The British in Africa* (London, Weidenfeld and Nicolson: 1971).

Leys, Colin, 'Sport, the state and dependency theory', in Hart Cantelon and Richard Gruneau (eds) *Sport, Culture and the Modern State* (Toronto, University of Toronto Press: 1982) pp. 308–12.

Leys, Norman, *Kenya* (London, Hogarth Press: 1926).

Lindblom, Gerhard, *The Akamba of British East Africa* (2nd edition) (Uppsala, Appelbergs Boktryckeri: 1920).

Livingstone, David, 'Climate's moral economy: science, race and place in post-Darwinian British and American Geography' in Anne Godlewska and Neil Smith (eds), *Geography and Empire* (Oxford, Blackwell: 1994) pp. 132–54.

Livingstone, David, *The Geographical Tradition* (Oxford, Blackwell: 1992).

Loy, John and McElvogue, John, 'Racial segregation in American sport', *International Review of Sport Sociology*, 5 (1970) pp. 5–23.

Lutz, Catherine and Collins, Jane, *Reading National Geographic* (Chicago, University of Chicago Press: 1993).

MacAloon, John, *This Great Symbol: Pierre de Coubertain and the Origins of the Modern Olympic Games* (Chicago, Chicago University Press: 1981).

Mackay, Duncan, 'King of the road Masya punches his weight', *Observer (Sport)* (18 September 1994), p. 15.

Mackay, Duncan, 'Ndeti and Pippig are still the bosses in Boston', *Guardian* (18 April 1995), p. 7.

Mackay, Duncan, 'A new world order', *Observer (Sport)*, 17 September 1995, p. 5.

Magnusson, Rooney, 'Rätt och fel; idrottstatistiken – exempel från den fria idrottens historia', *Idrott Historia och Samhälle*, Svenska Idrottshistorika Föreingens Årskrift (1983).

Maguire, Joseph, 'Preliminary observations on globalisation and the migration of sports labour', *Sociological Review*, 42 (3) (1994), pp. 452–80.

Maguire, Joseph, 'Sport, national identities and globalization', in John Bale (ed.), *Community, Landscape and Identity: Horizons in a Geography of Sports*, Occasional Paper, 20, Department of Geography, Keele University (1994) pp. 71–93.

Maguire, Joseph, 'Sport, racism and British society: a sociological model of English élite male Afro-Caribbean soccer and rugby union players', in Grant Jarvie (ed.), *Sport, Racism and Ethnicity* (Brighton, Falmer: 1991) pp. 94–113.

Maguire, Joseph and Bale, John, 'Introduction: sports labour migration in the global arena', in John Bale and Joseph Maguire (eds.), *The Global Sports Arena: Athletic Talent Migration in an Interdependent World* (London, Cass: 1994) pp. 1–24.

Mählmann, Peter, 'Perception of sport in Kenya', *Journal of Eastern Africa Research and Development*, 19 (1989), pp. 119–45.

Mählmann, Peter, 'Sport as a weapon of colonialism in Kenya: a review of the literature', *Transafrican Journal of History*, 17 (1988) pp. 172–85.

Mählmann, Peter, 'The role of sport in the process of modernisation: the Kenya case', *Journal of Eastern Africa Research and Development*, 22 (1992), pp. 120–31.

Mählmann, P., Asembo, J. M. and arap Korir, M. 'An analysis of sports in Kenyan educational institutions', *Journal of Eastern Africa Research and Development*, 23 (1993), pp. 160–75.

Mandell, Richard, *Sport: a Cultural History* (New York, Columbia University Press: 1984).

Mangan, J. A., *The Games Ethic and Imperialism* (London, Viking: 1986).

Mangan, James, 'Tom Brown in Tropical Africa: idealism and realism in the evolution of imperial education', in Norbert Müller and Joachim Ruhl (eds), *Sport History, Official Report of Olympic Scientific Congress* (Niedenhausen, Schors Verlag: 1985) pp. 119–26.

Manners, John, 'In search of an explanation' in Dave Prokop (ed.), *The African Running Revolution* (Mountain View, CA, World Publications: 1975) pp. 26–39.

Manners, John, 'Raiders from the Rift Valley', *Time* (9 April 1990) p. 55.

Marshall, L., *The !Kung of Nyae Nyae* (Cambridge, MA, Harvard University Press: 1976).

Martin, David, 'Simply awesome', *Athletics Weekly*, 23 (August 1995) pp. 7–9.

Massey, Doreen, 'Power geometry and a progressive sense of place', in Jon

Bird *et al.* (eds), *Mapping Futures: Local Cultures, Global Change* (London, Routledge: 1993) pp. 59–69.

Matson, A. T., 'Nandi traditions of raiding', in B. A. Ogot (ed.), *Hadith 2* (Nairobi, East Africa Publishing House: 1970).

Matson, A. T., *Nandi Resistance to British Rule 1890–1906* (Nairobi, East African Publishing House: 1972).

Matthews, Peter (ed.), *Athletics 1994* (London, Harmsworth Active: 1994).

Mazrui, Ali, *The Africans: a Triple Heritage* (London, BBC Publications: 1986).

Mecklenburg, Duke of, Freidrich Adolf, *In the Heart of Africa* (G. E. Maberley-Oppler, trans.), (London, Cassell: 1910).

Meinhertzhagen, Robert, *Kenya Diary (1902–1906)* (Edinburgh, Oliver and Boyd: 1957).

Middleton, J., *The Kikuyu and Kamba of Kenya: Ethnographic Survey of Africa*, Vol. V (London, International African Institute: 1953).

Miller, Austin, *Climatology* (London, Methuen: 1947).

Monnington, Terence, 'Crisis management in Black African sport', in J.C. Binfield and John Stevenson (eds), *Sport, Culture and Politics* (Sheffield, Sheffield Academic Press: 1993) pp. 113–28.

Monnington, Terence, 'The politics of black African sport', in Lincoln Allison (ed.), *The Politics of Sport* (Manchester, Manchester University Press: 1986) pp. 149–73.

Moore, Kenny, 'Sons of the wind', *Sports Illustrated*, 78 (8), pp. 72–84.

Moyes-Bartlett, Hubert, *The King's African Rifles: a Study in the Military History of East Central Africa (1890–1945)* (Aldershot, Gale and Polden: 1956).

Murray-Brown, Jeremy, *Kenyatta* (London, Allen and Unwin: 1972).

Mwaniki, Kabecca, *The Living History of the Embu and Mbeere to 1906* (Nairobi, East African Literature Bureau: 1973).

Ndejuru, Aimable, 'Studien zur Rolle der Leibesübungen in der Traditionellen Gesellschaft Rwandas', doctoral dissertation, University of Cologne (1983).

Ndoo, Philip, 'The Kenyan success', in Dave Prokop (ed.), *The African Running Revolution* (Mountain View, CA, World Publications: 1975) pp. 49–57.

Noronha, Francis, *Kipchoge of Kenya* (Nakuru, Elimu Publishers: 1970).

Ochieng, William (ed.), *Themes in Kenyan History* (Nairobi, Heinemann Kenya: 1990).

Okroth, O., 'The Amos Biwott story', *Sunday Standard* (11 March 1990) p. 29.

Osotis, R. M., 'The theatre in independent Africa', in William Ochieng (ed.), *Themes in African History* (Nairobi, Heinemann Kenya: 1990) pp. 209–17.

Peet, Richard, *Global Capitalism* (London, Routledge: 1991)

Peet, Richard, 'The destruction of regional cultures', in R. J. Johnston and P. J. Taylor (eds), *A World in Crisis: Geographical Perspectives* (London,

Routledge: 1986) pp. 150–72.

Penz, Otto, 'Sport and speed', *International Review for the Sociology of Sport*, 25 (2) (1990) pp. 157–67.

Philo, Chris, 'History, geography and the "still greater mystery" of historical geography', in Derek Gregory, Ron Martin and Graham Smith (eds), *Human Geography: Society, Space and Social Sciences* (London, Macmillan: 1994) pp. 252–81.

Pieterse, Jan, 'Globalization as hybridization', *International Sociology*, 9 (2) (1994) pp. 100–84.

Pieterse, Jan, *White on Black: Images of Africa and Blacks in Western Popular Culture* (New Haven, Yale University Press: 1992)

Pinaud, Yves, *African Athletics* (London, Charles Elliot: 1966).

Pinaud, Yves and Abmayr, Walter, *L'Athlétisme Africain, 1984* (Paris, Editions Sportive Africaines: 1984).

Pinaud, Yves and Abmayr, Walter, *L'Athlétisme Africain, 1993* (Paris, Editions Polymédis: 1993).

Popkin, J. M., *Kitabutab Bik che ng'ololi Nandi* (Nairobi, Macmillan: 1951).

Pratt, Mary Louise, *Imperial Eyes: Travel Writing and Transculturation* (London, Routledge: 1992).

Pratt, Mary Louise, 'Scratches on the face of the country: or what Mr Barrow saw in the land of the bushmen', in Henry Louis Gates, *'Race', Writing and Difference* (Chicago, Chicago University Press: 1986) pp. 138–62.

Prokop, Dave (ed.), *The African Running Revolution* (Mountain View, CA, World Publications: 1974).

Purahano, Kari and Vuolle, Pauli, *A Survey of the Needs of Sports Development Cooperation in Africa*, Reports of Physical Culture and Health, 57 (Jyväskylä: 1987).

Quercetani, Roberto, *Athletics: a History of Modern Track and Field Athletics (1860–1990)* (Milan, Vallardi and Associates: 1990).

Quercetani, Roberto, *A World History of Track and Field Athletics 1864–1964* (London, Oxford University Press: 1964).

Quercetani, Roberto, *International Athletics Annual 1966* (London, World Sports: 1966).

Quercetani, Roberto and Magnusson, Rooney (compilers), *Track and Field Performances through the Ages: 1929–1936* (Vol. 1) (Florence, ATFS: 1986).

Quercetani, Roberto and Regli, Fulvio, *International Athletics Annual, 1954* (London, World Sports: 1954).

Rail, Genevieve and Harvey, Jean, 'Body at work: Michel Foucault and Sport', *Sociology of Sport Journal*, 12 (2) (1995) pp. 164–79.

Ranger, Terence 'The invention of tradition in Colonial Africa', in Eric Hobsbawm and Terence Ranger (eds), *The Invention of Tradition* (Cambridge, Cambridge University Press: 1983) pp. 211–62.

Rayne, H., 'Turkana', *Journal of the African Society*, 18 (1919) pp. 258–65.

Reclus, Elisée, *The Universal Geography* (Vol. 13) (London, J. S. Virtue: 1876).

Richards, D. J. P., 'Athletic Records and Achievements in Relation to Climate, Social and Environmental Factors', unpublished master's thesis, University of Wales (1953).

Robertson, Robert, 'Mapping the global condition: globalization as the central concept', in Mike Featherstone (ed.), *Global Cultures* (London, Sage: 1990) pp. 15-30.

Rodda, John, 'Goodwill game for Kenyans', *Observer (Sport)* (24 July 1994) p. 7.

Roden, Paul, 'Baseball and the quest for national dignity in Meiji Japan', *American Historical Review*, 85 (3) (1980) pp. 511–34.

Rohé Fred, *The Zen of Running* (New York, Random House: 1974).

Rojek, Chris, *Decentring Leisure: Rethinking Leisure Theory* (London, Sage: 1995).

Roome, William, *Tramping through Africa* (London, A. and C. Black: 1930).

Rooney, John, *A Geography of American Sport: From Cabin Creek to Anaheim* (Reading, MA, Addison-Wesley: 1972).

Rooney, John, *The Recruiting Game* (2nd edition) (Lincoln, University of Nebraska Press: 1987).

Rosberg, Carl and Nottingham, John, *The Myth of 'Mau Mau' Nationalism in Kenya* (New York, Praeger: 1966).

Roscoe, John, *The Northern Bantu: an Account of some Central African Tribes in the Uganda Protectorate* (Cambridge, Cambridge University Press: 1915).

Ross, W. McGregor, *Kenya from Within* (London, Allen and Unwin: 1927).

Rothenburg, Tamar, 'Voyeurs of imperialism: *The National Geographic Magazine* before World War II', in Anne Godlewska and Neil Smith (eds), *Geography and Empire* (Oxford, Blackwell: 1994) pp. 155–72.

Routledge, W. Scoresby and Routledge, Katherine, *With a Prehistoric People: The Akikuyu of British East Africa* (London, Cass: 1968).

Said, Edward, *Culture and Imperialism* (London, Vintage: 1993).

Said, Edward, *Orientalism: Western Conceptions of the Orient* (London, Penguin: 1991).

Saltin, B. *et al.*, 'Aerobic exercise capacity at sea level and at altitude in Kenyan boys, junior and senior runners compared with Scandinavian runners', *Scandinavian Journal of Medicine and Science in Sport*, 5 (4) (1995), pp. 209–21.

Scherer, Joanna, 'The photographic document: photographs as primary data in anthropological enquiry', in Elizabeth Edwards (ed.), *Anthropology and Photography 1860–1920* (New Haven, Yale University Press: 1992) pp. 32–41.

Schneider, Harold, 'Pakot resistance to change', in William Bascon and Melville Herskovits (eds), *Continuity and Change in African Cultures* (Chicago, Phoenix: 1959) pp. 144–67.

Schumacher, Jack, *Die Finnen, das grosse Sportvolk* (Berlin, Wilhelm Limpert-Verlag: 1936).

Scott, John, 'Analysis of current aid initiatives and a process of effective intervention', in Pekka Oja and Risto Telema (eds), *Sport for All*, (Amsterdam, Elsevier: 1991) pp. 529–36.

Semple, Ellen, *Influences of Geographic Environment* (London, Constable: 1911).

Shaw, T. and Pooley, J., 'National success at the Olympics: an explanation', *Documents of the International HISPA-SHEPSA-AAPE Seminar* (Trois Rivieres: 1976).

Shorter, Aylward, *East African Societies* (London, Routledge: 1974).

Sillitoe, Alan, *The Loneliness of the Long Distance Runner* (London, Pan: 1961).

Smith, Anthony, 'Towards a global culture?' in Mike Featherstone (ed.), *Global Culture: Nationalism, Globalization and Modernity* (London, Sage: 1990) pp. 171–91.

Spencer, Paul, *The Samburi: a Study of Gerontocracy in a Nomadic Tribe* (London, Routledge: 1965).

Spurr, David, *The Rhetoric of Empire: Colonial Discourse in Journalism, Travel Writing and Imperial Administration* (Durham, Duke University Press: 1993).

Stoneham, C.T., *Out of Barbarism* (London, Museum Press: 1955).

Stovkis, Ruud, 'Sports and civilization: is violence the central problem', in Eric Dunning and Chris Rojek (eds), *Sport and Leisure in the Civilizing Process* (Toronto, University of Toronto Press: 1992) pp. 121–36.

Surin, Kenneth, 'C.L.R. James' material aesthetic of cricket', in Hilary Beckles and Brian Stoddart (eds), *Liberation Cricket: West Indies Cricket Culture* (Manchester, Manchester University Press: 1995) pp. 313–41.

Tatham, George, 'Environmentalism and possibilism', in Griffith Taylor (ed.), *Geography in the Twentieth Century* (London, Methuen: 1957) pp. 128–62.

Taylor, Peter, *Political Geography* (London, Longman: 1989).

Taylor, Peter, 'The state as a container: territoriality in the modern world-system', *Progress in Human Geography*, 18 (2) (1994), pp. 151–62.

Thiong'o, Ngugi wa, *Barrel of a Pen: Resistance to Repression in Neo-Colonial Kenya* (London, New Beacon Books: 1983).

Thiong'o, Ngugi wa, *Detained: a Writer's Prison Story* (London, Heinemann: 1981).

Thiong'o, Ngugi wa, *Homecoming* (London, Heinemann: 1972).

Thiong'o, Ngugi wa, *Moving the Centre: the Struggle for Cultural Freedoms* (London, James Currey: 1993).

Thiong'o, Ngugi wa, *Petels of Blood* (London, Heinemann: 1977).

Thomson, Joseph, *Through Masai Land* (London, Cass: 1968 – reprint of work originally published in 1885 by Sampson Low, London).

Throup, David, *Economic and Social Origins of Mau Mau* (London, James Currey: 1987).

Tidrick, Elizabeth, *Empire and the English Character* (London, Tauris: 1990).

Tomlinson, John, *Cultural Imperialism* (London, Pinter: 1991).

Tourist Bureau for the Belgian Congo and Ruanda-Urundi, *Traveller's Guide to The Belgian Congo* (Brussels, Information and Public Affairs Bureau: 1956).

Turner, Victor, *Dramas, Fields, and Metaphors: Symbolic Action in Human Society* (Ithaca, Cornell University Press: 1974).

Urch, George, *The Africanization of the Curriculum in Kenya* (Ann Arbor, MI: 1968).

Uweche, R. C., 'Nation building and sport in Africa', in Benjamin Lowe, David Kanin and Andrew Strenk (eds), *Sport and International Relations* (Champaign, IL, Stipes: 1978) pp. 543–50.

Vettenniemi, Erkki, 'The promised land of running', *Motion*, 2 (1994) pp. 101–2.

Vigarello, Georges, 'The life of the body in Discipline and Punish', *Sociology of Sport Journal*, 12 (2) (1995), pp. 158–63.

Virilio, Paul, *Lost Dimensions* (New York, Semiotext(e): 1991).

Wangeman, Björn and Glad, Bill, *IAAF Development Cooperation* (London, IAAF: 1990).

Watkins, Elizabeth, *Jomo's Jailor: the Life of Leslie Whitehouse* (Calais, Mulberry Books: 1993).

Watman, Melvyn, 'Keino: the world's most exciting athlete', *Athletics Weekly*, 19 (51) (1965), p. 16.

Webster, F.A.M., *Athletics of Today: History, Development and Training* (London, Frederick Warne: 1927).

Webster, F.A.M., *Why? The Science of Athletics* (London, John F. Shaw: 1937).

Weller, Henry Owen, *Kenya without Prejudice* (London, East Africa Ltd: 1931).

Were, Gideon, 'Cultural renaissance and national development: some reflections on Kenya's cultural problem', *Journal of East Africa Research and Development*, 12 (1982) pp. 1–12.

Whannel, Gary, *Fields of Vision: Television Sport and Cultural Transformation* (London, Routledge: 1992).

Wiggins, David, '"Great speed but little stamina": the historical debate over black athletic superiority', *Journal of Sport History*, 16 (2) (1989) pp. 158–85.

Young, Robert, *Colonial Desire: Hybridity in Theory, Culture and Race* (London, Routledge: 1995).

Younghusband, Ethel, *Glimpses of East Africa and Zanzibar* (London, John Long: 1910).

Index